Supervising the Doctorate

SRHE and Open University Press Imprint
General Editor: Heather Eggins

Current titles include:

Supervising the Doctorate

A Guide to Success

Second edition

Sara Delamont, Paul Atkinson
and Odette Parry

Society for Research into Higher Education
& Open University Press

Open University Press
McGraw-Hill Education
McGraw-Hill House
Shoppenhangers Road
Maidenhead
Berkshire
England
SL6 2QL

email: enquiries@openup.co.uk
world wide web: www.openup.co.uk

and Two Penn Plaza, New York, NY 10121-2289, USA

First published 2004

A catalogue record of this book is available from the British Library

ISBN 0 335 21263 8 (pb)   0 335 21264 6 (hb)

Library of Congress Cataloging-in-Publication Data
CIP data applied for

Typeset by RefineCatch Limited, Bungay, Suffolk
Printed in the UK by MPG Books Ltd, Bodmin, Cornwall

This book is dedicated to Amanda Coffey for being the easiest PhD student Paul and Sara have (so far) supervised.

Contents

Contents

Preface and acknowledgements

Writing this book is an act of hubris. No one with any sense would claim to 'know' how to be a successful doctoral supervisor, getting students through with friendship, integrity and emotional stability intact. The self-confidence of the doctoral supervisor can be destroyed by one 'failure': one person who fails to submit, or whose thesis is rejected by the examiners, or even one who never gets going but fritters the registration period away. We chose to write this book because we had done two research projects and our data on PhD students and their supervisors were extensive, because we had lived through a period of change in the British PhD, and because we felt our experiences were worth sharing.

We have of course learned a great deal from our own doctoral students over the years – not least from our mistakes, which they have had to suffer. Paul Atkinson would like to acknowledge in particular Barbara Adam, John Beynon, Robin Bunton, Amanda Coffey, Maggie Gregory, Andrew Lloyd, Evelyn Parsons, Andrew Pithouse, Susie Scott, Stuart Todd, Patricia Taraborrelli and Matt Williams. Sara Delamont would like to thank Mary Darmanin, Jane Pilcher, Michele Langlois, David Pearson, Teresa Rees, Jane Salisbury and Sue Sanders. Paul Atkinson and Sara Delamont have supervised more than seventy-five short (20,000) dissertations for five different masters' degrees, plus other MPhil and PhD theses. They have examined higher degree theses in twenty-eight different UK universities, plus three Australian ones, including EdD theses in two places. All those students and colleagues have contributed to the experiences drawn on in this book. Since the first edition of this book was published Sara Delamont has done a good deal of staff development on PhD supervision and examinations, in Cardiff, at a range of other British universities from Stirling to Plymouth, at the BERA Annual Conference, and for the Academy of Social Sciences initiative with the ESRC. We have also run workshops for PhD and EdD students in Cardiff and Stirling, in Finland, at the AERA and the joint Australian and New Zealand annual conference on educational research, and at two BSA summer schools in Cardiff and Bath Spa. We are very grateful to all those who have taken part in these courses, who have helped us to clarify our ideas. We are also grateful to the experts consulted by the publishers and to the twenty people who filled in a short questionnaire we sent to users of the book, who helped with this new edition.

The number of people doing higher degrees by research in Britain has continued to grow. Between 1996 and 2001 the total number of doctorates awarded annually rose from 10,214 to 14,115, an increase of 38 per cent. There is, therefore, more supervision to be done. Simultaneously, there has been a growth in the number of universities offering professional doctorates: that is programmes of coursework followed by a thesis of doctoral standard but MPhil length. We have had some experience of teaching on a professional doctorate. The best known is the EdD, the professional doctorate in education, but there is a range of others in the social sciences, and the EngD. The Humanities disciplines have not yet expanded their postgraduate qualifications into professional doctorates, and they exist in relatively few science disciplines. The policy context in all the English-speaking countries has also developed a good deal since 1997 and we have added a short chapter on the issues of institutional rules, national policies and the audit culture.

There has not yet been much research published on the supervision of the thesis stage of the professional doctorate, but what exists is incorporated in this book. A good deal of new scholarship has been published on the supervision and examination of the PhD since 1997 and we have woven that into this text. The research on which we draw extensively in this book has also been published in refereed journals and a monograph (Delamont, Atkinson and Parry 2000), since the first edition. The ESRC funded the research on which we have drawn in this book, with two grants: 'The academic socialisation of doctoral students in social science disciplines' (T007401010) and 'The academic socialisation of doctoral students in natural science disciplines' (R000233120). We gratefully acknowledge the support of the Research Council. The views expressed in this book are the authors' and do not represent the policy of the Economic and Social Research Council. We are grateful to Bob Burgess and Chris Pole for frequent discussions on both projects.

Sharen Bechares and Karen Chivers word-processed the original text for us. Angela Jones transcribed the tapes in the original research project. Mel Evans prepared the second edition, for which we are very grateful.

The chapter titles and opening quotes are taken from Dorothy L. Sayer's (1935) *Gaudy Night*, which includes many apposite remarks on the perils of academic life and research. The edition used is the 1972 NEL version, and page references are to that text.

1

A most persuasive piece of argument: introduction

> When I was at Flanborough College, examining for the professorial theses in York University, there was a man who sent in a very interesting paper on a historical subject. It was a most persuasive piece of argument, only I happened to know that the whole contention was quite untrue.
>
> (Sayers 1972: 330)

Supervising doctoral students is one of the most satisfying things that anyone in higher education can do. Watching a new scholar become an independent researcher, conduct a project, write up the results, present them at a conference and see the first publications is a wonderful experience. Guiding a new scholar into your specialism is intrinsically rewarding and the best way to ensure that your own work echoes down to the next generation and beyond. Building up a research group, with doctoral students and post-docs (postdoctoral fellows) is even more rewarding. Our aim in this book is to convey the joys of successful supervision, offer advice on how to maximize the chances of your students being successful, and foreshadow problems that can arise, by forewarning you and offering you both preventive measures and remedial ones. We hope that experienced supervisors can learn from the book, although newcomers are its main target. Our basic philosophy is that good, pleasurable supervision is based on self-consciousness, not intuition or flying by the seat of the pants. The whole idea of the book is that successful, pleasurable higher-degree supervision is based on making explicit to yourself, and to the students, what the processes and issues are. Many of the problems that arise stem from supervisors thinking that students know things they do not know, or vice versa, or both.

We have organized the book so that it follows the progress of a student through from starting out as a doctoral student to careers after the viva voce examination. Not all theses proceed in the linear way in which we have organized the book, but the linear structure works well enough for the book. Thus we start with how to ensure that the students get off to a good start, and end those chapters relevant directly to the process of supervision with the development of academic life after the viva. Then Chapter 11 opens up with the place of doctoral supervision in the career of the lecturer, and the role of the graduates in the academic department and the wider university. These issues take us to considerations beyond the intrinsic satisfaction of higher-degree supervision. Readers of this book will be acutely aware of the extrinsic rewards and pressures that bear on the supervision and management of graduate studies: postgraduate students, and their numbers, are regarded as indicators of success for academic departments and their universities. Successful completion does not only mean that an individual student is rewarded, or that an individual supervisor can share in the pleasure and can experience professional pride as a consequence. Completion rates are extremely important. Research councils and the Arts and Humanities Research Board (AHRB), who are the source of centrally-funded research studentships in the UK, increasingly demand high completion rates (usually submission of the PhD within four years of commencement) as part of their processes of recognition. Numbers of research students and the number of degrees awarded are part of the evidence required of all departments in the UK, as part of the funding councils' recurrent Research Assessment Exercises – on which depend the core funding of academic departments and their universities.

Throughout the text we have used vignettes and examples to emphasize particular dilemmas and solutions. The vignettes are composites of dilemmas that supervisors and students have raised during our research and at our workshops over 25 years. There are regularly arising dilemmas, and we have presented them as they could be presented at a staff development or career-planning session. We hope that they are useful to readers as stimuli for discussion in continuing professional development workshops in other universities. The protagonists are fictional, as are the thesis topics. We explain our examples below.

Imagine your university is having a staff development workshop on 'higher degree supervision' and everyone present has to outline a problem – as each supervisor speaks you hear about:

Vignette A: Work ethic

Dr Cassandra Reilly is from the Science Faculty. She says that because the university is in an exciting city with lots of night life, too many of the research students are 'party animals' who do not seem to be prepared to 'put in the hours' to get the work done. She and her senior colleagues in the research group are not puritans, but they do want the research students to come to work promptly, without hangovers, and put in their 8 hours. She does not know what to do to inculcate a work ethic. She is puzzled that the research students do not seem to love science or want to put in long hours.

Vignette B: Writer's block

Dr Atwood Taylor, from the School of Leisure and Tourism, says his biggest problem is students who develop writers' block. He says this has happened more than once. Currently Laurali Wright is stuck on her thesis on cultural tourism. She has interviewed over 100 couples who have taken an operatic cruise down the Danube about their tastes and hobbies. She wrote a literature review, and a methods chapter but is now frozen. Dr Taylor says he 'never' knows how to help such students.

Vignette C: 'Ignorant' supervisor in ancient history

Jules Harnest is being supervised by Dr Henrietta Francey. Henrietta says she is trying to be friendly and supportive, but she is ignorant of the methods Jules wants to use and the empirical area he is working on. He is keen to study nosebleeds in ancient Greek medical thought, and has been thoroughly enthused by scholars using computer software to work on ancient texts. She is not familiar with the literature on Greek medical thought, admits she is ignorant but sceptical about the use of IT in ancient history, but reports that the department is so small there is really no one else to supervise Jules: her colleagues are expert on the Hittites, Roman architecture and the early church. She is the expert on the Greeks, but her main interest is marine imagery in drama. Henrietta has not read the literature Jules is reviewing, and she reports that Jules is openly wondering how useful her comments will be. Henrietta asks the group how much research she is morally obliged to do on Ancient Greek medicine and whether she should go on an IT course.

By the time you and the workshop leader have heard about problems like this, being a PhD supervisor seems to be impossible. They might not be problems you have encountered yourself. You may find it hard to imagine a higher-degree supervisor being unversed in relevant aspects of the student's research – and in the laboratory sciences such a distance between supervisor and student is rare. You may find it hard to envisage that 'writing up' could be a major problem for any higher-degree student (although the problem is fairly widespread). Nevertheless, such problems, and a fair number of others like them, are quite commonplace in academic departments. Even if you have not had to grapple with such issues yourself, there is no guarantee that some such professional and personal problem will not occur in the future. Moreover, if you are going to mentor other academics, and you are going to train the next generation of academic supervisors, then you may find it useful to think about such issues. Indeed, it is one of the limitations of graduate work in the UK, that given its tradition of individual effort and apprenticeship, with little explicit reflection on the processes and products, we rely too much on our own experience, and too little on more general principles. The aim of this book is to offer some advice and suggestions for avoiding problems, and solving them as and when they arise. We are not focused obsessively and exclusively on 'problems' and the more negative side of academic supervision. We must reiterate that we regard successful supervision as intensely satisfying: the development of a successful working relationship with a higher-degree student is one of the high points of academic work. But such working relationships – however successful the outcome – are developed over time, and cover many facets of academic work. It is rare indeed for there to be absolutely no hitches, no hiccups, no disagreements. However gifted the student, however distinguished the supervisor, the process requires work and attention. When we discuss 'problems', therefore, it is not in order to depress the reader, or to suggest that the enterprise is intrinsically fraught or flawed. Rather, we wish to give our readers the opportunity to reflect on these issues in such a way as to avoid problems, and so maximize the personal and intellectual pleasures to be gained.

Let us take the third of our vignettes about the 'ignorant' supervisor. Suppose that Harriet Francey goes back to her department determined to tackle her problems. First, she sits down with Jules and comes clean about her problems. This clears the air between them and they agree on a set of compromises. Henrietta goes on an IT course, and then she and Jules attend a day conference on IT and ancient history, at which several experts are speaking. Henrietta discovers several old friends there, together with their doctoral students. Jules comes away with a useful list of doctoral students in other universities with whom he can network by e-mail, so that he can keep in touch with other people using the same analytic tools. Henrietta starts to use IT herself, and discovers that it can enhance her work. Her next book on Aristophanes starts to move faster as she deploys her new skills. She and Jules agree on a shortlist of central texts in ancient Greek medical thought that she can be expected to read, and she works through those. Meanwhile, she arranges for Jules to have a few meetings with a scholar in another university who is a UK expert in Greek medical thought, getting him a travel grant to go there. Jules relaxes, feeling more confident about Henrietta, and Henrietta starts to plan a paper on medical metaphors in Sophocles. When you meet Henrietta a year later and ask after Jules, she is reinvigorated and cheerful. Their action plan has resulted in a year's productive work for Jules, while Henrietta has nearly finished her book and written her paper. What were being presented as intolerable burdens for Henrietta have now turned into research opportunities.

This book presents data collected by the authors from supervisors and higher-degree students during two research projects, and the authors' own experiences, as supervisors and as the successful completers of three PhDs and one MPhil between them, to provide guidance on how a successful supervisor can maximize the student's chances of completing a thesis quickly and efficiently. The two research projects were conducted between 1989 and 1993 in the UK. The first was on social scientists (in Town Planning, Social Anthropology, Human Geography, Urban Studies and Development Studies), the second on science (Artificial Intelligence, Biochemistry and Physical Geography and Environmental Sciences). Data from interviews and observation gathered in these research projects are drawn on here. The findings from the projects are rehearsed in Delamont, Atkinson and Parry (2000). The available data include interviews with over 50 supervisors taped and transcribed. In addition to those research-based insights, we draw on a good deal of practical experience as supervisors and in working with graduate students in a variety of social sciences on their own skills and research problems.

The research base has grown considerably since we wrote the first edition, and we have incorporated some of the findings into this book, which therefore has more citations than its predecessor. We have also drawn on a chapter from an unpublished PhD (Pearson 2002) which presents recent data on how doctoral supervision is conducted in physics, chemistry, philosophy and music.

We have, for many years, run a course for doctoral students at Cardiff University. We have worked with students from sociology, criminology, psychology, education, planning and other disciplines (indeed, our direct experience is not confined to the social sciences, we also have experience with students in earth sciences, chemistry and pharmacy). We meet with those graduate students in a series of weekly workshops, in order to go over a number of core skills and processes over the course of a research project. These are intended to inculcate many of the 'craft' skills of academic life, and to help those selfsame graduate students to go on to become well-informed supervisors when their turn comes. We try to make those workshops as practical as we can, with handouts and worksheets. Some of these have been reproduced as figures in this book, such as Figure 4.1 in Chapter 4. We use them to illustrate our general points, and to share with our readers examples of the kind of resources that can be used in constructing such skills courses.

Throughout this book we have tried to blend advice for supervisors – places where we say 'Do this or your students will suffer' – and findings from academic research. We have offered advice only on points where our experience and the research findings are in agreement: that is where the experiential and the empirical are mutually supportive. Our basic belief is that supervising is a skill, or set of skills, that can be learnt, and improved with practice. We want this book to be a cheerful and optimistic one – our aim is to parallel the enthusiasm communicated by Becker's (1986) *Writing for Social Scientists*. For the second edition we have updated and rewritten the examples and the vignettes. The examples are based on real students and real colleagues we have dealt with in our careers, although we have changed all the details that could identify them. They are either positive stories with happy endings or rueful accounts of mistakes we or our close colleagues have made that could have been avoided if we had all been wiser.

We have written the book, and conducted the research that partly informs it, primarily in terms of the PhD and the thesis stage of the professional doctorate. The doctoral candidature, and the research processes that go with it, inform most of our discussion. Of course, such candidates and their concerns by no means exhaust the range of higher-degree work, or the kinds of supervision that may be involved. In addition to a relatively small number of Masters degrees exclusively by research (the MPhil in many cases), there are now very large numbers of taught Masters degrees that include a part-requirement dissertation (typically in our own institution with a limit of 20,000 words). The substantial growth in such Masters degrees in the UK has meant that supervision is now a much more pervasive aspect of academic work in virtually every department. The scope of such short dissertations is, self-evidently, much reduced from that of the PhD. The requirement of an original and major contribution to scholarship is not relevant. The conduct of major pieces of empirical research or the promotion of significant theoretical development are not feasible or relevant. Nevertheless, they do require supervision, and their supervision calls for at least some of the same skills as does that of doctoral students. Students at the thesis stage of the professional doctorate need supervision that is intellectually similar to that required by traditional PhD students, but as they are usually part time, and frequently in very demanding jobs, the practicalities are rather different. Our discussion of issues, problems and solutions should not, therefore, be seen as outside the sphere of relevance for academics concerned only with students at the Masters level. Many aspects of supervision are generic, and we are aware of that fact.

Ethics and confidentiality

Throughout the book there are illustrations taken from our experience, and examples from our research projects. All the illustrations and examples use pseudonyms for people and places. Sometimes biographical details have been changed to protect the student further – for example, a person who was a Welsh rugby international might be described as a 10,000-metre athlete. The informants from the two ESRC-funded research projects have also been protected by pseudonyms: all the supervisors are called Dr X, all the students have a forename and a family name. Thus Dr Throstle is supervising Jason Ingersoll. All the universities are also protected by pseudonyms. We have used some data from a study conducted for BERA (the British Educational Research Association) by Eggleston and Delamont (1983), and the students who responded to that survey are also protected by pseudonyms.

The structure of the volume

Chapter 2: 'Caught and held by a cobweb' shows how to help students move from their undergraduate or taught postgraduate phase into the research postgraduate phase. The specific focus will be on helping students design a *manageable* project: i.e. one that can be done single-handed in three years by a beginner.

Chapter 3: 'The balance between tradition and progress' is about a balancing act. Once the student has a sensible project, it has to be timetabled, planned and (if empirical) the research design has to be established. This chapter focuses on the delicate balance that a supervisor has to strike between ensuring the planning is done but not undermining the student's autonomy by 'taking over' the research.

Chapter 4: 'Old manuscripts' focuses on the literature review. This chapter shows how a good supervisor can ensure that the student reads widely enough, and writes an interesting literature review, while still getting on with the data collection. Many students 'drown' in the literature: the good supervisor is alert to that danger.

Chapter 5: 'Heavy and thankless task' deals with supervising data collection. The good supervisor, who will him- or herself have negotiated access, chosen methods, and done their own data collection, can help a student avoid the worst mistakes. This chapter focuses on how successful supervisors can deploy their own experience to help their students.

Chapter 6: 'Disagreeableness and danger' is focused on how the supervisor can keep up the students' motivation and work rate through the sticky patches. Completion of the project is as dependent on keeping up motivation and effort as it is on academic excellence. The difference between academic success and failure quite often comes down to perseverance and overcoming difficulties. The supervisor needs to be alert to potential problems, and needs to think about how to encourage students to carry on, surmount problems, and submit their work.

Chapter 7: 'Contorted corkscrew' is about the acquisition of a variety of tacit competencies, broadly concerned with judgement and taste in postgraduate research. In addition to technical issues of research design, data collection and so on, supervisors and students need to focus on broader issues of academic socialization within the relevant discipline.

Chapter 8: 'An emotional excitement' is all about writing. Turning data and notes into a completed thesis defeats many students. There are few books on writing, and nothing on how a supervisor can help a student to master writing, and even learn to enjoy it.

Chapter 9: 'A lack of genuine interest' deals with choosing examiners and preparing for the viva. Many candidates are scared of the 'unknown' aspects of doctoral examinations. This chapter explores how a good supervisor can reduce anxiety by organizing mock and practice vivas, and provide useful advice on handling the real event. It also addresses the vital issue of how to select appropriate external examiners, so that standards are maintained but students also get a reasoned verdict.

Chapter 10: 'The brave pretence at confidence' focuses upon how the supervisor should be 'moving them on': launching their careers. This chapter deals with the supervisor's duties to help students publish, build a strong CV, and seek jobs.

Chapter 11: 'A rather unpromising consignment' deals with selecting higher-degree students and building a research group. This chapter deals with the selection of research students: vetting applications, interviewing candidates, and matching students and supervisors to maximize the chances of thesis completion. Then it turns to the role that a research group plays in the career of the successful researcher.

Chapter 12: 'The very loftiest motives' sets the work of the supervisor in the context of institutional codes of practice, national standards and frameworks, and the audit culture.

International comparisons

We see these as the main issues with which a British supervisor has to be concerned. The institutional frameworks with which we deal – on the basis of our research and also from our professional experience – are from the UK. This is not, however, an exclusively British, parochial view. Internationally, there are regular debates about the nature of the doctorate. In the USA, for example, there has been the *Re-envisioning the PhD* programme (Nyquist and Wulff, n.d.) and the Carnegie Foundation for the Advancement of Teaching's set of reflections on the doctorate in a range of disciplines (Graff 2003). The American Educational Research Association had a special issue of their newsletter (Young 2001) devoted to debates about the doctoral preparation of educational researchers. Our perspectives are not applicable only to graduate study in UK higher education.

Notwithstanding national differences in funding, organization, examining, completion rates and completion times, many of the issues are generic and cross national boundaries. The evidence from other industrialized countries suggests that many of the basic issues are similar: indeed the findings of the most thorough cross-national study are that disciplinary identities are more powerful than national differences. That is, doctoral supervision in physics in Japan has more in common with doctoral supervision in physics in Germany than with history supervision in Japan. A brief summary of that programme makes our case for the international nature of basic supervisory problems, and serves briefly to locate what we have to say against that international backdrop. In 1987 the Spencer Foundation funded a three-year research programme in five countries (Japan, the UK, West Germany, the USA and France) on the ways in which graduate education and research were related (Clark 1993). The research programme produced analyses at the national level of 'the historical development of higher education and science' (p. xxii), and of the contemporary structure of funding, of research, and of higher education. More intensive investigation of archetypical disciplines – history to represent humanities, economics to represent social science, and physics to represent the sciences – took place in all five countries, with the addition of engineering in Japan and the biomedical science in the USA. The national level analyses were based primarily on published data, the intensive investigations on interviews with 'faculty, graduate students, university administrators, and, if necessary, personnel in research institutes' (p. xvii).

Clark's dream for this comparative study was that 'cross-national comparisons' would 'lead to a richer understanding' (1993: 378). He saw the main issues facing the five countries studied as the rise of mass participation in higher education, the labour market demand for advanced education, the expansion of knowledge and the increased government role in patronage and supervision of research. These four trends have led, Clark believes, to common tensions: between concentration and diffusion, between locating research in non-university settings and maintaining it there, and between bureaucratic control and autonomous competition. The five nations investigated during this Spencer programme vary considerably in the ways their higher education had responded to the four trends, and in the ways in which the resultant tensions were showing. Clark argues that, in 1990 'the future of British academic science is quite problematic' (p. 369), because the 'tensions between university and state is great' (p. 369). This prescient comment prefigured the various policy issues explored in our new Chapter 12. An expanded version of the British section has been published in Britain (Becher *et al.* 1994) as a separate monograph. Coincidentally, while the Spencer Foundation programme was drawing to a close, the British ESRC was launching a research initiative on the social science PhD which has also been published (Burgess 1994). Subsequently two projects on science PhD students and their supervisors were also funded by ESRC. In 1995 the UK finally had a substantial body of data on doctoral study, remedying a long-recognized deficiency (Winfield 1987).

Superficially, the five nations have very different systems of graduate education. France has the CNRS system, as well as the 1984 reform of the doctoral degrees which led to the single doctorate followed by the *Habilitation*. America has the largest and most diverse system. The Japanese section will probably be the most like *terra incognita* to readers who may be surprised to learn that Japanese graduate education 'is small and relatively weak' (297). Only 6 per cent of the first-degree graduates go on to do graduate work, and 'earning the doctorate is not a . . . routine part of the early stages of an academic career' (311) in the humanities and social sciences.

Shining through all the national differences are the commonalties of disciplinary cultures. The everyday experiences of a doctoral student doing physics are more similar to those of another physicist across countries than they are to a historian in her 'own' culture. Japanese history candidates experience supervision in ways very similar to historians in the other four countries. The supervisory cultures and the existence or absence of a laboratory setting for research, are more important for the life of the individual student than the particular nation state despite Traweek's findings on physics (Traweek 1988). The dilemma facing supervisors are very similar across the industrialised countries, and we hope this book will be relevant in all of them.

The problems of hypothetical supervisors opened the chapter. We end it with some real supervisors discussing their task, and the tensions they feel.

The problems of supervision

The scientists and social scientists we interviewed discussed sensitively how they had to find a balance between heavy-handed dominance and a 'hands-off' neglect of their students. Among our respondents were several who confessed that they were not good at handling the delicate balances required.

Dr Netley, a social scientist at Boarbridge, told us: 'It's very difficult to get the right balance between how much you teach them and how much you let them get on with it.'

His colleague, Dr Munsey:

If I feel the student wants to be hand-fed, i.e. he wants me to do half the work, that's not on. I look for the independence of personality in addition to motivation. They should be academically capable and phys-ically capable of doing the data collection and analysis, with some guid-ance obviously, but I'm not prepared to give up more than 10 per cent or 15 per cent of my time to a study if I find they keep knocking on my door every day, asking me to provide them with information and data.

These accounts of the supervisory relationship draw on contrasts of depend-ence and independence on the part of the research student. Dr Coltness, of Tolleshurst, was adamant that: 'supervising is extremely difficult, let me say that. I think its the most difficult part of my work. It's the part I enjoy least because I feel I don't do it well enough.'

Central to Dr Coltness's doubts was the delicate balance:

how much should you be spoon feeding? Should they be doing it them-selves? Should I be in the library sussing out things? How much rewriting? Do you go through it with a toothcomb? . . . There are no guidelines at all. So I find it very problematic. How much to help the weaker ones, how much to try to keep up with the brighter ones. They are so different, they're not off-the-peg.

Dr Danson, a natural scientist at Forthhamstead, described this process: 'Once we've decided on a topic and an area of work then I think the student will gradually put more and more into the project on his or her initiative, I mean it's not a doctorate of being a technician, it's a doctorate of philosophy.'

This is a particularly important distinction in a laboratory discipline: suc-cessful researchers have to be autonomous: 'Therefore you're not actually wanting someone to do something and then tell them to do something else. You're wanting them to come back with ideas, and indeed, from then on guide the project in particular areas.'

Perhaps the most detailed reflection on supervision we collected emphasized the changing nature of the student–supervisor relationship over time. One of our informants, Dr Shannon, a social scientist at Chelmsworth, emphasized how the relationship between student and supervisor can, and must, change over the student's registration period:

> I do think its quite a difficult process for both parties, supervisor and student. And it changes over time. It's a very personal thing. To begin with the supervisor's in quite a strong position in defining and directing students, and they're relatively subordinate at the beginning, willing to accept your advice and direction.

For Dr Shannon, the student needs to outgrow that early phase, so:

> as the student gets more and more into the subject, that relationship begins to change, because they develop an expertise which the supervisor is no longer sharing. Also they develop a view about their intellectual property which is separate from their supervisor. And it's a bit like a growing-up process, an intellectual growing-up and it leads to conflicts at a certain point in time, as the student develops that independence.

For Dr Shannon, the time when the balance begins to shift can be likened to the stormy adolescence of the candidature:

> I've always found there's this period in the middle where there is that conflict, like my relationship with my daughter, where there is a change occurring, and it's quite difficult as a supervisor to begin to 'let go' almost. You feel they're not ready for it, they're not in control, and that leads to a degree of conflict which can be overt, or could not be overt. Sometimes people will avoid seeing you – it's like that.

Dr Shannon said she had observed this period of conflict between colleagues and students.

> I've seen that process sometimes with colleagues, where people don't seem to be able to complete, and I think it might need to be overtly addressed. And I think the most successful candidates are when you can be relatively open about that, get through it and then move to completion. But otherwise you can get stuck in that phase when the supervisor still tries to over-direct, over-control, and the student tries to pull away and develop their own interests. And if you're not careful you can get bogged down – the student doesn't know how to progress and you're not giving them the sort of advice they need to get through.
>
> I don't know if other supervisors have felt this, but I do think there's this shifting relationship which is actually quite difficult to cope with.

While Dr Shannon was more articulately self-critical than many of our respondents, she was typical in her concern to do the job well. Most of our respondents talked at length about the pleasures and pains of supervision, and about their strategies for helping students. They discussed selection, upgrading from MPhil to PhD, told stories of catastrophes and successes, and were self-critical. Some of them found it enormously rewarding, such as

Professor Brande, a geographer from Hernchester, who expressed the task as follows:

> I think the most important thing you can do as a supervisor is to really give them a love – it sounds curious, that word, but I think it's the right word – for what they're doing, and a sort of motivation, because I think that research is a desperately lonely business.

Dr Gastineau, in development studies at Gossingham:

> DPhils are terrible things, and I don't yet know a DPhil student who didn't go through a financial crisis, a mental crisis, a supervisor crisis or an emotional crisis, that's why it's such as appalling system.

Dr Jelf at Eastchester, a social scientist described his ideal student: 'The ideal student will write regularly, be a good friend, won't mythologize the PhD as a lifework, will be a source of stimulus to your own work.' This book is intended to help supervisors diagnose and deal with the crises and build good relationships with PhD students so Dr Jelf's ideal is more often obtained.

Conclusion

If the reader has recognized anything we have raised hitherto, then he or she will already be aware of the diverse issues that confront the contemporary academic who must tackle the demanding intellectual and personal task of overseeing the development of graduate students. As we shall have reason to mention later in the book, the transition from undergraduate to postgraduate can imply major changes – not only in status, but in styles of work, intellectual problems, confidence and self-esteem. Likewise, the shift from undergraduate teaching to postgraduate supervision can imply similarly significant shifts in professional tasks and preoccupations. Neither undergraduate teaching nor postgraduate supervision comes 'naturally'. The latter is not simply a direct extension of one's own research activity either. It is an important aspect of academic work in its own right. It is, moreover, a key feature of academic departments and of most academics' core duties. The institutional organization of postgraduate work has been the subject of considerable attention in the UK in recent years. The research councils have encouraged more systematic attention to the quality of postgraduate provision, and the success of graduate students. The proper preparation of graduate students for their own research, and for their own future role as researchers and research supervisors, has been the topic of considerable debate and some degree of innovation in the UK: the introduction of Masters degrees aimed at the transmission of research skills and methods is but one aspect of such policy reviews. The professionalization of higher-degree work should have had a direct impact on academics' perceptions of this aspect of their professional role. Higher-degree work cannot be based – even if it ever should have been – on ad hoc or implicit criteria, approached casually in the interstices of the working week. It demands and deserves to be treated seriously as a set of commitments and demands on a par with other teaching and scholarly activity. It is our ambition to make some contribution to the processes of reflection and personal development that will help the academic – whether experienced or novice – to approach such challenges and to reap the rewards that go with them.

2
Caught and held by a cobweb: getting the student started

> a tortoise-shell butterfly, fluttered out into the brightness of the window, where it was caught and held by a cobweb.
>
> (Sayers 1972: 10)

Introduction

It is hard to recognize how terrifying the new status of 'PhD student' can be for a person starting out. Even if the student has been an undergraduate in the same university, the role and status are new, if he or she is in a fresh department and university then everything is strange. The supervisor has to ensure that the students get started academically, find their feet in the institution, and adjust to the status. We have used the image of the butterfly caught in a cobweb here because many bright, clever undergraduates are paralysed by the almost invisible demands of graduate work. Just as a cobweb may only be visible in some weather conditions, so too the constraints of higher-degree work can catch the unwary graduate. The supervisor's job is to clear the students' flight path. This chapter has four sections. First it deals with setting up a productive working relationship with the student, then with what are reasonable expectations for you to have of them and vice versa, then it addresses some common problems that arise in the first few months of a candidature. Finally it addresses two unspeakable issues: sex and lies.

Managing your supervisees

Having a reasonable experience with higher-degree students is dependent on their relationship with you, and, if there are any, with the other supervisor(s). You need to sort out a good working relationship with your supervisee. Relationships have to be worked at, and discussed, because most of the problems stem from a failure to set out the expectations both parties have for the relationship, agree them, or agree to disagree. A few supervisions devoted to discussing the best ways to work together will not be wasted. As the needs of the student will change over time, the ground rules of the relationship may need to be renegotiated periodically, but it is most important to set up guidelines early on so that the student knows what to do, and how to work with you. Consider these three vignettes of different 'management' and relationship problems, brought to a university staff development workshop.

Vignette D: Clash of personal style

Revd Dr Jesse Vardallo is from religious studies. He says that his biggest problem is with two students, Caron Mallory and Spencer Donne. Both, he complains, are hopelessly disorganized, and discourteous. Both regularly 'forget' appointments, miss deadlines, arrive without vital pieces of paper, lose things, forget to back up their work. He tells of wasted hours in his office waiting for one or the other to arrive for scheduled meetings, and his mounting irritation at their 'slapdash' activities.

He keeps appointments and hits deadlines: what can he do to make them 'grow up' and be reliable?

Vignette E: Arrogance or ignorance

Dr Lloyd McGown, from the Hispanic Studies section of modern languages, says he sympathizes with Jesse, but has an equally tricky problem. He is new to supervision, and his first PhD candidate, Arthur Grasemann, is supposed to be working on the Brazilian novelist, Jorge Amado. Lloyd is interested in the topic, and was looking forward to close intellectual involvement. Arthur, however, is proving resistant to supervision. He tries to avoid supervision, will not discuss his work, and keeps saying that he knows what he is doing, what his thesis will cover, and 'just' wants Lloyd to read the draft chapters before he submits. Lloyd is worried about completing the university's official monitoring forms – and is not sure how to get Arthur to share his ideas.

Vignette F: Over-dependence

Dr Orania Papazoglou is next to speak – she bursts out that she came with one problem in mind about writing, but Lloyd's problem reminds her of a worse one she faces. She is in Education, and has a new EdD student, Christianne Lewis. This woman did well on the taught courses during Stage One of the professional doctorate, but seems unable to function at the thesis stage. Christianne is supposed to be evaluating a change in the anti-bullying policies in two schools using focus groups with pupils, and individual interviews with teachers and parents. However she seems unable to take responsibility for her own thesis. She keeps e-mailing Orania to ask for advice, not on specific details but at the level of 'what should I do *now*?'

> Orania asks the group: what can she do to get Christianne to be autonomous?

In each of these vignettes, we can see that the parties have never sorted out the basics of the relationship. In this chapter we set out guidelines for making explicit how the relationship is going to work, to try and avoid such clashes and misunderstandings.

A good starting point is to get hold of Phillips and Pugh's (2000) *How to Get a PhD* (3rd edition) read Chapter 8 yourself, and Cryer (2000) *The Research Student's Guide to Success* (2nd edition) and read Chapter 6, then get your student to read them, and then devote part of a supervision to discussing them. Because they are student-centred books you may find them offensive, but this makes an excellent basis for sorting out how you and your student will work together. Cryer includes the responsibilities of supervisors according to the National Postgraduate Committee (p. 59). Leonard's (2001) *A Woman's Guide to Doctoral Studies* has a similar chapter (5) and for female students, especially those from out with the UK, that may be a better place to start. Middleton (2001) contains useful data too.

It is easy to forget that students may not know what a PhD *is*. Colin Ives, an anthropology student, confessed to Odette that:

> A lot of mistakes I've made are the result of me not asking questions and people not putting me right – they presume I must know . . . I didn't know the PhD was meant to be an argument, as Dr Durtham said, its meant to say something. I thought it was meant to be one of those old-fashioned monographs, a collection of information. When I was an undergraduate I used to think a PhD was one of those articles you get in *Man* or something, a 10,000 word article, I used to think 'they must be PhDs'.

Colin discovered what a PhD was, not by reading some in the Kingford library but: 'I just happened to be reading a book, the prospectus, one day, and saw 100,000 words and thought, "That's really long" and nobody bothered to tell me, and nobody has told me.' Note that Colin did not *ask* about thesis length, but waited to be told by 'someone'. He had not read any recent theses in the library, nor been briefed on the requirements. He was in his third year when we interviewed him.

The growth of taught courses for doctoral students may reduce the number of students like Colin, but only if the course includes some very explicit coverage of very basic 'facts'. Our experience is that those students like Colin who most need explicit coverage of basic issues like length, structure and function of the thesis, are most resistant to taught components, regarding them as 'irrelevant' to their own individual project. A wise department makes sure that some basic material is covered in a course, that a document with fundamentals is issued to all students, and that a supervisor also deals with them. Similarly, supervisors who wish to survive their careers unscathed by appeals and complaints will ensure that their students have, and are urged to read, the formal rules governing the degree for which they are registered. However, this does not ensure that students hear, far less that they understand, what is covered.

As we reach our first example, we can use it to explain that term. Our examples are essentially cautionary tales or success stories or tips, drawn from our experience, the cautionary tales very heavily disguised to protect our former colleagues and students. Vignettes are left open-ended, in examples we stress the moral of the tale and the lessons to be learned.

Example 2.1: Two cue-deaf students

Vivienne Harnsberger was a part-time student, registered for an MPhil. She attended the compulsory classes on survival skills and study skills, she had the departmental graduate handbook, and regular supervision. However well into the third year of her registration she began sending Paul e-mails headed 'My PhD'. We saw her together, so there was a witness, and pointed out gently that she was registered for an MPhil, and if a student wanted to apply for an upgrading that there were formal bureaucratic procedures to be undertaken, and that the normal deadline, 18 months into the candidature for a part-time student, was long gone. She seemed amazed. We got out the departmental handbook and showed her the relevant pages. She still seemed amazed. She had clearly never registered any of the verbal material, nor read the handbook with any understanding.

Equally cue-deaf was Kent Holland, who was employed as a temporary lecturer and registered for a PhD as a staff candidate, supervised by a senior colleague. He too had attended our survival skills classes and at least one of our public mock vivas. However, when he submitted his thesis he was thunderstruck to be told he would have two external examiners and no internal: he had been registered for five years and never internalized a basic fact about his assessment, even though we regularly stressed it in class.

What follows are, first, some guidelines for a good relationship and, second, reasonable expectations, which may prevent you discovering after several years that you have a Colin Ives on your hands.

Guidelines for a good relationship

Discuss with the supervisee how the two of you will work, separately and together. Explain how you like to work with your PhD students, and see if they are going to be able to fit in. If they seem recalcitrant, find out why, and reach a compromise. Some may seem trivial – but trivia often wreck relationships. For example:

The best time of day to meet

Are they morning people or night owls? Which are you? Would 7.00 a.m. be a good time? Would 6.00 p.m. be better? Resolving this will enable you to discover their biorhythms – watch their faces when you suggest 7.00 a.m. – and their domestic circumstances. If there is a new baby, a crack-addict teen-age child or an elderly parent to be cared for, you need to know, so you can plan realistic meetings. Similarly, if your student is circuit-training twice a day, or too hungover to focus before lunch, or coaching A level candidates every evening you need to know that too. In the end you and the student need to find a regular slot, at a time of day when you are both awake and alert, so you can supervise the student. If you are a morning person, and the student only wakes up after dark, then an alternating slot may be the best compromise: one week you are awake and the student is not, the next you are flagging but the student is bright eyed and alert.

Example 2.2: Mutual convenience

Justin Quincy was doing the professional doctorate in social work, and at the thesis stage got a lectureship in a university, Mallingford, several hundred miles away. Justin was financially stretched by the move, over-whelmed with the new workload, and we worried that he was never going to get his thesis finished. We persuaded Justin to discuss the issue with his new head of department, armed with a note from us volunteer-ing to come to Mallingford to contribute to the department's staff development programme or seminar series. His new head of depart-ment, anxious for Justin's thesis to be completed, paid Justin's rail fare to Cardiff three times, twice paid for his supervisor to travel to Malling-ford, to do a staff seminar and to conduct a staff development event for practice tutors in the catchment area, and also paid for Justin to go to a conference at Castleton where he could meet his supervisor who was giving a paper there. These six meetings, with regular e-mail contact, got the thesis finished on schedule.

Scheduling the meetings

Initially a new student needs a weekly meeting, even if it is brief, because it is too easy for a novice to drift. However it is sensible to discuss, probably termly, whether the meeting schedule is meeting both your needs. A longer gap may not be harmful, but given that there are inevitably periods when you are not available, about thirty supervisions a year is a sensible target. If you are not going to have a regular, timetabled slot then the issue that must be settled is: who will set up meetings? and if it is the student, how? If you are senior and have a secretary, does the student see her to fix a supervision? If not, does the student bang on your door? Leave you a note? Phone you at home?

These may seem pathetic questions, but students cannot know how to arrange to see you unless you explain and set the rules. It is all too easy for a student to drift, hoping to catch you in the corridor, when they really need a supervision. The following comment, made by a man doing a PhD, is not unusual:

> Four tutors have supervised my study. Supervisor No. 1 left to take up an appointment overseas after one year. Supervisor No. 2 left to take up an appointment elsewhere after one year. Both were extremely busy men. As a part-time student I was loathe to take up their time. When writing or telephoning for infrequent appointments I seemed to be in rather the same position as a National Health hypochondriac with ingrowing toenails pestering a neuro-surgeon. I'm sure the supervisors did not intend it to be so.
>
> (Jimmy Thesiger, a PhD student in Education)

An agenda

It is an excellent idea to have an agenda for supervisions, agreed in advance. It is important, though, to decide who decides the agenda? Here the sensible answer is probably both of you. Sometimes you need to set it: to say clearly: 'Next week, please bring X and we'll discuss it.' At other times, the student needs to set it, so you ask, 'What do you want to focus on next time?' and then follow the agreed agenda.

Mechanics: confirmation and cancellation

One of the worst things about supervision is the broken engagement. For a supervisor a 'no-show' student is absolutely maddening, especially at 7.30 or 8.00 at night. For a student the 'vanished', absent supervisor is simply horrid, especially if the student is a part-timer who has travelled into the university at some trouble and expense. All supervisor–student pairs need firm arrangements written down, and clear cancellation arrangements. Undergraduates may never have needed an appointments diary: as a doctoral student they do. You may need to recommend buying an academic year diary, carrying it, and entering appointments. One which has lots of useful addresses in it would be a good buy. This is one big advantage of supervising mature students, and busy professionals on the professional doctorate: they have diaries or electronic organizers and expect to use them. Once they have a diary, and the habit of entering meetings, you can *negotiate* the mechanics of confirming and, when necessary, cancelling and rescheduling meetings. When such arrangements are not made, there can be confusion and bad feeling over broken, or missed appointments. Sometimes, however, a more complicated cancellation arrangement is needed.

Example 2.3: Paul's confirmation policy

Paul has a clear confirmation policy with all part-time higher-degree students. They phone Paul's home the evening before the supervision appointment to confirm it. This has two functions. If Paul has to cancel, he can do so, rearrange the meeting, and deal with any immediate problems on the phone. If the student cannot attend, he or she can cancel, reschedule and seek telephone help. If the supervision is confirmed, both Paul and the student explicitly remind each other they are going to meet. This means both turn up, and if either has to prepare, there are still a few hours before the actual supervision to do so.

The annual cycle

What is your annual, termly, weekly, cycle like – when will you be free to concentrate on them? Research students cannot be expected to know, unless you explain, that when you have a Research Council grant application to prepare, or 100 exam scripts to mark, or a major conference paper to write, you have less time and attention for them. A few minutes explaining what are the pressures and deadlines in your annual cycle always pays. Make sure they know when your busy times are, and set up the formal, longer meetings for the quieter periods. Learning about deadlines for grant applications, conferences, marking and examining is an important part of their socialization, so explaining your annual cycle is not only sensible, it counts as part of their training. A discussion of your annual cycle should also help them plan theirs, so they do not book their holiday for the same week you need them for intensive supervision.

Mutual availability

Sort out a timetable of the first term, first year, and whole thesis period – check mutual availability. It's no good them relying on you, the supervisor, reading 50,000 words in July if you are going to be in Australia. It is particularly important to be open about long absences – maternity leave, sabbaticals, field trips – and serious disruptions like being head of department – or dealing with the A level results and admissions in August. Then, if the student is worried about not being supervised you can agree to set up telephone or postal supervision, or bring in a second supervisor, or set up a support system for your absence.

Expectations for the relationship

Try to be as explicit as you can about what you hope to provide for the supervisee: methodological help, advice on the literature search, theoretical ideas, help with computing, visits during foreign fieldwork, de-bugging of equipment, practical tips, good references when they are applying for jobs, or tea and sympathy. If possible, try to be equally explicit about what you cannot, or will not, provide. If you are acutely aware that your computing skills are inadequate, say so, and promise to help the student find the computing skills and advice they need from elsewhere. If you are ignorant of the academic literature on a topic, the student needs to know how to seek help from a colleague to make up for your ignorance. If you hate conferences, do not go to them, and cannot put the student in contact with networks in the discipline, they need to appreciate your efforts to despatch them with your colleagues to make this up to them.

During the research project, Odette interviewed a woman who expected very close, friendly relationships with doctoral students. Dr Challoner, at Tolleshurst, described her intensely 'personal' supervisory style as follows:

> All my students come over for dinner, they know us as individuals and as a family. Eunice, who comes from Canada, has spent two Christmases with us. Bill, who was a Zambian student – his grant ran out and he had nowhere to live so he lived with us for six months to finish. So I guess my style is different.

It is particularly important to have clear expectations about the student's writing, and communicate them to the student. Be clear about when written work is expected, when they will get it back, and the sorts of help you will give with it. This is particularly important with students whose first language is not English. If you are not prepared to correct grammar, stylistics and spelling, then the student needs to know this early on, and you need to steer them to a source of help. Losing student work is unforgivable. Keeping it for weeks is nearly so. If you *know* these are faults of yours then stress that they must *always* keep back-up copies, and the two of you must work on scheduling you enough time to read, comment on, and return what written work they hand in.

Keeping a written record of the supervisory experience signals that you have high expectations of it: that you expect it to last. Keep an agreed record of decisions you have both taken, and make sure you keep a copy in your files. This is particularly valuable if you are ill, or on sabbatical, or away for any reason, and a substitute supervisor has to be involved. The coming of e-mail has revolutionized this aspect of supervision. First, it is relatively easy to e-mail a student after each meeting with a set of bullet points about what was covered, and what each of you will do before the next meeting. If the supervisor keeps a copy, there is a clear record of how carefully the supervision was done. Alternatively, the student can be made responsible for e-mailing their record of the supervision back to you with the action list. Either pattern can work well. The action list provides the agenda for the next supervision. It is also invaluable if you end up involved in an appeal or other legal/disciplinary proceedings. It will also help the student when they write up the thesis, because key decisions will be 'minuted', in your files and in theirs. If there is a supervisory panel, minutes can be e-mailed to all members of it when they are not at meetings.

The supervisor will, depending on the discipline, probably hope that the student will generate publishable findings. It is also useful to decide what will happen about publications by the students (whose name goes first, etc.) early on, long before there *are* any publications. In humanities and social sciences it is not usual for research students to publish much before submission, nor is it usual for the supervisor to be included as an author on conference papers, or publications before or after submission of the thesis. However in science and technology, where joint publication is much more common, the student needs to be made aware of the conventions of the discipline, the laboratory, and the research group. If the custom of the lab is that *all* publications carry the professor's name, and the supervisor's, the sooner the student understands that, and the reason for it, the better. Sorting out this issue allows you to set out the expectations that the student will finish, will produce publishable work, will succeed, and to explain the politics of publication for the individual, the research group and the department.

Expectations: reasonable and mutual

The more you sort out your expectations the better the relationship is likely to be. As part of the negotiations of a relationship, you have a right to set out your expectations for student conduct. Figure 2.1 sets out a number of such expectations, which might form the basis of an explicit departmental code of practice:

Figure 2.1:   Reasonable expectations

A supervisor can expect a PhD student to:

1   turn up to appointments, prepared for them;
2   write regularly, and share the draft material;
3   tell the truth about work done and not done;

---

4   keep in touch – socially, practically (holidays, sickness, change of address, etc.) and academically;
5   most importantly, do the research tasks that have been mutually agreed and scheduled.

In return, the student can have the following expectations for their supervisors:

1   Regular supervision. A reasonable student can expect to see his or her supervisor twenty to thirty times a year (if full time), for a private, one-to-one discussion of the research.
2   Written feedback. A student can expect to have draft material read, and returned with *written* comments in a reasonable time.

If you are not doing the things in Figure 2.1 your students will have legitimate grounds for complaint.

Praise and criticism

In the early stages of a supervisory relationship it is very easy to destroy a student's self-confidence by criticism, or give them a false sense of security by too much praise. Students can expect an evaluation of their progress, constructive criticism, and advice and reference to others for some kinds of help (e.g. a specific method, a particular theory). Because criticism always hurts, it is important to discuss how necessary it will be for you to criticize them, how you will try to be constructive, and how you will try to praise their successes too. Using some examples of how you have been constructively criticized in your career is often helpful.

In the next section some of the problems supervisors and students face when starting out on a new candidature are discussed.

Problems and difficulties in the starting-out phase

There are several sources of problems in the starting-out phase. They include those problems that are due to the inexperienced supervisor, the inexperienced student, and the failure to get the relationship going. It is important to remember that for many students doing a higher degree involves them in structuring their *own* work for the first time in their life (Hockey 1994b). Most have come from school, where their time and their curricula were very largely structured by teachers (and parents), to an undergraduate degree where time is organized and deadlines are quite short. The full-time student suddenly has an apparently unlimited time horizon, and a task of overwhelming and unknown complexity. The part-time student has to find time in a life that is probably full anyway and schedule the academic task. Encourage your students to read Chapter 4 of Cryer (2000) on 'settling in'.

One of the biggest problems is that many supervisors are inexperienced (Hockey 1994a). Dr Morrow, a social scientist at Boarbridge, described her early inexperience – 'so six months after I'd arrived I was supervising three people which I found deeply terrifying' – in order to contrast it with her current expertise – by the time of our research. In most British universities there are no requirements that supervisors are trained, or that they learn to supervise by doing so jointly. Dr Morrow's experience – she got a lectureship in geography and was immediately allocated three doctoral students – is common in arts and social sciences. In science and technology the new supervisor has almost certainly been helping doctoral students throughout her career as post-doc, and is more likely to slide smoothly into the role. If you are a new supervisor it is worth asking if your university has a training course, and if not, applying to be sent on one elsewhere. Failing that, a discussion with a popular or successful supervisor in your department, or a meeting of younger staff over lunch to discuss tactics, should help you get started.

The vital thing to recognize is that new students will, inevitably, flounder in the first weeks, and it is the supervisor's job to give them some tasks, guidelines and activities. Dr Morrow had to learn that this was an important role for the supervisor and by the time of her interview she was much more confident in her supervisory skills:

> when the student starts they feel very lost and lonely . . . poor students with a desk and a filing cabinet, and they were sitting there looking at it and what were they supposed to do next? So I'd always try to give them something to do – read certain articles, review them in written form. And that's something I know about myself, I'm not very good and commenting on verbal discussions – I need something in writing, however scrappy. Then having got some flavour of how they work and where they were at, I would try to set various projects for a term's duration.

In this way, Dr Morrow aims to respond to the individual student, but also to set up a framework. Similarly Dr Palinode, lecturer at Portminster in an applied social science, described his own PhD experience at Boarbridge: 'I know supervision is always problematic, it's a problematic relationship, but the quality of supervision I had at Boarbridge, I didn't think was very good at all.' Dr Palinode's use of 'quality' here does not seem to depend on special connotations of quality assurance and the like. It seemed to reflect more the lack of attention and lack of direction he had experienced as a doctoral student. He stressed that he had been lost and isolated, especially in the early days of his doctoral experience:

> I think you need to be able to talk to a breadth of people who are not necessarily close to your subject but understand generally, and can give information that can help, rather than being in the lost position I was

. . . But the first day you arrive, there you are with a blank desk and you think, 'What do I do now?' And I spent the first six months deciding what I was going to do . . . I think it's quite important to be settled in, and for people to help you early on. I think the doctoral programme, although you can't see it at the time, is quite useful – it depends – it could be argued that you should do a year's research, understand the processes of doing it and then do a research methodology programme, and then do the PhD.

Dr Meade, now on the staff at Boarbridge, claimed that when she did her doctorate there several years before: 'when I was doing mine it was very much being thrown in at the deep end . . . it was a jump from undergraduate work. I started off with one supervisor here – excellent academically but in fact just let me carry on in my own sweet way.' Similarly, a lecturer in artificial intelligence at Illington, Dr Panthing, said he began with a total lack of knowledge of what a British doctorate should be:

> I would say also I did not have a clear idea of what a PhD was . . . I had not read enough of them . . . I never had a clear, I don't think I had a clearly focused problem . . . I was always sort of exploring a lot of things, and I didn't have a clear question in mind that I was attempting to find the answer to . . . I think in effect I probably had about enough work for two PhDs.

He juxtaposed that past lack of understanding with the experience he has today, as a supervisor. Dr Panthing says of his work with doctoral students: 'I try and help them firmly identify a problem, explain to them that their research field is a life-time occupation, but the PhD is just a milestone and should be focused. Get it done, get it over with, and move on.' This is a typical contrast between the lecturer's own past biography, when no proper guidance was provided, and his own supervisory role offering proper advice and support.

It is easy to think that a bright, high-achieving undergraduate will become a bright high-achieving doctoral student by magic. A department's concern to attract good students, and the limited choices open to doctoral candidates may have unintended consequences:

> the 3rd year undergraduate cannot be expected to know how anxious many departments are to attract good students and that this sometimes leads them to give too rosy a picture of their ability to ensure that a student working in a particular area will have the necessary facilities and be supervised by someone with sufficient knowledge in the field.
>
> (Rudd 1985: 64)

Certainly we found, in more than one case, students who had been high-flying undergraduates were not necessarily suited to the exigencies of doctoral research. The following account, provided by a home recruit whose registration period had elapsed, suggests self-recruitment is not without it's own risks: 'I was a star pupil in my (undergraduate) year, and I think that has a bearing upon my difficulties because I'd always been able to do it and everybody thought I'd be able to carry on like that.'

In the following comments from doctoral students, the first four interviewed by Odette Parry in the early 1990s, the fifth writing for Eggleston and Delamont (1983) in the early 1980s, reveal how unsettled new doctoral students can be.

Ben Safford described his first months as: an unsettling experience, '. . . the whole thing seems very daunting, you don't know where your niche is, or if there is one for you'. Bryan Faul said, 'I suppose I expected a lot more structure,' and Nick Minakis commented, 'You tend to be thrown in at the deep end,' echoing generations of his predecessors. Laurence Fournier, a third-year, captured the student's dilemma: 'a lot of them have the idea of being suspended between a student who just absorbs things, and an academic who produces it, and that suspension gives them all kinds of paranoias and neuroses – suspended between these two stools.'

Finally in this section, we offer a long extract from a written response to an enquiry about postgraduate problems. Michael Seaton was a doctoral student in education responding anonymously to a request from BERA.

> Working in isolation in comparison with the situation as an undergraduate. This was a problem I was not remotely equipped to deal with because as an undergraduate I had worked alone whenever possible, always choosing dissertation work in preference to lecture courses, and thrived on it. I obviously failed to realize how important I had found being part of a group, both in terms of exchange of ideas and for reasons of 'ego' or morale – affirmation that my work and ideas were acceptable or even good, recognition that when I didn't understand something nor did a lot of people. The second big problem was my expectations of myself. I find it impossible now to work for hours every day, to make a real onslaught on the work as I used to when an undergraduate. This caused me weeks of total panic, a feeling that I had completely lost my ability to work. I think I have gone some way towards realizing that this is due to the different nature of the work, but it is a recurring problem and still sometimes seems overwhelming. I was not at all prepared to solve this problem and I had worked extremely hard as an undergraduate and thoroughly enjoyed doing so. I am working towards solving it by congratulating myself when I work a five-hour day rather than feeling a failure because it isn't twelve hours. This 'psychological' approach doesn't always work! Another problem is a feeling of insecurity in academic terms due to carrying out research which is supervised and will be examined in a department (or part of one) in which the discipline (history) is different from that in which I did my first degree (sociology and education). I am rather nervous that this leaves me particularly vulnerable to attack.
>
> A more practical problem than all of these was the initially enormous one of how to actually go about carrying out a piece of [historical]

research. This problem related not to the research topic, how to develop it, etc., nor to any profound theoretical or methodological problems, but extremely simple things like, well where do I go, what do I look at? The only way to describe this adequately is that for the first few desperate weeks I felt I wanted someone to say, look, next week take the number ten bus and do . . . (whatever). My supervisor and other members of the department were always helpful and friendly, offering constructive advice, but *never* on that level. I felt nobody remembered the experience of not actually knowing 'how to do research'. Of course one can't be spoon-fed, in fact I probably seek minimum guidance from my supervisor, but I do feel that some sort of 'Idiots Guide to Starting Research', either written or verbal would have been a great help in that initial period.

These are all problems which I sometimes feel are solved and which at other times threaten to drive me to navvying as an alternative! The biggest help is the knowledge that most research students feel the same way.

I sought help mainly from friends and from lecturers I knew well from my first university – simply because I didn't want to 'impress' my supervisor – who is always sympathetic and helpful – with my obvious stupidity!

The professional doctorate does not necessarily reduce these problems, because the shift from the 'taught' phase, when the student has an external structure, to the thesis stage, can leave the student struggling with the lack of structure.

Confidence-building and confidence-tricks

No matter how able the student, there are times, especially in the early periods of the research, when the supervisor may have to build and support the student's self-confidence. Indeed, in many cases, the supervisor's main task is to reassure and motivate the student rather than supplying detailed advice on the content of the thesis itself.

Imagine yourself in a staff discussion of postgraduates and hearing about the case in Vignette G.

Vignette G: A lack of self-confidence

Dr Jamie Smuth, from the English department, tells the group about his student Mirelle Feldster who began a PhD with him six months ago, to do a study of gothic influences in the fictional work of Winifred Holtby. Dr Jamie Smuth has just told her to redraft the chapter that she had been working on for four months – on Holtby's war service and the literature of the First World War. Mirelle wept and ran out of the room.

> Dr Smuth was paralysed with embarrassment, had no idea of what to do or say, but discovered from another student that Mirelle is under the impression that he thinks she is incapable of the level of work needed for a PhD. She believes that she is probably not clever enough to do a PhD, and keeps worrying that she is not doing the right things. In fact Jamie is excited about Mirelle's work, and thinks she is perfectly capable, but does not know what to do next.

Jamie Smuth obviously needs to signal more clearly the nature of his criticisms: he needs to find ways to separate his comments about this particular piece of work from any negative estimations of his student's general abilities or the nature of her chosen project. He also needs to make more clear the general standards or criteria he is adopting. A student needs to know that searching comments that are based on the highest possible standards of scholarship, intended to bring the student's own work up to that very high level, are not intended to imply that he or she is entirely incompetent and 'not up to it'. It is hard to realise how insecure many students are about their own potential to achieve higher degree standards. It is enormously easy to destroy their fragile self-confidence and perhaps to demoralise them. The vignette we have just provided is a dramatic one, but not impossibly so, as Example 2.4 shows.

Example 2.4: Owen Griffith

Owen Griffith was a PhD student of Lucien Bex. One day Meredith Crale, a PhD student of Paul's, found Owen in the men's lavatory, ripping up his thesis draft and burning it in the handbasin, strip by strip. Owen had decided, after a supervision in which Professor Bex had criticized one of his chapters, that he might as well destroy his work and 'pack it all in'. Meredith seized the remaining draft by force and took it to Paul's office for safe keeping. Paul found Professor Bex and persuaded him that Owen was in need of either an explicit recommendation to withdraw, or an equally explicit statement that he really was capable of a PhD and that this weak draft was only that. Professor Bex had had no idea that Owen was so vulnerable.

The experienced, successful supervisor knows that there are times when the student must be told that the work is fine and that they are doing well, because it *is* fine for that stage of the registration and the student must move ahead. Criticism, even unvarnished realism, can at such points demoralize and demotivate. The American sociologist Harvey Sacks once pointed out that in everyday life 'everyone has to lie'. Tact and reasonable behaviour dictate that we do not always tell the whole truth. In that sense, supervisors often have to 'lie'. You may be fortunate enough always to supervise students of outstanding ability, whose work never falters, and who never lose momentum or suffer from any doubts. In such circumstances, there is no need for careful management of the stark truth, perhaps. In many cases, however, there is need for a more strategic management of advice and criticism. Judicious 'white lies' will allow the student to move on, and if he or she is really any good they will see that more needs doing later. (We return to the development of academic judgement and insight in Chapter 7.) We are not suggesting that the supervisor should blindly encourage students whose work is clearly inadequate, or who are heading in quite the wrong direction. Clearly, such delusion is in nobody's interests, and misdirected work needs to be aborted at the earliest opportunity. Equally, no supervisor should express totally inappropriate approval for work that is clearly below par. But advice and criticism need to be managed in order to encourage the competent student to develop sufficient self-confidence to embark on and sustain several years of demanding, independent work. The wise supervisor will cultivate phrases such as, 'I'm very pleased with this', 'This is coming along well', or 'This is an excellent basis for the PhD', which are unambiguously favourable, but omit the qualification 'for a person in the first six months', or 'when it has been revised six or eight times'. The sensitive supervisor will realize that, at the wrong time, thoroughgoing and detailed criticism of work in progress can undermine the student and bring the progress to a dead stop. Most students, like most academics, need to have their self-esteem supported: supervisors need to cultivate skills of confidence-boosting. Failure to do so can damage the working relationship and hold up progress.

We are not advocating an abandonment of critical standards in supervisors. As we have suggested, purblind enthusiasm for anything and everything, however poor, is clearly inappropriate. But students need the clear and supportive endorsement of their supervisor, who in turn needs to be able to distinguish between authoritativeness, even assertiveness, and damagingly negative criticism. Students need to be given 'permission' to embark on their research, while guidance and evaluation need to be applied with a careful touch. One needs to bear in mind that even the most able of students need reassurance about the quality of their work, and that if they do not get it, they are unlikely to progress. (The same applies to most of one's academic colleagues, of course.)

Sizing up the student: cue-consciousness and the supervisor

There is one further issue that the good supervisor may wish to address early on in the relationship. That is, sizing up whether the student is 'cue-conscious' or 'cue-deaf'. These terms derive from research on final-year law students studied by Miller and Parlett (1976), adapted by Eggleston and Delamont (1983) for higher-degree students in education. Miller and Parlett divided the law students into three types: 'cue-seekers', 'cue-conscious' and 'cue-deaf'. The cue-seekers were the fewest in number, and they 'deliberately interacted with the system'. In other words, they asked staff about the form and content of their examinations, they found out who the external examiners were and what they specialized in, and they set out to impress the lecturers with their ability and level of interest. The cue-conscious were alert to hints about assessment, but took no active steps to acquire such organizational knowledge. The 'cue-deaf' did not believe that impressing staff was relevant nor did they hear cues when given out. They believed that hard work and virtue were rewarded. The cue-deaf tried to 'revise everything' because they had not heard any of the guidance about selectivity and did not trust themselves to spot topics. The cue-seekers used the data they had amassed to inform very selective revision strategies. So, for example, a cue-seeking student would look at past papers, and then say to a lecturer, 'Regina *v* McKay hasn't come up for several years, has it?' to try to test whether it was worth swotting up that case. The cue-seekers were disproportionately successful in getting first class degrees.

Eggleston and Delamont (1983: 39–45) used the same threefold categorization to characterize research students surveyed for BERA. Twenty-one of 84 respondents were classified as cue-deaf about the examination of their degree. We have already quoted the example of an extremely cue-deaf research student, Colin Ives, earlier in this chapter. We shall return to the appropriate ways to handle the cue-deaf student in later chapters. Here we wish to stress that it is useful to decide quite early on whether a new postgraduate student is at the cue-seeking or cue-deaf end of the spectrum, because if she or he *is* cue-deaf then the supervisor may need to make many aspects of the whole higher-degree period more explicit than might otherwise be necessary. These personal or intellectual styles are not absolute differences, and do not have to be thought of rigidly as if they represented personality types. But they capture some differences that can have far-reaching consequences for how students approach their work and how a supervisor needs to work with them. Just as the anxious student, or one whose self-esteem is fragile, needs careful encouragement, so the relatively cue-deaf students may need to have things spelled out for them rather more explicitly than might otherwise be the case. A failure to appreciate the nature of cue-deaf student styles can lead to misunderstanding and frustration on both sides. The supervisor may assume that a student will have 'picked up' what he or she needs to know about procedures, obligations and so on; but the student may fail to do so, and may feel aggrieved if the supervisor did not explain things with sufficient clarity.

Personal and working relationships

The relationship between a higher-degree student and his or her supervisor can take many forms. We have already suggested that it is necessary to establish clear, productive and mutually convenient arrangements for the supervision.

Without a firm basis for everyday work, supervision is likely to become frustrating and difficult for all parties. Beyond that, the degree of personal commitment is likely to depend on personality, the nature of group dynamics in the research group, the department or the faculty. Some research students and their supervisors establish close collaborative relationships, and personal friendships that may last for many years after the higher degree itself has been completed. Indeed, the networks and invisible colleges that characterize a great deal of academic work are often formed on the basis of such relationships. The stream of higher-degree students you supervise, and the research groups you may build around you, can form the basis of long-term collaborative arrangements. Those networks are part of the successful academic's 'cultural capital'. Such relationships and their value are not confined solely to the academic works. Research students from industry, public sector agencies and so on can also be extremely important members of the research network – again, providing opportunities for further collaboration, research access, professional advice and so on.

Active research groups, with a critical mass of higher-degree students, post-docs and more senior academics are more characteristic of the natural sciences than the humanities or social sciences. (We return to the issue of fostering research groups in Chapter 11.) Here it is worth noting that the existence of a formal research group – often vital in providing the right working environment in the laboratory disciplines – provides a framework for the promotion of more sociable and personal working relationships as well. The development of graduate schools and formal training provision in the humanities and social sciences may help to provide similar kinds of social environments. Nevertheless, in those latter disciplines, the higher-degree student's work and progress are more likely to be based in more individualistic relationships with one or two academics.

In all cases, but especially when the supervision is based primarily on a one-to-one relationship, it is important to establish at an early stage whether it is 'working'. Crucially, if it is not working out productively, then remedial action needs to be taken as soon as possible. It is standard practice in contemporary quality systems for there to be an explicit procedure for a change of supervisor. Admittedly, in small departments, and with highly specialized research interests, this may not always be easy. But it is more useful to recognize and address problems at an early stage than to press on regardless and to ignore clashes of personality, working styles, intellectual orientations and the like. In the subsequent chapters of this book we shall be introducing a variety of 'problems' and their possible solutions, and we shall not dwell on them here. It should, however, be possible for a student and her or his supervisor to address any identifiable problems and incompatibilities without blame or recrimination: it should be seen and handled as a practical issue concerning good working practices. A head of department, or director of graduate studies, or sub-dean, or whoever is responsible for such matters should have procedures to hand, and should be empowered to intervene constructively.

It is clear from our interviews with students and supervisors that the degree of personal friendship and commitment varies enormously. Some supervisors keep their students at arm's length, and restrict themselves to formal relationships. Others enjoy and encourage greater degrees of friendship and intimacy.

That brings us to one potentially delicate set of issues: sex and the supervisor. It arises in a minority of cases, but it does arise nevertheless, and can crop up in three possible ways: sexual harassment, sexual relations between student and supervisor by consent, and sex in the project.

Sexual harassment

In the BERA research, Eggleston and Delamont (1983) were told of one sexual harassment case by Geraldine Marsh, who wrote:

> My original supervisor has a reputation for making passes at female students. When this happened to me, I found offence was taken when I gave what the supervisor considered to be the wrong answers to his questions. The relationship grew worse, and I changed my supervisor.

In our experience, we have known one male lecturer who behaved in a way that distressed three women higher-degree students, one of whom claimed that when she refused his advances he withdrew supervisory help. There can be misunderstandings in this area: men may not realize that their behaviour is harassing, especially if they are from a different culture, class or religion from the student. There is the occasional disturbed student who sees sexual harassment where none existed, or where none was intended. It is hard to be friendly, sociable and supportive in a relationship with a power dimension. In general, those who wish to avoid accusations of sexual harassment should never touch a student unless invited to, be very careful when telling jokes or using endearments, avoid asking about students' personal and emotional lives, and try to ensure that social events and travel together are chaperoned. The problems with sexual harassment overlap those of consensual sexual relationships with students.

Sex and the student

There is a power dimension to supervision which complicates the idea of any *consensual* sexual relationship between student and supervisor, either gay or straight. Our feeling is that if a sexual relationship develops the student ought to have another supervisor. The guidelines for doctors and patients are a useful model for supervisors who feel an intimate relationship developing.

Sex in the project

There can be problems if the project is about sex, and/or if the supervisor and student disagree about sexual issues. Phillida Salmon (1992: 115) recounts a case of the latter kind:

> Another student whom I undertook to supervise was an apparently pleasant and conscientious person who brought evidence of high academic ability. Nonetheless, there was something about his research approach which made me feel very uncomfortable. Unwisely, I ignored these feelings. It was not until we had been working together for two years that it became obvious that his interest in his young women subjects was a prurient one. At this point I withdrew from a supervisory role which I should never have taken on.

Issues of sexual conduct are merely extensions of the more general issues we have been alluding to. They concern the establishment – the negotiation – of appropriate expectations, boundaries and mutual obligations within the supervisory relationship. They also serve to underline how significant the relationship is between the higher-degree student and the supervisor. It is not necessary to develop unduly intimate personal relationships in order to recognize that there is a strong element of mutual dependency inherent in the process of higher-degree work. The student is often dependent on the supervisor, not just for the formal aspects of the research – such as access to research facilities, technical advice and specific oversight of the work – but also for a host of less visible things, such as personal support and confidence-building, personal contacts and network-building. The supervisor's task is often one of striking a series of balances, between involvement and detachment, between directing students' work and letting them have their head. We turn to some aspects of that 'delicate balance' in Chapter 3.

3

The balance between tradition and progress: designing and planning a project

> It is rather difficult for us of the older generation to hold the balance
> between tradition and progress – if it is progress.
>
> (Sayers 1972: 44)

Introduction

The title of the chapter comes from Sayers but the theme is echoed in many of our interviews with social scientists and natural scientists in British universities and former polytechnics about their supervisory experiences with PhD students. Dr Crupiner, a geographer from Tolleshurst, told us: 'it causes a lot of angst to me creating a delicate balance between letting them do something which is their own and giving them a good topic.' This was the most succinct statement of one of the dilemmas facing the social science and natural science supervisors we studied between 1990 and 1993. Dr Crupiner talked of his 'angst' in creating a delicate balance between letting doctoral students pursue work which is their own and 'giving' them a research topic. Other academics constructed their accounts in terms of similar tensions and dilemmas. They described tensions and balances at every critical stage of the research process: not only topic choice, but also research design, data collection, analysis and text production. At all stages supervisors expressed a pull between their desire to exercise tight control and to allow the student the freedom that comes from non-interventionist supervision. The academic staff variously express the tensions and contradictions between the imposition of supervisory control on the one hand and granting of licence to students to pursue their own ideas on the other.

Dr Nuddington, a social scientist at Boarbridge, said he was much less directive than some of his colleagues:

> I have colleagues who will lay out a very clear-cut routine for the student
> to stick to – I'm a little bit more casual than that. I don't really believe in
> regimenting the students too much, because if I do that I'll impose my
> will on them too strongly – it's supposed to be their PhD not mine.

For the natural scientists, who were more likely to have teams of doctoral students and post-docs working on closely-related problems around a funded project, there was a tension between the individual thesis topics and the overall research programme. As Professor Nankivell, a natural scientist at Ottercombe, explained to us:

> In my mind I constantly try and weigh up the balance of supervision that is required and I've come to the conclusion that it depends on the individual, especially with my experience with the MSc person who needs his hand held all the time. Now I could have been really blunt with him and kicked him out but that wouldn't have benefited him but it would have benefited me because I would have got the research done that I had hoped, so I'm always balancing my own intentions, research in hand and trying to develop the individual's research skills and I find it a difficult balance to strike.

The appropriate balance between organizing the PhD for the student and watching them sink or swim on their own has been altered by the policy change. Today the funding bodies are imposing sanctions on institutions whose students do not submit inside the time limits. This was leading some of our respondents to report they had altered their supervisory pattern. One such was Dr Crupiner, a social scientist at Tolleshurst:

> sometimes a PhD student doesn't want to see you because they want this to be their own stuff and there's always a dilemma about saying to a student, 'This is a great topic, this is what you should do' and I'm more inclined to do that these days because of the time limit, whereas in the past I'd avoid it. It's caused a lot of angst.

Similar views on the increasing pressure from ESRC and the difficulties of the delicate balance can be seen in the interview with Dr Wishart, a social scientist at Latchendon:

> the PhD programme should really be a marriage of your interests and the student's interests. You develop together. Now I'm conscious of the pressures that are coming from the ESRC to churn over PhDs in terms of three or four years, but I perceive the PhD as something that is essentially your starting point in a long career . . . As a supervisor I'm not saying, 'You must produce Chapter One in four weeks, get them all done in ten months.' I much prefer to allow people to choose their own pace and in a sense to me that's a part of the learning process of being a PhD student. I think it's a lonely existence for many but I think they have to push at the limits, they have to engage the supervisor. I can push them to a certain extent, I can say, 'OK, what have you been doing for the last two or three weeks?' but in the end I'm going to put barriers in their way and they're going to have to jump over those barriers. I'm not necessarily going to demonstrate how to jump over those barriers. Some are smarter than others in terms of how they proceed with the problems of jumping over those hoops. Others are less certain and need more direction, more of a helping hand.

What must be avoided is described from our interview with Dr Mincing, a natural scientist at Ottercombe, who described his own experience as a student: 'my supervisor . . . hadn't had any experience of PhD students before and he took on four at the same time. And we all sat there in his room for the first year virtually doing nothing, twiddling our thumbs and accomplishing very little indeed.'

This chapter is about helping students and supervisors away from 'thumb twiddling' towards making a productive start on research design and the production of the thesis. If the student has courses to attend, then discussing the content of these, and any written or oral assessment requirements associated with them, provides a ready-made agenda for early supervisions. Going over the course content will serve three functions. First, it enables the supervisor to check that the student is actually attending the classes! Then it gives the supervisor an idea of the content of the courses and how far they are relevant to the individual student. Finally, the candidate's response to the courses will be revealing about the student's strengths and weaknesses: if he or she sees all discussions of ethics as irrelevant, or rejects all coverage of methods other than the one that has been chosen, then the supervisor has to widen her or his focus.

A checklist for early supervisions

The following issues are sensible ones to focus on in early supervisions, when you are overseeing the students' early days. In the handout we use in Cardiff we state that when choosing a thesis topic: 'There are six main criteria to bear in mind, and you should discuss your topic, bearing all six criteria in mind, with your supervisor as soon as s/he is allocated to you.' These six criteria are enjoyment, timetabling, thesis length, feasibility, methods and theoretical perspective.

Will I enjoy working on that topic?

Students have to be strongly motivated to complete a thesis. They must be allocated to or choose a topic that interests them and fires their imagination. If the thesis subject bores them, it is not likely to get finished. A good supervisor asks a student some searching questions about motivation to investigate their particular topic, and expects the student to evaluate their own commitment to the topic. It is important not to confuse your own enthusiasm for a research topic with a student's. Beware of attributing your own intellectual and personal agenda to your graduate students. Equally, one's own agenda should not be allowed to pour cold water on students' research plans inappropriately.

Timetable

Second, the supervisor is likely to be more experienced than the student, and therefore more realistic about the timetabling of research projects. Ask the student to focus on the following: How long the student has got to finish the thesis? By what date does it have to be handed in? What are the earliest and latest dates for submission? When do you and the student actually plan to complete it? Then encourage them to draw up a timetable, and think about designing a project that fits into the time they have. In our own classes with graduate students, we find it helpful to work with specimen research timetables like those given below, full of deliberate mistakes. In class, we have the students work through such a timetable, find the ten mistakes, and learn from them how to make their own realistic schedules. A realistic timetable is a great help: an unrealistic one is depressing, so ensure that they review theirs regularly and keep it realistic. The three specimen timetables reproduced here – one for a social survey, one for a piece of geographical fieldwork, the third for a history project – have been carefully designed to be riddled with common faults. If all of them are wrong for your students, it is not difficult to prepare one that will allow them to 'spot the mistakes'. We have not spelled out all the errors here, but the most obvious ones in the social science project include concentrating too much data collection over Christmas and New Year, and leaving out any time for piloting the computer analysis of the questionnaire results. The geology one includes doing fieldwork at high altitude when snow would be several metres thick. The history one fails to allow any time for getting access to the archive. All three have the common flaws of a literature review that stops too soon, and a 'write up' that starts too late.

Length of thesis

The supervisor has a duty to prevent the student embarking on an overambitious programme, which would involve collecting far more data than anyone could ever use. The supervisor knows the word limit and should know roughly what size and shape of project will fit neatly into that word length. Get the student to focus on: What is the maximum length the thesis can be? Plan the research so it can be written up properly within the word limit. As the supervisor you should be able to help the candidate plan a study that can 'fit' into the limit prescribed for the relevant degree registration. As is shown by the example of Colin Ives in Chapter 2, it is easy to think students know what a thesis is and can plan their own work accordingly.

Figure 3.1: Proposed timetable for social science PhD programme

Specimen – faulty timetable for a survey of health workers

	2004		2005						2006						2007					
	OCT	DEC	FEB	APR	JUN	AUG	OCT	DEC	FEB	APR	JUN	AUG	OCT	DEC	FEB	APR	JUN	AUG		

1 Literature review
2 Establish contacts with community, identify social and health services, community workers
3 Prepare pilot questionnaire –
(1) Design
(2) Translation
(3) Pre-test
(4) Administer
4 Main research –
(1) Refine questionnaire
(2) Organise fieldwork
(3) Administer
(4) Editing and coding
(5) Computer analysis
5 Analyse research findings
6 Assembly and writing of thesis

Figure 3.2: Proposed timetable for earth science PhD programme

Specimen – faulty, timetable for research in Switzerland

	2004		2005					2006					2007	
	OCT	DEC	FEB	JUN	AUG	OCT	DEC	FEB	APR	JUN	OCT	DEC	FEB	APR
1 Literature review	——	——												
2 Pilot fieldwork at 3,700 m		——	——											
3 (1) Analyse pilot results				——										
(2) Plan main study					——									
4 Main data collection at 3,700 m							——							
5 (1) Sort and classify specimens										——				
(2) Code data											——			
6 Computer analysis												——		
7 Analyse findings													——	
8 Assembly and writing of thesis														——

Figure 3.3: Proposed timetable for history PhD programme

Specimen – faulty, timetable for a biography of Elizabeth Twining

	2004		2005				2006				2007		2008
	OCT	DEC	FEB	APR	JUN	AUG	OCT	DEC	FEB	APR	JUN	AUG	OCT	DEC	FEB	APR

1 Literature review: published works

  (1) Twining family

  (2) Victorian philanthropy

  (3) Middle-class women

2 Access

  Negotiate access to archives

  Prelim. visit to archives

3 Time in archive

4 Analysis of notes made in archive

5 Write thesis

Example 3.1: Too much

Peter Rosen was registered for the EdD. The word limit is 40,000 words. His original supervisor retired, and Peter was transferred to Sara. She discovered that he had drafted 100,000 words of his thesis but had not yet analysed his data. It was a miserable start to a new relationship. Sara warned him about the word limit, and encouraged him to analyse and write up his data. However, eventually they had to work out how to cut the 100,000 words down to 20,000 to leave room for the results.

Feasibility?

There is also the issue of feasibility. Novices may have no idea about the related issues of practical feasibility and 'political' feasibility. Ask the candidate to consider the following kinds of questions and be brutally realistic: Will you be able to get to the fieldsite? Will the data be available? What lab equipment will you need? What advice is available? What software exists? As a supervisor you may be more alert to practical and political problems than the students. Going out into the field to do geological data collection, for example, can take much longer than a novice imagines. Theo Karras, a geology PhD student at Ottercombe, found that on his first field trip, 'it took a long time to actually – just to get my eyes to be able to see things in the rocks that you are meant to see,' which meant he was more realistic in his plans for his next one although he foresaw new problems: 'I think I'll have to hire a car because its a very big area and I'll have to drive . . . and I've explained all that to NERC and they've said they don't pay for cars.' Supervisors, more advanced students and post-docs may be helpful at the planning stage. Encourage the student to discuss the practicalities with more experienced colleagues.

For social scientists negotiating access to a setting, or drumming up enough respondents is a typical problem of feasibility. In the South Wales area, local education authorities in the 1970s and 1980s would not allow anyone to conduct research involving IQ tests, or inquiries asking pupils to rate their teachers' abilities. Knowledgeable supervision could prevent a student from wasting time designing projects based on either focus.

Example 3.2: Impossible topic

Gus Daly thought he wanted to do his professional doctorate thesis on the illness narratives of ileostomy patients (that is people who have had their ileum surgically removed, and have to manage a bag instead). He had a sympathetic consultant to help him get ethical approval, and went to meet a group of potential informants at a regular self-help meeting, and fixed up a pilot interview. However, when he came to focus on the illness narrative of this patient, and his notes of the meeting, he felt repulsed. Gus and Paul agreed this was not a sensible thesis topic, if he could not stomach the 'gory details' and procedures.

Methods

The fifth criterion is the choice of research methods. The student needs to be able to master the necessary methods, to enjoy using them, *and* to have intellectual confidence in the results that these methods generate. Ask the student to focus, honestly, on the following: Does their topic involve methods of data collection *and* data analysis that they (a) *believe* in? (b) can use, or can learn to use? They need to select a method of data collection they trust, that they can learn to be an expert in, and methods of analysis they believe in and can master (with help). Such methodological choices are especially pertinent in the social sciences and some aspects of the humanities, where epistemological issues are contested, and methods of data collection and analysis carry with them a good deal of theoretical and philosophical freight. In the natural sciences, choices of method are normally rather different kinds of consideration. Normal scientific practice rests on methods that are more taken-for-granted within particular networks or research groups. For the graduate student the issues are more likely to confront them as practical ones: Is the correct technique for my chosen problem available in this lab, or in this group? Where do I go to learn new techniques, if I need to? Here the task of the supervisor is more likely to involve checking that the student has either mastered the necessary techniques, or is receiving the best possible advice and training. Similar issues arise quite frequently for the social-science supervisor and student, and indeed among humanities students as well. Students may have to cope with particular skills in acquiring data: the historian may need to learn or improve a foreign language, the specialist knowledge required to decipher manuscripts, computer software and so on; the social scientist may need to acquire skills in a variety of data collection techniques, and analytic procedures – including computational skills. Not only is it important for the supervisor and the student to establish what methodological skills will be needed, it is even more important that they jointly establish *how* they will be acquired. Formal training courses cannot be guaranteed to cover all the necessary issues, and supervisors need to recognize that they are not omniscient, and need to seek out the best sources of help and advice for their candidates. In the laboratory sciences, expertise is often passed on from postdoctoral researchers to the new generation of research students, while the supervisor offers more general advice. In other disciplines too, up-to-date methodological advice may be available most readily from research fellows and other junior academics.

Theoretical perspectives

The sixth criterion may not apply in all disciplines, but in many there are theoretical perspectives to be considered. The student needs to be happy about their theoretical perspective, intellectually committed to it, and able to master it, before the thesis is too far advanced to change either the theory or the research design. Again, this is especially significant in the humanities and social sciences, where broad theoretical and epistemological issues are hotly contested. In such contexts, 'theory' has a very different function from that of most laboratory science, and implies a general perspective, determining choices of problem, choice of approach, identification with a particular intellectual tradition, and so on. For many students, it is unrealistic to speak of a 'choice' of orientation on this scale. By the time they embark on graduate research work, many have become committed to a particular intellectual style, and have adopted a theoretical 'position'. In our view, indeed, graduate students become identified with such theoretical stances too early and too firmly, adopting them as articles of faith rather than subjecting them to critical scrutiny. Often, of course, the working relationship between student and supervisor is founded on a commonality of perspective, and such shared views are not always conducive to a critical reflection on fundamental assumptions. Nevertheless, students need to be encouraged to work critically within particular paradigms, and to resist the adoption of a given perspective while remaining in ignorance of alternative, even competing, orientations. Enthusiasm and blind faith are not the best foundations for scholarly inquiry, and a supervisor may have to act as devil's advocate and sceptical inquirer in order to force the student to reflect on her or his chosen perspective.

The importance of ethics

Students may not realize the importance of ethical issues. Social science research students for example, may not realize how carefully they need to protect their informants. Students do not have to intend to behave in unethical ways in order to find practical difficulties: the unintended consequences of research – especially on controversial issues – often call for a good deal of careful thought. Inexperienced students may find it hard to think through all the possible ramifications and implications of their work. Supervisors need to ensure that their students are thoroughly acquainted with ethical guidelines and requirements – especially formal guidelines relating to laboratory work (especially with animals), professional codes of conduct, legal requirements (such as the Data Protection Act in the UK, and similar legislation elsewhere), the requirements of national or local ethics committees, and so on. Students whose experience does not extend beyond the undergraduate degree, and who have never had to undertake independent research, may well need explicit and systematic reviews of ethical guidelines and their practical consequences. To some extent, such considerations also spill over into more general considerations concerning the 'politics' of the research. Where a research problem has special topical importance – and that can arise in many disciplines – students may need to think about the possible consequences, public and personal, of the research.

This is an area where a student may learn from a 'cautionary tale', such as Example 3.3.

Example 3.3: The external's brother

Ralph Paton had conducted interviews with twenty admissions tutors to architectural schools as part of his PhD. Sara, one of the externals, noticed nothing amiss. However, the other external, Ruth Kettering, opened the viva with the complaint that the respondents had not been carefully enough disguised: one was her brother, a well-known architect, and she was sure everyone in architectural education would spot him immediately. Ruth referred the thesis for Ralph to redraft in ways that would disguise her brother.

The doctoral training now required in the UK includes a compulsory course in research ethics, but students may not necessarily apply what they have learnt to their own work. Because some of the ethical issues can be foreseen by the supervisor, they can be discussed and planned for at this early stage. If the project will need an animal licence, or involve the Data Protection Act, this needs to be discussed at the outset. The student can also start to write about the ethical issues while they are fresh in both your minds.

Research design

When your students design their thesis projects, you should also ensure that they are thinking ahead. They should be planning the general shape of the eventual thesis as well as making a rough timetable of the kind we have already recommended of how they are going to research the topic. Get your students to show both to you as their supervisor and get an agreed research design, thesis plan and work schedule. These will need regular review, and probable revision: it is helpful to discuss the plans and timetable at regular intervals throughout the life of the project.

Because research design is extremely subject-specific, there is little generalized advice that we can give. However, it is always important for the supervisor to remember that students are novices, and will not necessarily know how to design a piece of research in their discipline: they are being supervised in order to learn how to design and conduct research. It is often helpful to get students to argue against the particular techniques they plan to use – in other words, to understand the limitations of whatever methods they choose. In a laboratory context, they need to learn from recently completed post-docs about how their external examiners challenged the research group's approach, in order to help them gain a broader perspective on the pros and cons.

In the social sciences there are, quite literally, hundreds of books on research methods, and many on design, so the supervisor can encourage students to use the literature to inform their decisions. Social science students may need your expert guidance on how data generated from the different methods are analysed in order to start learning the relevant tech-niques. Social scientists also have to think carefully about sampling, negotiat-ing access to a research sample or population, ethical issues, as well as choice of method and design. Increasingly the supervisor needs to warn about how long some procedures will take, and about the need to keep a diary record-ing the processes of decision-making and the design phase. Both arts and social science students need to be writing even at this early stage, and we have suggested some appropriate writing after the next section, which deals with access, and is primarily for social scientists.

Helping them get access

Frequently a student can get access to the data/research site/population without help. However, it is nearly always useful to encourage them to discuss access with you, and to write up that phase as they go. The handout repro-duced as Figure 3.4 is used primarily for supervisors in the social sciences. Because access to a research population is so crucial to social scientists, we run whole classes on that topic.

For humanities disciplines, the relevant material may be in the public domain, but if it is not, the student may need the supervisor's help. If you were supervising a historian trying to write a biography of Elizabeth Twining, and you had been at Oxford with one of the current generation of the family you can write an introductory letter for your student. One example of pro-viding help through an 'old boy' network is the case of the Bassington-ffrench archives.

Example 3.4: The Bassington-ffrench archives

In the 1970s Mary Debenham, a colleague of Sara's, was writing a book about the nineteenth-century education system of Norwich and Ches-ter. The Bassington-ffrench family had been pioneers of technical schooling in Chester, and Sara had known William Bassington-ffrench at Cambridge. She wrote to him, and he passed on the request to his grandfather, Thomas. Mary Debenham was able to do a life-history interview with Thomas, who recalled his father and grandfather setting up the technical school, *and* get access to private family papers.

Figure 3.4: Access (handout for students)

Getting access to do your research can be time-consuming, needs care, must be discussed with your supervisor, and must be documented. It should be written up as you go along while the scars are fresh. Text-books on ethnographic methods spend whole chapters on access – e.g. Hammersley and Atkinson (1995) *Ethnography: Principles in Practice* and Burgess (1984) *In the Field*. Books on questionnaire design don't usually discuss access so much. Even if you plan a questionnaire study, read one of the chapters in an ethnography book on access to sensitize yourself.

Basic points to bear in mind

1   Does your study need to go to an ethics committee or an LEA committee, or into any bureaucracy? This needs *checking out* – you need to discover what the rules are, and what procedures have to be followed; *then* you need to allow time to go through such hoops; *and* you need to discuss with your supervisor how to present yourself to that bureaucracy.
2   Who are the gatekeepers for your research? Ask around to see if particular named people will make the decisions, and see if anyone you already know has connections to them. If someone in the department was at school with the gatekeepers, or your old headteacher knows them, or they did an MEd here, or the gate-keeper's spouse was in the same cricket team as your supervisor's cousin . . . use the network.
3   Think carefully about how letters are written. Should they be hand-written or word processed? From home or college? (Make sure there are no spelling mistakes!) How much should you say about the project in the initial letter?
4   If you are going to meet a gatekeeper, think carefully about how you dress for it. Your self-presentation could lose you the access.
5   Don't make promises you can't/won't keep.
6   Remember access is a process, not a single event.
7   Keep a diary of the process, keep copies of all documents.
8   Write up the access negotiations as you go along while they are fresh.
9   Read some accounts of access proceedings. There is a good one in Linda Valli's (1986) *Becoming Clerical Workers*, and another in G. A. Fine's (1983) *Shared Fantasy*. (The access processes are often in the methods appendix.)

Many novice researchers in arts and social sciences are caught out by the length of time that negotiating access can take. As funding bodies increasingly press universities to get students to complete in three years, there is less time to spare for lengthy access negotiations. Paul's own career shows how times have changed.

Example 3.5: Prolonged access

When Paul was starting his PhD he began access negotiations with a Scottish medical school, asking to do participant observation on the wards. He eventually got access (Atkinson 1981, 1984) but it took a year. In those days of relaxed attitudes to submission dates this was not seen as a major problem by Paul or his supervisor – Paul waited, doing other things. Today, no supervisor could allow a student to 'waste' a year.

For many students the design phase is followed by a hiatus, and they can lose momentum. While some supervisors like the student to work on the literature, for others, the step after design and starting access is a pilot study. In science disciplines the student may need to learn to use, or start to build, the equipment needed for the experiments. Our preferred 'next step' is to encourage students to start writing parts of the methods chapter, and we discuss that next.

The methods chapter

For many social science research students the methods chapter is a good one to write early on, and a useful test for the supervisor. If the student needs help with writing, the sooner the supervisor is aware of that the better. Equally, if the student writes well, praise for the draft material will be a great motivator. Encouraging the student to plan and draft the methods chapter early on is a wise move. We use the handout (Figure 3.5) with an attached worksheet (Figure 3.6). To help social science students think about what their methods chapter can and should contain, we ask them to role play being an external examiner, and to discuss in small groups what they would expect to find in a thesis. The worksheet reproduced as Figure 3.6 is obviously designed for sociology PhD students: the second example is a reference to Barbara Heyl's (1979) work, the others are invented. Both figures can be easily adapted by a group of colleagues to fit many disciplines.

Figure 3.5: The methods chapter/appendix

Somewhere in the thesis there must be a discussion of your methods – a whole chapter/part of a chapter/an appendix.

This should contain four elements:

1   Discussion of the academic literature on the method(s) you used.
2   Reference(s) to at least one other study that used the same method(s).
3   An account of how they worked when you used it/them (which should be *honest* but not self-indulgent).
4   Copies of all your research instruments – in an appendix.

Items 1 and 2 are necessary to show that you have studied the literature, 3 and 4 are essential for anyone who wants to replicate your study.

1   Make sure that you show that you have understood the pros and cons of the method(s) you have chosen. All methods have advantages and disadvantages – you need to show that you realize that.
2   There are two kinds of literature you can refer to here – *either* published studies *or* the 'autobiographical' accounts people write – both are useful. Methods are usually discussed in the appendices of published books – check them out as you read.
3   It is difficult to get the balance between reporting what you did in sufficient detail and being too fussy/detailed/boring. In the first draft, put down everything and then get your supervisor to help you cut it down. Don't pretend it all went smoothly according to the text book if it didn't but equally try not to make yourself look too incompetent.

Write early and write often
This methods chapter is one that you can start writing early in the registration period. As you take each step, write a draft section about it. Doing this while it is fresh in your mind and filing them carefully is very prudent and sensible.

A flying start

If a student undertakes all the tasks suggested in this chapter, by the end of their first three months of registration they should be aware that they have made a flying start. Remember to praise students explicitly for the fact that they have made a good start – they cannot know they are doing well unless you tell them. As we emphasized in Chapter 2, the establishment of a sound working relationship, the building of trust and mutual confidence and the

Figure 3.6: Worksheet on the methods chapter

Imagine you are the external examiner for a set of theses. One of your jobs is to vet the methods chapter. Taking each of these examples, make a checklist of what information you would need/expect to find in the methods chapter.

1 A survey, using a postal questionnaire, of primary head teachers in two LEAs on their attitudes to race and gender equality.
2 Life-history of a brothel-keeper (madam) using several interviews.
3 An analysis of diaries kept by sweetshop owners.
4 Open-ended interviews with people coping with migraine.

establishment of sound routines are all important ingredients in building the foundations of successful supervision. In this chapter we have stressed various ways in which that foundation can be built on: getting students off on the right footing and establishing the basis of the research itself. While higher-degree students should not feel pressured into premature fieldwork or other kinds of data collection, it is clear from many of the interviews we conducted, as well as from more anecdotal evidence from colleagues, that it is all too easy for research students to drift and for valuable time to pass unproductively. Moreover, if students start to feel aimless, or feel that their work is not progressing, then self-confidence can be damaged. If, on the other hand, students can be encouraged to make a 'flying start' then confidence will grow, research plans can be progressed realistically, and supervisor and student will both feel positive about the research process.

4

Old manuscripts: the literature review

after a fruitless rummage in a cupboard . . . she dragged out an ancient
trunk, unlocked it and flung back the lid. A close, cold odour. Books.
Discarded garments. Old shoes. Old Manuscripts.

(Sayers 1972: 9)

Introduction

Whatever the discipline, the doctoral student has to get to grips with the
literature, and learn how to find it, read it, assimilate it and write about it.
This chapter deals with helping the students to find the literature, make a
permanent record of it for themselves, read it intelligently, and write the
review of the literature. It also deals with teaching them to cite and prepare
reference lists correctly.

It is easy to overestimate the level of library skills that students have. In the
research we have done, we regularly find students who did not know that
inter-library loans existed – or other *basic* things, like where the back numbers of journals were shelved. All departments should organize sessions on
library and information use run by specialist staff from the library or information centre: if yours does not, then you should fix up training for your
own students. However, it is only reasonable to discuss with the librarian what
can be covered: the best librarians in the world will not know what your
students need unless you have run through relevant issues with them. Setting
up training sessions with the specialist librarian(s) is always beneficial to
students, especially if your university is not in the same city as a copyright
library.

Helping the student with finding the literature

Encourage your students to make friends with the relevant library and
information staff. Warn them always to be polite, patient and remember to
thank library (and computer centre) staff and to acknowledge their help in
everything they write! Failure to get such personnel on the student's team
can cause missed opportunities. When a good relationship is established,
there can be far-reaching consequences. When Sara worked in the School of
Education at Leicester University the specialist librarian, Roy Kirk, was active
in the professional association, LISE (Librarians in Schools and Institutes of

---

Example 4.1: Sins find you out

Dr Jonathan Marder says, loudly and publicly, that reading the literature is a waste of time: that creative scholars are making the field at the frontier not reading the past. Experienced colleagues know this is a rhetorical pose: he has actually read and internalized much of the canon of his field: penology. His PhD and DCrim students sometimes treat what he says literally: in the past three years two of his PhD students have had their theses referred for inadequate literature reviews. Dr Marder does not regard a dutiful and thorough literature review as important, so never enquires whether his students know the field – indeed he seems to assume they share his mastery of it and do not need to rehearse it.

Education). When Roy, Sara and one of the library staff – Barbara Barr – discovered that there was no published bibliography or union list of histories of girls' schools, Roy got LISE to sponsor Barbara to research and produce one which they then published (Barr 1984). That union list is still the basic research source for anyone working on the history of women's education. Here a close working relationship between a young scholar and experienced librarians had benefits for everyone.

Example 4.2: Belle Flanagan

Belle Flanagan is one of the university's great assets. A passionate archaeologist herself, she is a long-standing librarian in the archaeology library, and publishes on local archaeology and librarianship. She loves helping students track down material: thesis after thesis contains a heartfelt acknowledgement to her professional and personal support.

Many undergraduates have not become familiar with the range of periodicals in the discipline, so research students need to find out which are the most important journals relevant to their thesis: by asking not only you, and the specialist library staff, but also post-doctoral researchers and your colleagues. Discussing the newest journals, the most authoritative ones, which ones are in the hands of small cabals, which accept a wide range of perspectives, is an important part of orienting students to the literature. You can help by discussing where you publish, which periodicals you subscribe to yourself, and which ones you have to get on-line or on inter-library loan, and why. This is often the first opportunity to talk about the learned societies and about academic publishing houses.

Other theses

Undergraduates will probably not have used theses before, so this is another category of literature the research student needs to focus on. There are three categories of theses that it may be helpful to steer your students towards. Your own doctoral thesis is often fascinating for your students: to see how the field has changed, to realize you yourself were once a rank beginner, and to remind them you were young yourself once. If you were a PhD student at the place where you now teach, your students can read it easily. If not, then you might put a copy in the postgraduate room, or offer to lend it to selected candidates. If there are publications from your PhD, such as journal articles or a monograph, you can suggest that your students might compare the thesis and the publications to see how the same data appear in the two formats (Richardson 1990).

The second category of theses your students need to read is successful ones in their discipline in their university. They need to get a feel for the length, format, style and scope of past theses in the university where they are registered. Try to steer them to excellent examples, and discuss their responses to them. Again, if there is a recent graduate of the department who has published from the doctoral research, the doctoral student can compare the thesis and the publication(s). If your department or research group has produced several 'generations' of doctoral students developing a research tradition, explain to the new student that external examiners will look for the local school of thought in their literature review. The third category of theses the student may need to consult is those in other British (and American) universities. Steer them to British theses which are listed in the *Index of Theses*, and American ones which can be traced from *Dissertation Abstracts International.* The library staff will be delighted to show postgraduates how to use these indexes.

Abstracts

Undergraduates are unlikely to have used any of the online or published abstracts. Most libraries subscribe to several sets of abstracts and post-graduates should learn to use them. These are useful but a student can be swamped by the sheer volume of previous scholarship. Two respondents to the Delamont and Eggleston (1981) survey, from the same university, reported that

> Students pioneered and established a link with the ERIC information retrieval system with help of computer centre staff. Department didn't want to know until the feasibility work was done.
>
> (Charles Enderby)

> The literature search remains a never-ending headache. The infinite extendibility of the academic enterprise means it is very difficult to know

when to stop. What is a reasonable literature search very much depends upon the topic and the problem. I am extremely ambivalent about specialist indexes as they are both an aid and a torment . . . The library here is very poor . . . Access to the literature is fairly straightforward. Although I do have to shamefacedly admit that I have never come to terms with *Dissertation Abstracts International.*

(Ronny Devereux)

Online and computer searches

It is important that your students find out how to do computer searches, how much they cost, (if anything) and what they are allowed to do, paid for by the department. The facilities here and their capabilities are changing so fast that your students may be ahead of you already, but they may not. If this is an area where you feel fully confident you can show your students what to do, but if not the specialist librarians are best placed to help them – your role is to remind them to ask nicely!

This is an excellent topic for a seminar or workshop with the students doing theses sharing their search strategies. If there is a taught course, with sessions taken by the library, it can be followed up by academics. If not, a good supervisor can usefully get all his or her students to pool their ideas. As the technology changes, it is plausible for a supervisor to plead ignorance of the latest wrinkles, and appear to be asking students for help – thus ensuring that they get clued up. You will know you are succeeding when they start to bring you references for your work that you have missed.

The literature search is a good opportunity to start the student's acquaintance with the politics and practicalities of publication in your discipline. If your field now works mainly by e-mail and electronic publishing, if pre-prints are vital, if conference papers are central, if certain journals are much higher status than others, this is the time to help the student discover that for himself or herself. Sooner or later the research student needs to know which are the best sources of new ideas in the specialism, and looking for literature is one way to learn that.

Helping the student with taking notes

The student may lack skills in taking notes on their reading, perhaps not knowing what to record, and they may be hopeless at organizing and storing their notes on what they have read. It is important that you help them to recognize that the quality of their thesis will depend on how adequately they research the field in which they are going to write it. The quality of the notes they take on what they read is an important part of mastering/mistressing any field. Figure 4.1 provides a checklist of things students in social science should put into their notes, which we give out at Cardiff. It should be straightforward for any supervisor to produce an equivalent in his or her discipline.

Figure 4.1: Specimen checklist on note-taking

Your notes should always include:

1   Full bibliographical details

    (a) The full name(s) of the author(s);
    (b) the title of the book/article;
    (c) the date published originally (so you know if it is an old, or a new study) and of the edition you are using;
    (d) publisher, place of publication (if it is a book);
    (e) name of the journal/book and page numbers (if an article).

2   The Library catalogue number (e.g. LC5146.H27) so you can find it again! (And even the ISSN or ISBN number).

In addition you should check, and note:

3   Is it an original study, or a report of other people's work? (primary or secondary source)
4   Is it empirical (has data in it) or theoretical or polemical? (argumentative)
5   What methods were used? (e.g. computer modelling, experiments, field measurements)
6   What theory is cited?
7   What are the author's conclusions? (i.e. what did she find out/prove?)
8   On what date was the research *done* (may be many years before it was published).
9   The number of informants/subjects sampled, the response rate(s). The breakdown of the sample by age/race/sex, etc.

Many of the items in Figure 4.1 may seem crushingly obvious. However, students frequently have no idea they will need all this information if they cite the publication in the thesis. Most undergraduate students have never looked at the technical bits of a book, or journal, such as the ISBN or ISSN. Encouraging new postgraduates to focus on such things helps their career. Our experience is that few students have ever noticed that books have ISBNs, or got into the habit of recording all the details of a reference. A workshop on the practicalities of note-taking and recording all the details is a good point for British supervisors to introduce the CVCP categorization system for collecting publication details from universities, and explain it (Figure 4.2).

Figure 4.2: CVCP publication categories

1 Authored books
2 Edited books
3 Short works
4 Conference contributions, refereed
5 Conference contributions, other
6 Departmental working papers
7 Edited works, contributions
8 Editorships, journals
9 Editorships, newsletters
10 Journal letters, notes, short papers or abstracts
11 Academic journal papers
12 Professional journal papers
13 Popular journal papers
14 Official report
15 Review articles
16 Reviews of single academic books
17 Other publications, research
18 Other publications, research equivalent
19 Other media, research
20 Other media, research equivalent

The CVCP categories, which have been used since the mid 1980s, are a relatively straightforward way of classifying publications and other outputs. All the universities in Britain collect a list of all the output of all the staff each year, and the categories are also used in the periodic British government Research Assessment Exercises. Most of the categories are self-explanatory, but it is worth quoting the explanations of the three types of journal article:

> Journal paper (Categories 11–13)
> The three categories provided, academic (Category 11), popular (Category 13) and professional (Category 12) are meant to cover all possibilities. An academic journal (Category 11) normally contains research papers aimed primarily at the academic and research community. The paper will normally be refereed, but may not be. A professional journal (Category 12) is normally aimed at practising members of a profession and mainly contains papers informing members of current developments in the profession rather than communicating research results. Such papers will not normally be refereed by the academic and research community, although they may be.

Clearly Category 11 is the high-status one in academia, but it can be useful to publish things in Category 12 because that is a form of dissemination to users and beneficiaries, or Category 13, because popular journals pay fees.

Categories 17 or 18 are designed to include music scores or scripts. Categories 19 or 20 can include performances of music or plays and works of art such as sculpture or paintings. Other possible entries here are architectural or engineering designs, or maps or software. Each year institutions collect data on publications and other outputs, classified by the RAE Unit of Assessment, the CVCP category and the authorship fraction attributable to that institution.

Supervising the student's recording of the literature is a good point to introduce discussion of software, of back-up systems and horror stories about lost quotes. There are several good software packages available for storing references and also for keeping indexed notes on the literature. It is useful to get the student an introduction to one or more of these, to see if they are enthused by them. If the student prefers to keep notes on file cards or on paper or in notebooks, ensure this *is* a genuine preference and not computer phobia. Either way, stress (repeatedly) that computerized records need to be backed up and the back-ups kept safely in a different place from the originals, *and* that hand-written records can, and should, be photocopied or carboned, and the back-ups put in a safe place. Remind the student of this periodically. Our department has a safe, in which we ask, even urge, students to place their back-up disks, but few of them bother except when there has been a burglary, or theft or fire that has destroyed the work of a fellow student. Stories of colleagues wasting hours trying to track down a quotation or citation that is central to a text but which has got detached from its proper origins serve as cautionary tales.

Example 4.3: Connor Bantry

Connor Bantry's EdD had been a long time in the making. Head of a difficult school, with his most trusted deputy away ill, Connor had had multiple extensions. In the end the thesis preparation was rushed: there were 27 missing citations, 38 citations were incomplete, and there were four different styles of presenting the items mixed up. The thesis had to be referred to have the bibliography done properly. Because that was essential the external insisted on several other additions and alterations as well.

When we tell this story to our students they are sceptical about it, so it is necessary to set up concrete examples of the miseries caused by lost citations to drive the message home. If you or a colleague can afford to employ a new PhD student to check the bibliography of one of your articles or books for publication and there are some missing references, this is a neat way of training them to be more precise themselves without them noticing.

Finding the literature and recording it is not the end of the story.

Helping the student to read

Professional librarians can help the student find relevant literature, and they or the local computing experts can help them to record it. Only the supervisor can train the student to read professionally, in a way different from their successful undergraduate reading strategies. Researchers are, first and foremost, readers. The appropriate sources, and the techniques of reading them in science can be learnt in the research group: perhaps by hearing a more advanced doctoral student or a post-doc pull together the key issues in the relevant journals. Gilbert and Mulkay (1984) provide an account of how journal articles on oxidative phosphorylation were read by other leading and young biochemists. The doctoral student has to learn how to read the relevant literature, and write coherent accounts of it. In the humanities and social sciences, reading, defining relevance, and producing the review of the literature is a more diffuse task with more scope for individualized styles of attack. The literature review is not only a ritually positioned chapter in the thesis: that review is also the source of hypotheses and the entry to other worlds. Delamont (2002) devotes a chapter to reading which can be recommended to social science and humanities students, but there is no equivalent guide for science students. For arts and social science students there are three types of reading to be done: reading on the topic, contrastive reading and analytical reading. Novice students need to recognize the three types and plan their reading to mix them. Reading *on* the topic is the only kind that most people think of doing, yet it is the least interesting. Students need to be encouraged to do all three types. Delamont (2002: 10–30) offers worked examples of the three types of reading relevant to five different educational research projects. Here we have exemplified those three types with a sociological topic, a history project, and a literary one which leaves readers in other disciplines to imagine their own.

A sociological research project

Eileen Brent is going to study the Corfiot community in Cardiff. There are about 25,000 people of Greek and Greek Cypriot origin in Cardiff, within that is a substantial Corfiote minority some of whom are unusual in being Roman Catholic not Greek Orthodox. Eileen's reading *on* her topic is pretty obvious: material on

1 Corfu, the Ionian islands, Greece and Cyprus;
2 on Greek emigrants to Britain, Australia, the USA, and Canada; and
3 on other 'Mediterranean' immigrants to the UK such as Cypriots, Maltese, Italians and Portuguese.

Her supervisor should be able to steer her to those literatures without difficulty. Eileen's reading for contrast might include

1 the literature on other immigrant groups from other faiths and ethnic groups such as Muslims from Pakistan or Rastafarians from Jamaica;
2 the literature on Roman Catholic versus Greek Orthodox beliefs;
3 studies of other multi-racial ports, such as San Diego;
4 novels of exiles and minorities.

Her reading for analytic categories might include whatever anthropological or sociological theorists she and her supervisor have agreed upon, plus those espoused by the leading authors of other studies of ethnicity in the UK and especially in Wales.

A historical research project

Greta Onlsson is planning to centre her PhD on the life of Elizabeth Twining (1805–89), an educational and biological pioneer. Her reading on her topic will clearly include everything on Elizabeth, her sister Louisa (the pioneer of social work/workhouse visiting) and their family; Elizabeth's friends and colleagues, her enemies and opponents, and the pupils who attended the school she ran. The reading for contrast might include histories and biographies of male educational and biological pioneers; of women equivalent to Elizabeth in the USA or Australia; or studies of other commercial 'dynasties' such as the Bulmers, Cadburys or Rothschilds. The analytic categories would probably come from feminist history, or from self-consciously anti-feminist history.

A literary research project

Donald Ross is going to study images of science, scientists and engineers in the novels of Trollope, Mrs Gaskell and George Eliot. His reading on the topic will start with the novels (probably in Trollope's case only a selection of them), central texts of literary criticism and histories of 'popular' science in the nineteenth century. The reading for contrast might include histories of science and engineering in other periods (such as Ancient Greece) or other cultures (such as China); contemporary literature with scientific or engineering themes; or studies of other issues in nineteenth-century fiction (such as slavery, or illness, or religion). The reading for analytic categories would be literary theory.

 The general message of this section is that students need guidance on how to read appropriately for their discipline. They need to understand how scholars in their field read and assimilate the relevant literature. Some students read too widely, and need to be brought back to the central purpose of the thesis. Others bitterly resent time spent on anything not *directly* relevant to their own definition of their topic, as this respondent of Rudd's (1985: 93):

One was offered, for example, texts to be read by beat poets like Alan Ginsberg, or novelists like Norman Mailer, who interesting writers though they are, didn't seem to me, and still don't seem to me, to have the level of seriousness of Herman Melville, or Nathaniel Hawthorne or of Mark Twain.

If this man's supervisors had good reasons to expect him to read Mailer and Ginsberg, they had not explained them clearly, or convinced the candidate. Enthusing the student to read creatively and professionally does not get the literature review written. That is your next task.

Helping the student with writing the literature review

Do get the student to check – by looking at some relevant theses in your area – how many words are usually spent on reviewing the literature in successful past theses. In a 20,000-word MSc thesis it may only be about 2000–3000 words. In a 40,000-word MPhil, or EdD thesis reporting an empirical project, 5000 words will probably be ample. In an 80,000-word PhD, 7000 words on the literature may be plenty. Many theses have reviews that are too long and unfocused. Of course if the whole MA or MSc thesis, or even the whole MPhil or professional doctorate thesis, is an exegesis of 'the literature', these guidelines would not apply. Students will probably need to make the first draft of the literature review at least twice or three times the length of the version that appears in the final thesis.

Example 4.4: The off-putting review

Sara was the examiner for Keziah Dane's PhD thesis at Castleton. There was no word limit for doctoral theses, and Keziah's had come in about 120,000 words. The literature review was about 190 pages long, and gave a very bad impression of the thesis. The original research was of doctoral quality, but it was proceeded by the 190 pages of incredibly dull, dutiful recapitulation of previous work. The structure was chronological, from 1918 to 2000, there was no critical perspective, and no care had been taken to relate the literature to the empirical work which, eventually, followed. It was neither use nor ornament.

The problem with helping novice scholars prepare their literature review is that very few research students have thought about what the finished product is for. You need to explain that the literature review should: (1) show the reader that the student is capable of searching for relevant material, summarizing it, arranging it by some theme, and relating it to his or her own work; and (2) show that his or her study is original *or* is a principled, conscious replication of a previous one.

Few students recognize that displaying the ability to synthesize the literature is one of the skills they will be judged on. Yet the evidence is that many examiners see that synthesis as a crucial part of a good thesis (we give examples in Chapter 7). The supervisor can alert the student to the main dangers associated with the standard thesis literature chapter. There are three main dangers. People can leave things out, be out of date, and be boring. Try to ensure that your students avoid all these dangers using the following strategies:

- To stop them leaving things out. Remember to ask your supervisees, the library staff, other people, to keep their eyes open for all studies relevant to all the people you are supervising as well as encouraging the student to do the same. A colleague may spot something relevant to your student in a journal, but will only tell you or your student if you have encouraged them to do so.
- To stop them being out of date. Remember your students need to keep reading. They cannot review the literature at the beginning and leave it. They should keep reading until the thesis is finished and then prepare for the viva. Journals are crucial, so encourage them to keep an eye on *Current Contents* and its equivalents in your discipline, as you do.
- To stop them being boring. This is the worst danger. Help your student to arrange their review by themes, not just in long lists or sequences. Encourage them to highlight the findings that are relevant to their thesis. Most importantly, the supervisor has to train the student to be critical of the literature not just report it.

This may be particularly difficult for students who have been educated in the Islamic/Koranic tradition, or the Confucian/Mandarin one. In both these ancient educational systems, apprentice scholars are required to memorize and absorb the work of masters for many years, and are not expected to attack and criticize the scholarly corpus. Eickelman (1978, 1985) has written eloquently about the Islamic/Koranic tradition, while Wilkinson (1964) and Hayhoe (1984) explore the Confucian/Mandarin one. Moving to the robust Anglo-American tradition, where young scholars are required to criticize the publications of leading authorities, can be confusing. Supervisors can become frustrated by an over-reverent tone, suspect a lack of ability in the student, or worry about plagiarism, when they receive careful summaries of published work rather than the robust criticism they want. Students can be perplexed by the cool reaction to their painstaking efforts. Neither party realizes that these are different scholarly traditions meeting in mutual incomprehension. Once a supervisor has read about the student's own scholarly tradition, he or she can discuss with the student what the differences are and help the student learn to produce UK-style texts. If you are supervising students who have been educated in countries with a Koranic or Confucian scholarly tradition, then it is well worth spending some time reading about it: an understanding of a different tradition leads to an improvement in supervisory skill. You will be able to open up the differences in traditions for explicit comparison.

When a student does a good literature review it is a very satisfying product. At best it can lead to a publication.

Example 4.5: Bartholomew Strange

Sara was the external examiner of a PhD by Bartholomew Strange. It was an excellent thesis, and fell into two potential books. The empirical material was ideally suited to a monograph which his supervisor, Professor Leidner, was able to place with a publisher. Sara could see that the literature review and methods chapters contained an outstanding overview of how one particular data collection and analysis method had been used in three different ways in related disciplines. She knew that a leading scholar, Anthony Cade, was planning a series of methods books, into which Bartholomew's work would fit perfectly. After the viva, Sara wrote to Professor Cade, and he commissioned the book from Bartholomew. In the years since his two books were published, Dr Strange has had a very successful career as an expert in the area of his methods book.

Not all literature reviews can become books, but many of them can generate a research note or a journal article, perhaps written with the supervisor. This is worth exploring with promising students, because it provides a real incentive to think about the literature, and if an article is submitted, the referees' comments provide useful feedback on the thesis, even if the article is rejected.

Teaching citation and referencing

The literature review is an excellent point or stage to train the student in citation and referencing. These are skills candidates will need, and the sooner they learn them, and deploy them automatically, the better. There are three aspects to this: the technicalities of citation, the politics of citation, and the construction of the reference lists and/or bibliography. It is important to explain to students why these things matter, because most undergraduates will not have been forced to master the technicalities and will be innocent of the politics. This section deals with the technicalities first, and then the politics. It may be necessary to warn, or even threaten, students with the possibility that their thesis could be referred for an inadequate or incorrectly presented bibliography. This may even be the appropriate place to raise the spectre of plagiarism: and ensure that the student knows that the best way to avoid accusations of plagiarism is to be meticulous about citation.

Unpicking a student's citation problems may also reveal more serious issues, as in the case of Alice Ascher.

Example 4.6: Plagiarism or poor citation?

Alice Ascher was doing a 20,000-word thesis at the end of a Masters degree. In her literature review, she appeared to have got her citations wrong, confusing contributions to edited collections and secondary references. Her bibliography was full of entries such as: 'i.e. Smith, 1926 cited in Jones, 1989: 32'. As Sara tried to help her sort out her citations, it became clear that the literature review was full of citations to readily available sources Alice had not read first-hand, and indeed had been written without any first-hand knowledge of several key sources central to her theme. Discovering and unpicking that mistake, and sending Alice off to read the original texts of her central authors took several weeks. Then Sara discovered that Alice was apparently unable to distinguish primary sources from secondary ones or from textbooks, or recognize the difference between writing a book and editing one. Trying to ensure that Alice understood plagiarism then had to be built into several more sessions. Here an inadequate list of citations was the warning signal about underlying scholarly problems.

Many students have not realized that what they are doing when citing references, and need to have it explained that a reader in fifty years' time should be able to trace everything they used from the bibliography. The best way to reinforce this message is to show them how maddening it is to try and trace the sources of a sloppily-referenced text in your own field (we leave it to you to make the selection!). Teaching a class on referencing while writing this book we found a Masters student who was reordering co-authors and co-editors into alphabetical order for her bibliography. So, if she wished to cite Field and Abraham (1999) she was putting Abraham and Field (1999) in her text and bibliography. Students may also need to have the issue of intellectual ownership explained to them: they will not know 'naturally' the difference between the author of a paper, the editor of the volume it appears in, the translator of a foreign text, or the compiler of a bibliography unless the nature of these different scholarly tasks is made explicit for them. Both these aspects of intellectual ownership and the consequences of ignoring them make excellent topics for student workshops – preferably based round an exercise relevant to the discipline. The case of Peter Brichter (Example 4.7) can be used: again, you may need to rewrite it as a subject-specific example.

Students whose first language is Arabic, or any other where the family name precedes the forename may find referencing in English very confusing, and need to have it explained. It is not obvious to a Saudi Arabian that 'Banks, Olive' and 'Olive Banks' are the same person, and that the author goes

---

Example 4.7: Intellectual property

Peter Brichter had done research on internet chatrooms where fans of Australian football debated their passionately-held views. His supervisor discovered, when reading an advanced draft, that Peter had been very casual about distinguishing two sets of data (that is, what the fans in the chatrooms said spontaneously and what they said to him when he conducted online interviews with them) and his citations conflated serious academic sources with popular journalism about the AFL.

---

under 'B' in the bibliography. Students from other cultures are not always able to sex authors from their forenames, either, and their use of 'he' and 'she' when referring to authors often needs careful scrutiny. British students are not necessarily able to sex Americans from their forenames either, and this too needs watching.

We have found it useful to run a class on referencing technicalities with a worksheet which we go through in class. Ours is reproduced as Figure 4.3, and is clearly designed for a sociology/social policy department where theses are referenced using the Harvard system. It is fairly easy to produce an equivalent exercise for other disciplines, using the APA (American Psychological Association) or Biomedical referencing systems, or those required for legal, humanities or linguistic research.

The politics of citations in scientific disciplines have been studied by sociologists of science (e.g. Edge 1979) but there has been less research on how scholars in other disciplines use citation. In many disciplines researchers have found citation being gendered: publications by women are less likely to be cited than those by men (Cole 1979). If you suspect that any of your students are recapitulating that pattern, a departmental workshop on sexism in your discipline, perhaps led by an outside speaker may be in order. Many supervisors may never have thought about their own citation strategies or read anything about how citation works in their own field. As you lay bare your own practices, you may discover more about yourself and your speciality than you wanted to know. Delamont (2003: 25–7) reports an examination of the citation patterns in two areas of social science. You and your graduate students may even be able to produce equivalent analyses of your own specialism which could be publishable.

Figure 4.3: Exercise on bibliographies and referencing

Spot the mistakes in each of these, and either write it out correctly below, or list the mistake.

1   Jenni Williams (2001) *Spot Removal.* London: Hotline
2   Franklin, B. J.; Williams, P. Q.; and Marshall, Z ( ) (2000) *Readings on Spot Removal.* Boston:Little, Brown & Co
3   Andrews, Z. (1996) Chaos in the Streets, New Zealand Journal of Street Studies Vol 2 No 3 pp 210–236.
4   Castenada, John Antigone's Struggles Los Angeles: Feminist Press Inc.
5   Pithouse, A.J. (1999) 'Thoughts on Radical Social Work', *British Journal of Radical Thoughts* pp 12–17.
6   Delamont, Sara (1976) 'Beyond Flanders' Fields'. In Stubbs and Delamont Explorations in Classroom Observation Chichester Wiley pp
7   Zonabend, Michelle (1974) *The Enduring Memory*
8   Gage and Berliner (1984) Educational Psychology (Second Edition)
9   Berliner, D et al (1986) Teaching Teachers Thinking Journal of Education for Teaching Vol 19 No 4
10 Adamson, David (1992) 'Understanding machismo and caciquismo'. *Iberian Studies* Vol 7 No 1 pp 1–27.
11 Penny Jones and Mary Smith ( ) 'Policewomen in Corsica'. In M. Levi and A. Smith (eds) European Policing in the 1990s University of North Carolina Press.
12 (look at 13 as well)
    Walton, R. (1985) Entry Requirements for the UCC course in social work' *Social Work Today* Vol 38 No 2 pp 75–80.
13 Walton, R. (1985) *Prison Reform in Ghana* Manchester.
14 Paul Atkinson The Clinical Experience Unpublished PHD thesis Edinburgh
15 Beale, Dorothea (1892) My first thirty years at Cheltenham reprinted in D.Spender The Educational Pioneers (1987) London Virago

'There isn't any literature'

Occasionally a student will complain that they cannot find any literature on their topic. This may be because they lack vision, and are defining their topic too narrowly, and you can reassure them and demonstrate how to use the literature there is. If the student is defining the parameters of their literature searching in order to 'fit' their own specific topic very narrowly, then indeed, there will be little or nothing to show. If such a narrowly defined search throws up a good deal of research literature, then the student may find it hard to identify an original and significant topic for their own thesis: a crowded research field may prove hard to penetrate and some redefinition of the problem may be in order. More likely is the phenomenon whereby students define their interests so specifically that systematic searches suggest little or no literature. In that case the supervisor's task will be help them rethink the task: as we have suggested already, to search more creatively, looking more laterally for creative comparisons, contrasts and the like.

If, when you have exhausted all your ingenuity, you are forced to agree that there really is a lack of literature on the student's topic, you may need to show them how to write creatively about that absence. A genuine absence of research literature in a specific field can provide the student and supervisor with a creative opportunity. Gaps in the research coverage can provide very telling information about the preoccupations, biases and blind spots of the research community. They may be indicative of genuine oversight of important problems and perspectives. The ambitious and creative research student can often make capital out of a negative result in searching the literature. If the absence is a significant one, it can be used to mount a principled criticism of the present state of the field. A publishable research note may be the outcome. In any event, a creative response to the presences and absences in the literature can be used to construct literature reviews that actually map the current state of the art.

Throughout this chapter we have tried to indicate a number of ways in which the research student and the supervisor can approach the task of literature searching and reviewing. Our general message is that this set of tasks, which are sometimes seen as tedious chores, can be approached professionally and creatively. A failure to think positively about 'the literature' can readily lead to the sort of dull writing that too often mars the finished thesis. Experienced external examiners will probably be familiar with at least some theses in which the student has indeed approached the job in a mechanical and ritualized fashion. The result can be a dutiful but uninspiring aspect of the work that adds little or nothing to the final product. A more thoughtful approach to the tasks, that combines thorough inquiry with a more creative approach, can be a significant contribution to the thesis in its own right, whether or not it appears as a separate 'literature review'. Rather than stultifying, the result can be an empowering overview of the state of the art, and help to place the research student's own work firmly in its proper intellectual context. It is the task of the supervisor, along with providing specific advice on searching, reading, bibliographic work and so on, to help the student to see the wood for the trees: to help them to *use* the literature to hand as part of the research process; to link the student's own work to key issues and themes in the discipline; to derive and to explore ideas through the literature rather than passively reporting it.

5

Heavy and thankless task: overseeing the data collection

> The confidante has a very heavy and thankless task. It's not surprising if
> she goes mad in white linen. It's more surprising if she stays sane and
> sensible.
>
> (Sayers 1972: 142)

The supervision of data collection is clearly a key feature of the research
process, and may be one of the most problematic areas of the project. If all
goes well, of course, it may prove one of the most satisfying too: there can
be few more exciting aspects of the supervisor's work than to see good
quality data that put flesh on the bones of a previously schematic research
design.

It is in this phase of the project, too, that prior training in methods and
careful preparation of the research student pay handsome dividends.
Equally, all parties need to be mentally and emotionally prepared for the
possibility that data collection procedures will not go smoothly. Problems of
some sort are common – to be expected in general terms, but unpredictable
in practice – and should not be allowed to lead to unnecessary loss of confidence, or to the abortion of the project entirely. Gumport (1993: 265)
reports of Physics PhD students in the USA:

> A student might need help with techniques of instrumentation, meas-
> urement styles, or design of equipment; there may be a leak ... One
> faculty member said, 'I have to set up the harder parts of the experiment
> myself. But when it breaks, they fix it.'

One of the students Gumport interviewed captures the highs and the lows of
the data collection phase of a physics PhD: 'Some days you are a peon. Other
days you know how ... and you're King for a day.' This chapter is about
supervising through the days of peonage and the days of majesty.

Equally, student and supervisor alike need to remain flexible in their general approach. Data collection in all disciplines is unpredictable. The natural
sciences are no more immune from problems in getting their experiments to
work and in deriving useful data than the social sciences. Thought, therefore, needs to be given to how various contingencies might be dealt with and
how research designs or data collection methods might be modified if
insurmountable problems are encountered.

The following town planning student, Glen Madson from Portminster, found out the hard way about adequate preparation for data collection, and reflected on his own lack of prior experience:

> I know I made one major cock-up in the first year by approaching a particular firm about its relationship to its union. And if I'd had any kind of research training I wouldn't have done that. It was innocent, but it wasn't interpreted that way and it cut off my access to that firm completely. And because I really wanted to do that firm, I was really upset. It had taken me six months to get some kind of access and I blew it. OK, it was common sense, but common sense that had to be learned. It's difficult doing research in organizations and in retrospect I was very sloppy, but that's because I didn't have any training.

Here Glen may overestimate the degree to which prior training can guard against adverse eventualities and accidents. Nevertheless, his rueful comments capture some of the feelings and experiences of graduate students in facing their data collection.

Glen's comments also remind us of issues of timescale. Data collection, at the best of times, can be a protracted process, irrespective of the method used. It is often labour-intensive, and graduate students – unless they are part of some larger research project, with a linked studentship – have limited resources. Often they have only their own labour-power. For the part-time research student, problems of time and resources can be especially pressing. For the social science student, for instance, the negotiation of access can be a time-consuming task in its own right (and we have already drawn attention to that through the example of Paul's access problems – see Example 3.5). Access to data can, indeed, be a problem for research students in any discipline.

Example 5.1: Access

Richard Gatoire was scheduled to collect the data for his PhD in earth sciences on Monserrat. Everything was set up for him when the volcano erupted, and the capital, Plymouth, and much of the island had to be evacuated.

Research students in the social sciences, in our experience, all too often plan data-collection phases that would take a medium-sized research team, with funded support, a fair time to complete. In our experience, students are far too ambitious. Ambition is commendable, but over-optimistic estimates of time and effort are not to be encouraged. A corollary is that students often plan to collect more data than they will be able to use productively.

Although one should encourage students to realize that their thesis is not the final point of their research career, and that the research they do now will stand them in good stead in the future, most supervisors will recognize the

In training our own graduate students, we base our advice on the following maxim: 'Take your first research design, and your first estimate of how long data collection will take. Halve the volume of data you envisage, and then double your estimate of time. You may then have a more realistic and feasible plan.'

syndrome of too much data. Students who have been able to complete the data-collection phase of an empirical project all too often drown in data. We shall return to such drowning later in this chapter. For now, we want to link it to these preliminary remarks: students and their supervisors should be encouraged to think realistically and pragmatically about the scope of data collection. A well-targeted, well-designed empirical project is likely to yield data that the student will be able to cope with, analyse productively, and turn into a successful thesis. By contrast, any attempt to tackle a research question by overwhelming it with huge amounts of data is likely to end up by simply overwhelming the hapless student. To a considerable extent, the general issue relates to *confidence*. Too much data can be collected if the student and the supervisor are not sufficiently confident – in the precision of the research design, the significance of the research questions to be addressed, the student's analytic capacities, and so on. The temptation to cover all the angles, or to collect data simply because 'It would be interesting to see if . . .', betrays a lack of assurance about the research process. We feel one of the most important things that a supervisor can impart is that sense of confidence: to collect the right kinds of data, with an appropriate research design.

How much data? Students – especially in the social sciences – are often preoccupied with this question. It seems to be especially pressing for candidates preparing for the shorter dissertations associated with taught Masters courses and the thesis for the professional doctorate. But it is an issue for higher-degree students of all kinds. The methodologist, of course, will recognize how such questions are unanswerable in a vacuum, and how they might be addressed for particular research designs. The experienced supervisor will also recognize, however, that such questions are recurrent even among students who have had the advantage of research methods training.

In the social sciences, we are often asked by nervous students questions such as, 'How many informants should I interview?' Our answer is predictable: 'It depends on what you want to do.' We find ourselves explaining that a modest volume of high-quality data that are analysed in considerable depth and with methodological precision and sophistication will often be far better than a lot of data that are superficially analysed. We remind them of the adage offered by Harry Wolcott, the American anthropologist of education. Wolcott points out that he only studies one of anything at any given time: one village, or one school, or one school principal. 'But Harry,' he says people say to him. 'What can you learn from just one?' 'As much as I can,' he tells them.

This is a useful maxim for students and supervisors to keep in mind, no matter what their discipline. What is important is what you can learn, not the sheer volume of data that are collected.

Getting started and keeping the faith

One of the most important functions the supervisor can perform is to maintain the student's confidence and enthusiasm. This is, of course, true throughout the research student's career (and may need to extend beyond the formal end of the candidature, as a career progresses) but it is often especially significant during the early period of empirical work. If things were easy, and research problems were soluble as soon as we approached them, then research would be much easier than it really is, and there would be little need for research training, the whole apparatus of research studentships, fellowships, supervision and examination. Research is hard and it is messy.

In sociology and social anthropology, beginning students are often disappointed to discover that the social worlds they observe do not readily yield up research problems and analytic concepts. In particular, students who have been reared on the kind of ideas that are more characteristic of undergraduate courses and textbooks find it hard to adjust to the diffuse reality of the social world. They look in vain for their cherished ideas ('hegemony', 'patriarchy', 'anomie' or whatever) and they discover that social worlds do not come neatly packaged in such terms. They see ordinary people doing more or less familiar mundane tasks. They collect data, but often become fretful and insecure because they cannot 'see' problems or processes. It is very easy for the novice student to lose confidence early in the empirical phases of the research project in the face of uncertainty or a lack of clarity in the initial results.

The phenomenon is by no means confined to research students in the non-experimental disciplines. Experimental psychologists and natural scientists will normally have been socialized into a 'puzzle-solving' view of laboratory work in the course of the undergraduate training, and even in a Masters programme. While students are exposed to the laboratory, and learn practical lab skills, the kinds of experiments they perform are often more in line with the kind of science taught in secondary schools than with the kind of work that they may encounter for the first time as research students in their own right. A number of authors have now commented on this distinction between research and the quasi-experiments that are characteristic of scientific pedagogy. The latter may more usefully be thought of as demonstrations or recapitulations. Undergraduate students are not expected to 'discover' new phenomena, nor even to explore established phenomena from a novel angle. The majority of experiments that are performed in university laboratories are not aimed at novelty. Students may be discovering things for themselves, but they are usually following well-trodden paths. They reproduce the taken-for-granted knowledge of 'normal science'. They and their teachers usually know that provided they follow the recipes of laboratory technique, and are reasonably careful in executing their work, then they will approximate to the 'right answers' in their practical work. Moreover, pedagogical demonstrations can be constructed and carried out because the 'correct' answers are predictable (at least to the teachers concerned).

In contrast, when postgraduate research students start to embark on their own research projects, then they are very likely to encounter novel experiences: among them the fact that their experiments – their equipment, perhaps – will not 'work' in the way that their undergraduate laboratory recapitulations 'worked'. They cannot rely on their teachers stage-managing the laboratory setting so as to ensure positive results, nor can they recover failures by recourse to the kinds of pedagogical repair described by Delamont and Atkinson (1995): in other words, one cannot wish away failure by tidying up results, or going over what 'ought' to have happened, or what 'in fact' is the case.

All our biochemistry respondents had completed a practical (laboratory based) project in their final year of undergraduate study, but as a biochemistry supervisor confirmed. 'At undergraduate level the experiments are designed to work, that's why they're chosen.' Many postgraduates come to doctoral research poorly prepared because the differences between undergraduate and graduate science are largely unanticipated.

Whereas at undergraduate level, students expect their experiments to work, at postgraduate level they can never be certain. Biochemistry supervisors recognize the difficulties experienced by postgraduates in coming to terms with this uncertainty. The biochemistry postgraduates acknowledged a lack of preparation for postgraduate work, despondency, and sometimes panic when their experiments consistently failed. The following description of initiation into PhD work is provided by a biochemistry doctoral student and is representative of the accounts provided other postgraduates;

> The first thing I had to do was make an RNA and I kept failing. It took me three months before it started working. The thing about biochemistry is that often nothing works and the only thing you can possibly do to come to terms with that is to grit your teeth and carry on trying. It came as a big shock to me that nothing worked.

The realization that the outcomes of laboratory work are by no means certain, accompanies a growing concern among postgraduates that there is nothing predictable about doctoral study and there is no guarantee that PhD requirements will be met;

> It's that it's suddenly for real. You're not playing any more but that it's completely open ended and there is no guarantee that it's going to work. It's three years of your life and it could easily go down the toilet.
>
> (Biochemistry student)

PhD students involved in experimental laboratory work felt frustrated because initially 'you can't get something to work' and 'you can get to your wits' end trying to get something to work'. We also learnt how, just because an experiment has worked once, there is no guarantee that it will work at any time in the future: 'When you run a test you might do it once and it works. You do it four or five times more and it doesn't work' (Biochemistry postgraduate).

Although one explanation for this was the sheer volume of variables involved, 'for a single experiment there may be six or seven variables, for a complicated one there could be hundreds', this does not explain why some experiments work first time and others don't: 'Sometimes you'll do something for the first time without any rhyme or reason it will work, and other times things that should work won't.' We also learned how once a particular experiment has worked, then in most cases it always works: 'It's funny because if you're having trouble getting something to go, when it does finally go it will work routinely.'

Learning to cope with the insecurities associated with scientific work formed an important part of the process of PhD work, particularly among our biochemistry respondents. There are a number of strategies or ways in which postgraduates learn to rationalize initial failure. One of these is by understanding that it is not personal; it happens to everybody. In reaching this understanding the role of 'significant others' (the supervisor and other members of the research group) is crucial:

> PhDs get bad patches when things don't work out in the expected way. They can't see where it's going wrong and they don't have any results. They mostly appreciate that this does happen and not just to them.
>
> (Biochemistry supervisor)

Another way in which students come to terms with failure is to interpret it as a fundamental component of scientific training which is ultimately resolvable. The immediate realization that initially nothing works is gradually replaced by a certainty that in the end it will work. Although coming to terms with initial failure is seen as a 'totally demoralizing process' it is nevertheless recognized as part of learning the ropes and therefore constitutes a crucial component of 'lab experience'. Coming to terms with uncertainty therefore constitutes an important benchmark for PhD students: 'You either learn to accept that nine times out of ten things in the lab don't work; and if you can cope with that you'll be all right.'

It is when PhD students first begin to produce results in the laboratory, that their previous worries and insecurities are overshadowed and despondency gives way to a growing conviction that ultimately their experiments will work:

> When you get your first results, you get really excited. You probably get more excited with the first results than any you get after. You're really pleased. And slowly you come to terms with things not working.
>
> (Biochemistry student)

Once students come to accept the unpredictability of scientific research then it becomes a manageable component of their work:

If you make plans it's always on the basis that everything will work, which of course it doesn't. You could say at the first attempt there's a 50/50 chance it will work, but that's being generous.

(Biochemistry PhD)

The attitude expressed above, namely 'everything goes wrong but you have to remember that's not all the time' was shared by all our respondents in biochemistry and was accompanied by the conviction that 'once it's started to work then you're on your way'.

We do not want to exaggerate the difference here. It is a well-established feature of academic disciplinary cultures that research problems in the laboratory sciences are usually well specified, and research students are not cast adrift on totally uncharted waters. Research problems are typically formulated and handed down from one generation to the next. In natural sciences, for instance, one generation may establish one set of experiments, or solve one kind of problem. The next generation may then go on to refine the techniques, solve the next line of problems, develop new techniques to derive further research topics and so on. In some labs the former generation, now postdoctoral researchers, supervise the day-to-day work of the next, who are the postgraduate students.

For all that careful preparation and the cascade of problems and techniques within the laboratory, however, beginning students frequently encounter problems. Sometimes they seem not just tricky, but unpredictable and whimsical. The natural world does not appear to research students to yield up its problems and solutions any more readily than the social world.

If the research student in most disciplines were easily discouraged, then they could very easily give up the whole enterprise at an early stage. On the other hand, we know that perseverance carries rewards. For the majority of students in the social sciences and humanities, patterns and results do emerge: the relevance of general theories and major concepts does start to become apparent. Likewise, equipment in the laboratory sciences does start to work, and the folk wisdom of the sciences is that once an experiment starts to work as it should, then results start to come. And once that process starts, things rarely go wrong again in a major way. Cracking the problem is itself unpredictable. Sometimes the breakthrough can come from a critical incident, or from a particular piece of reading, or from a more-or-less random modification to the equipment. It is difficult to foresee just what will start to unlock the process. And, one must admit that sometimes things just never get ungummed, and the student can never get everything to work properly, or can never quite see the analytic pattern.

What is important is for the supervisor to maintain a productive balance between optimism and realism, and to shore up the student's confidence should it wobble. Purblind encouragement is clearly dangerous: no supervisor should push a student to carry on banging their head against the proverbial brick wall. If things seem to be going wrong, then one must entertain the possibility that they really are going wrong and will not get any better. If a student does turn out to be pursuing a problem that cannot be cracked, trying to study an organization to which access will not be forthcoming, or trialling a technique that really is not ready to be implemented, then the supervisor's job may be to help him or her to undertake a realistic appraisal of the situation, to review what has been learnt from the project to date, and to apply those insights to a reformulation of the problem, or a new research design, or whatever it will take to rescue the student and her or his project. On the other hand, the supervisor needs to be alert to varieties of 'data-collection blues'. If the problems of data collection seem to be routine, reflecting the normal vicissitudes of research, then the supervisor's role will be different. In such cases, the most important job is to maintain impetus, to help the student to work through the various disappointments and frustrations. A good deal of postgraduate supervision can be described as a kind of 'confidence trick' – repeatedly persuading students that they can get the equipment to work, and that it will one day soon, that the results will start to come, that they will start to find themes and patterns in their field data, and that their laborious work in the archives will start to yield significant results as well as huge volumes of dull records.

Student research projects are, in different ways, acts of faith. As school students and as undergraduates we have to have faith, and we place our trust in our teachers. We have faith that the problems we have been set are soluble and are within the compass of our existing skills and knowledge. As research students we outgrow that elementary form of faith. Now research student and supervisor alike have to embark on the research project as an act of renewed faith – believing that research is possible, that new results can be obtained, and that a serious contribution to knowledge will be the outcome. The oversight of data collection, especially – but not exclusively – in the early phases, requires of many supervisors that they help to maintain that level of belief. This, of course, depends on the kind of mutual trust that we discuss elsewhere. The student must trust the supervisor if he or she is to take real heart from such encouragement, or if there is need for a radical evaluation of the project.

We have, incidentally, discussed these issues almost exclusively as if the research process were an empirical one in a conventional sense. It needs to be emphasized that similar considerations apply to purely theoretical work. The investigator in the laboratory, the social scientist in the field, or the social historian in the archive may sometimes envy the pure theorist. It is true that data collection in the normal sense of that phrase is not a major problem for the theorist. That does not mean, however, that a student and supervisor may not face similar problems. The contrast between undergraduate and research work is often just as stark. The undergraduate 'theorist' learns fairly standard ways of reading and writing, acquiring a critical rhetoric to mount sustained commentaries on leading figures in the field (as one might well find in philosophy, cultural studies, critical theory or sociology). These are, more often than not, grounded in the pedagogical devices of teachers' questions, rather than researchers' questions. The transition from such recapitulation of critical commentary to the requirement to engage in original theorizing, or to cast original light on theory, can be a major one, and may be no less fraught than any other first steps. Here, too, the supervisor needs to temper a critical engagement with the candidate's ideas with the ability to sustain his or her self-belief. The student has to have faith that an original voice will be found, and an original contribution to the scholarly literature will be the result.

Drowning in data

As we have already suggested, initial difficulties in getting started, and getting the research to 'work' can often be paralleled by an apparently opposite problem – drowning in data and information. These are not absolute antitheses. The same problems give rise to both phenomena. The problem is especially common among social scientists. They may have had difficulty in setting up the project, gaining access and so on. But all too often they end up with reams and reams of data. The same problems seem to result – though in somewhat different guises – irrespective of whether the candidate is collecting qualitative or quantitative data. To some extent, in at least some projects, too much data is probably inevitable. Where research is exploratory, and the research design to some extent open-ended, it is virtually impossible to collect just the right amount of data. Indeed, it is hard to see what that might mean. The young anthropologist who spends a year or eighteen months in the intensive study of a given social setting can never judge from the outset how much is 'enough'. In any case, in such research contexts, the thesis is but one outcome of the research, and the young scholar may have few chances of such long-term immersion in a field site in the course of an entire career. The data gathered must last well beyond the period of doctoral candidature and submission of the thesis itself. They will be the basis of many subsequent publications. The problem is by no means confined to the social sciences, however. Historians may often find themselves 'drowning' in their archive or other source material. Physical scientists too may amass a great many experimental data, once their equipment is up and running.

On the one hand, the growing pile of data is welcome. It is a visible reminder of the progress of the research. Concrete results and documentary materials provide some guarantee that the research is proving 'successful'. The accumulation of lots of data can provide the fledgling researcher with the equivalent of a 'security blanket': it is a guard against the uncertainties of research in the widest sense. The results themselves may be intrinsically exciting and satisfying. Research student and supervisor alike can become engrossed in the results as they emerge. After all, there are few highs that are more satisfying than to make a genuine discovery, to demonstrate a new technique, prove a theorem or whatever.

On the other hand, the accumulation of data can all too readily leave the student (and the supervisor) floundering. When the original research proposal was formulated, things probably had a certain simplicity. A preliminary review of the literature, or a more worked-up research design will probably have suggested some well-defined research problems. The collection of substantial amounts of data is quite likely to make things seem a good deal more messy. Even in the 'precise' disciplines, measurements are unlikely to be perfectly consistent. Correlations are not always statistically significant; not all results exactly fit the curve; distributions have outliers. When the student becomes over-involved in the minutiae of data and results, then she or he may find it hard to see the wood for the trees. Furthermore, it may be emotionally hard to give up some of those hard-won data, and students may cling to them so tenaciously as to lose a sense of discrimination.

The supervisor's role at this point has a good deal to do with helping the student to achieve some sense of discrimination. She or he needs, perhaps, to distinguish once more between what is important and what may be discarded: to exercise judgement over results that may be discarded, those that are significant, and those anomalous results that might just be the germ of the next exciting project. If a student has become unduly attached to the data and the findings, then a good supervisor will have to find a way to help discard some – or at least to put them on the back burner, ready to be visited once more when the thesis is safely in the hands of the examiners, or the degree safely awarded. (Getting the student to let go of the completed thesis may also be a problem, and we shall return to that topic also.)

Academics from all disciplines talk of the need for the gentle control of students who are wild or over-ambitious. One of David Pearson's (2002) respondents, Dr O'Connor, exemplifies this view of the philosophy PhD:

> I'd say clarity of focus is a very important issue because my experience is that students are sometimes over-ambitious in what they think can be accomplished within a PhD. And maybe this was okay ten or fifteen years ago when people could take about ten years over a PhD . . . We had somebody who . . . wrote about two-hundred thousand words in about seven years and then had to spend the next two years editing it down to a hundred thousand words. [laugh] You can't do that any more. . . . The tendency with inquiring minds is always to push outwards – 'Oh that's interesting; let's follow that up; that's a nice idea; what does so and so say about that?' And there's always the tendency with the thing to expand and the more it expands the more unmanageable it gets and the less likely it is that it will be finished in four years. So it's got to have limitations and it's got to have a clarity of focus.

There is often a crucial juncture in the research process when the supervisor needs to help the candidate step back momentarily from the day-to-day grind of data collection and analysis. It may be opportune to schedule a seminar presentation, or a brief written working paper, used as a vehicle to establish a sense of what is really important, what needs to be focused on in the thesis, what issues will engage most readily the attention of the academic community, what will be regarded as especially publishable, and so on.

Whether or not such formal procedures are adopted (and many programmes have regular reviews and presentations built into them, of course) it is important to help the student gain an adequate perspective on the work, to see the overall shape and pattern that can emerge, or is emerging, and to concentrate on the essentials. Poorly constructed theses are often characterized by unnecessary detail. Self-confidence is, again, vital. The student who is unsure of what the thesis is really about, or is not secure in its significance, may be tempted to try the kitchen-sink strategy – including everything that has been done, rather than constructing a selective and purposeful set of analyses.

It is crucial in this context that the supervisor's greater experience, and greater awareness of comparable standards across different institutions, can be invaluable. The supervisor should be in a position to provide just that sort of critical and well-informed distance that a review requires, while maintaining the student's trust in that critical process.

How close is the supervision?

There is no right answer to this question, but the degree of involvement of the supervisor in the actual processes of data collection is an occasional problem or dilemma for the conscientious supervisor. In the ordinary run of things, it is impossible in the majority of cases for a supervisor to be closely involved in the day-to-day, hands-on collection of data in most disciplines. Data collection is arduous and time-consuming, irrespective of whether the research is based on the laboratory, fieldwork, the library or the archive. Full-time students barely have enough time and energy to devote to their own work. Busy supervisors have little opportunity to oversee and interfere at the level of detail, even if they wanted to, or if they should. Pearson (2002) interviewed at least one chemist who supervised the data collection very closely.

> Dr Phillips (chemistry): They have to have the judgement of knowing when they can do something on their own bat without talking to their supervisor about it and when it's appropriate to come and ask and that's a balance that has been learned and for each student it will be different. Some are very capable and have an instinct as to what is safe and what can be done; others are not. And this is one of the great differences between organic chemistry and PhDs in other subjects: it's quite common for a supervisor to go and see a student even in the second year three or four times a day because maybe they're concerned about what they're doing or they want to ensure that the experiments are efficient in that they're not doing things that are a waste of time. It depends on the supervisor, but if you're conscientious you can easily do that.

In many laboratory sciences the 'everyday' oversight of data collection is done by fellow students, postdoctoral colleagues and technicians rather than the supervisor. Under these arrangements the research context revolves around mutual support and sharing of materials, skills and equipment. An important feature of this model is a continuity of practice in that skills, equipment and topics are passed down through the ranks of postdoctoral researchers and research students.

These arrangements occur where the research structure revolves around one supervisor or research director with doctoral students and postdoctoral researchers working in his or her area on topics that are to some extent related. In this context a specific set of research related patterns emerge which inform the 'habitus' of the group. This model was offered to us in contrast to the 'traditional' model of PhD supervision in the social sciences: 'The difference between us and social science is that we tend to do PhDs through team work' (Geography supervisor). Because supervisors or research directors tend to have several PhD students at any one time they take a back-stage role in regard to practical day-to-day supervision of students:

I think my leverage, what I contribute is not sitting there and doing research myself but creating the possibilities for other people to do it and trying to shape the direction of what gets done.

(Artificial intelligence supervisor)

The supervisor's main role as research director means that assistance with everyday problems concerning the research are resolved elsewhere:

I don't tell her (the supervisor) the ins and outs of problems, I tend to talk to other people, call in the knowledge of others in the department.
(Biochemistry Post Doctoral Researcher)

The PhD students see the research group environment as mutually supportive:

There are other people working on different things but there are similarities in our work, e.g. mathematics, methods and computing. There's no explicit link between projects but we almost totally rely on each other for support. Its a reciprocal arrangement that people respect rather than a role which people take on.

(Geography doctoral student)

Where group members are working on different research problems there are still overlaps in the materials and techniques which they use:

We're all working on the same sort of areas, we use a lot of the same assays and substances . . . a lot of the substances I make will be used by other people as well. If I invent a method to make something easier then they'll use it as well.

(Biochemistry doctoral student)

Less experienced members of the group rely upon the more experienced members: 'If things keep going wrong then usually someone who gets it right will sort of go through the experiment one day with you' (Biochemistry doctoral student).

Under arrangements like these the supervisor provides guidance on the framework and direction of research while experienced group members such as postdoctorate researchers or doctoral candidates more advanced in their work, help the inexperienced PhD students on a day-to-day basis:

> Well, what I like to do with students; when I was a post-doc in the lab, I liked to work very much on my own. Because it suits me. So I encourage people to do the same, I give them their own head. Because of the numbers I couldn't always be looking over their shoulders anyway. If they need day-to-day help there are others like the post-docs in the lab and they can help them. I tend to give specific advice to students. They have a definite programme I'm not there to tell them how to use an instrument they can find someone else for that.
>
> (Biochemistry supervisor)

Given the numbers of doctoral students per supervisor (which can be as many as ten at any one time), it would not be feasible for supervisors to take full responsibility for training graduate students: 'Most of the training of the PhDs is the responsibility of the post-docs. We couldn't do it otherwise' (Biochemistry supervisor).

The doctoral students we talked to described the very different expectations of individuals within their research groups: 'I use my supervisor to sort out my structure and any individual problems only when I feel it is appropriate and when I can't get it from Dave or someone else' (Geography doctoral student).

The supervisor is seen as above the day-to-day functioning of the research group members: 'I think we have a really healthy research environment. We don't always, or often, even, take our problems to our supervisors. We're a well-established group working along the same lines' (Geography doctoral student).

Because of this, PhD supervision is seen as a collective responsibility:

> I work within a group . . . a whole group of people, research associates, PhD students and technical help and consultancy help. That makes about 10 people. So for fieldwork problems or day-to-day things I don't have to go to my supervisor. There's all sorts of people to draw from who did similar PhDs, and who've come through here. So its like a big supervisory group.
>
> (Geography doctoral student)

Where relationships with the supervisor break down, this collective support can rescue the PhD as described below:

> We had to dig ourselves out of a dodgy situation so we pulled together and were able to help each other a great deal. It was a kind of collective survival, in the face of a staggering lack of supervision.
>
> (Biochemistry doctoral student)

The collective support of the research group also functions as a buffer, for the PhD students, against failure: 'It was a large group which was my saving. I felt I could go to anybody in the group. If I had been isolated I would have been terribly demoralized and I would probably have given up' (Biochemistry postdoctoral researcher).

The onus of supervising the burden falls upon postdoctoral researcher:

> I think the post-docs give day-to-day guidance. My role as head of the lab is a psychologist. Experiments don't always go well and I need to cheer them up. Especially the PhD students when nothing seems to be working.
>
> (Biochemistry supervisor)

Postdoctoral researchers often take on this role as a matter of course, 'After all, it was the way I was trained.'

> One thing you do get as a post-doc is troubleshooting other people's problems and you do generate a feeling for what is likely to make the difference between something working and not working.
>
> (Biochemistry postdoctoral researcher)

Postdoctoral researchers themselves acknowledge this change of role and their responsibilities in this respect: 'Recently my role has changed. I'm now a research associate which means I'm a stepping stone between PhD students and their supervisor' (Geography postdoctoral researcher).

Although it was acceptable practice for postdoctorate researchers to supervise PhD students on a day-to-day basis it is nevertheless an unofficial line of responsibility: 'There's two PhDs working on the model. Here I am the direct line of unwritten responsibility. Its not in my contract and I don't really see it as my role. But I help them and sort it out' (Geography postdoctoral researcher).

The type of PhD organization that we have just described is only possible where certain conditions prevail. The two crucial features are group size and continuity of research. Only where there are sufficient numbers of postgraduates (at different stages of research) and postdoctoral researchers can the team or group model of supervision operate. Also the group or team structure depends upon a continuity of funding which allows for several individuals (students and postdoctoral researchers) working in the same area both simultaneously and in succession. Under these conditions, topics or projects can logically follow on from each other with new PhD students developing the work of previous students. In this way a pedagogic continuity operates as skills and equipment are handed down through the research group. If we apply Hacking's (1992) analogy of the strand or rope we can see how the interests of group members are mutually intertwined in a linear process through which the work of individuals is shaped and developed. However, the supervisor is ultimately responsible for the intellectual quality of the PhD student's work, and cannot abrogate that responsibility.

Some research of necessity takes place at some remove from the supervisor's gaze. Social anthropology probably provides the most sustained examples of distant fieldwork, although other 'field' disciplines such as geography and earth sciences can also depend on distant data collection. Anthropology is probably unique among disciplines in placing such a heavy emphasis on such 'fieldwork', and in stressing its solitary nature (collective 'expeditions' or research groups are not the norm). We have explained this at length in Delamont, Atkinson and Parry (2000). In such cases, the supervisor and the student need to establish considerable degrees of trust in each other, and a degree of faith that the fieldwork will prove successful, despite whatever vicissitudes and intellectual problems may ensue. Anthropology supervisors try to ensure regular contact from 'the field', through letters and reports from their students. This is not always possible, however, and contact may become quite attenuated, as in the case of Nina Yeager with whom we open Chapter 6.

6

Disagreeableness and danger: keeping up student motivation

If you have put anything in hand, disagreeableness and danger will not turn you back, and God forbid they should.

(Sayers 1972: 209)

Introduction

This chapter deals with one of the hardest and most diffuse tasks that faces the supervisor. PhD students very often go through sloughs of depression about debt and poverty, isolation, thesis problems, and poor employment prospects, which the supervisor may be able to alleviate. They also have problems with supervision which the supervisor may not recognize, and may or may not be able to solve. Take this story about an anthropology student, told to us by Dr Feste (University of Kingford).

Yes, this is the woman I'm seeing through to the end, who's actually been supervised as far as I can tell, by everyone else in the department . . . Well, she started with not a very coherent idea with Jeremy Styles, I think – she's doing ideas of procreation and birth – and it wasn't coherent when she started out, and she was moved on to both Ian Felgate and Ralph Dorroway, both of whom she did not get on very well with, and she seems to have been through several other people, and ended up with Carolyn Brackenberry after seven or eight years – it's been a long drawn-out saga, and Carolyn's managed to get her through to the point where she's almost ready to submit. Everything's just about ready in draft, and she [Carolyn] had to go on leave, so rather than saying 'take another nine months' she arranged to bring her to me, so that she would finish by 30 June. Which is the ESRC deadline, although she's missed it by several years, as far as I can tell. The department had more or less written her off, and its quite clear from her fieldwork material, as Carolyn Brackenberry pointed out, that she was not adequately supervised at various points, so that questions the supervisor would have said, 'Have you asked your women this?' particularly as she was right here in Scotland, are missing from the material, because there was no one there to suggest things, so there were gaps, which even if you're in the field, you write to your supervisor and get a letter back saying, 'Try this' etc.

And she's had great blanks of supervision where she was on her own so it has been a problem.

All such stories have two (or more) sides – as we can see if we match Dr Feste's account with that of the student herself, Nina Yeager. As she tells her own story:

> When I moved to Kingford there was a trend in Kingford anthropology that appealed to me . . . Here there was an interest in the anthropology of the emotions, and that sort of thing and I think that's very central in the problems I've had as a postgraduate student.

Nina had been a postgraduate for 'eight or nine years', and this is her account of her supervisory problem. We have put the supervisor's names in brackets for the reader.

> My supervisor [Jeremy Styles] went away for a year – I talked to him in the summer and he agreed to be my supervisor and he went away that year. So the first year I started off with someone else [Ian Felgate] for a year, who I felt I had a similar approach to, so that wasn't a problem. Then when he [Jeremy Styles, the original supervisor] came back I moved back to him, that was the arrangement, but then after a year he got a job in another university so I moved back to the man I'd started off with [Ian Felgate] as a temporary arrangement, but after a year he went on sabbatical.

By this point Nina had already been enrolled for five years and her first two supervisors were both absent from Kingford, one permanently. She should, as an ESRC-funded full-time student, ideally have finished her work at least a year before. However Nina's story has another three years to run:

> So I was then moved to another person [Ralph Dorroway] who I worked with for six months, and who's gone somewhere for a few months, so I'm now temporarily with someone else [Carolyn Brackenberry] but in the meantime I hope to finish. So that's an end to it.

Nina then outlines her problems as she sees them:

> . . . apart from all these changes . . . the first two supervisors, really, I think belonged to one school, then I changed to a supervisor of a different school and he found a lot of problems with my work, some of which I think were because I had had poor supervision. The people were interested but not very directive at a time when I needed more direction.

Odette asked Nina to run through the 'natural history' of her PhD, and this revealed a raft of other problems. Nina explained that she had spent 1984 'trying to sort out the questions that I needed to ask' before fieldwork. However,

> I got pregnant in '85 . . . I had problems with the pregnancy, so apart from having maternity leave, anyway, I also had time off because I

couldn't work after the fifth month ... I had a miscarriage and my mother was ill, then I was pregnant again ...

Nina had not had financial problems, because her husband supported her and the two children. 'We came to an understanding that I have had the children in my thesis time and therefore he would fund me afterwards so I'd get it finished.' Having two infant children had prevented Nina from taking much part in the intellectual life at Kingford, such as the postgraduate writing group. So: 'the isolation of it is difficult. I know you get involved in an area that's very much your own, so in a sense up to that point you're intellectually isolated.'

Clearly most postgraduates do not have two children, a miscarriage and a sick parent all in four years, or indeed, four or five different supervisors. However, nearly all students hit some problems: repetitive strain injury, glandular fever, eviction, parental divorce: as well as the thesis-related problems. All the stages: pre-fieldwork, data collection, analysis, writing up: had their problems and their pleasures. One of our geography students, Eunice Lester, in the final stages of her PhD told us:

> I'm constantly amazed because at each point of the research process somebody will come along and say this is the worst part of the whole process – from research question formulation right up to now! And somebody just said to me they felt really sorry for me because this is the most demoralizing and lonely part etc., etc., etc ... And it has been a lonely process. There are ups and downs. There are times when I'm sick and tired of reading my own prose, I don't want to do it any more. But I'm feeling positive at the moment.

This chapter contrasts some of the different problems facing science and humanities postgraduates, then outlines some strategies the supervisor can use to help students face them and resolve them. First we deal with supervisory problems, then data collection and then more personal obstacles.

Supervisory problems

Precisely because the relationship between a research student and their principal supervisor is so important, disruptions to that relationship are very damaging to the progress, and the quality of the thesis. In this section we deal with some causes of disruption and some precautionary strategies. Disruptions to the supervisory relationship can be intellectual, personal, or structural. If the relation has broken down intellectually or personally, a change of principal supervisor is probably the best solution, and the sooner it happens the better. Such a change should *not* be treated as a tragedy or a failure on either part. Academic partnerships should be seen as business relationships which can run out of steam, not as marriages with emotional baggage.

Example 6.1: Willow Pugh

Willow Pugh had done an MSc in the department, part time, and then enrolled for a part-time PhD with Dr Bonnie Indermill. After five years the supervisor–student relationship had broken down. Willow was demotivated and not doing any work. Dr Indermill found this annoying and saw no purpose in arranging, from her perspective, pointless supervisory meetings. Willow decided that she needed a fiercer, more directive supervisor and it was agreed by all parties that she should transfer to Sara. Sara's more directive, robust and intrusive style forced Willow to think about what the obstacles to progress were, and to focus on ways to address or circumvent them. One obstacle was untranscribed tapes: Willow persuaded her boss to pay for some commercial transcription, and to buy a transcriber Willow could use. Once the tapes were being transcribed the thesis could move forward.

The case of Nina Yeager at the beginning of the chapter shows how sabbaticals and research leave can be disruptive to the personal relationship between student and supervisor and to the intellectual continuity of the project.

Worse is the supervisor who leaves for another post, especially if that job is abroad and the student cannot transfer with the supervisor. Worse still is the incapacity or death of the supervisor, because the disruption to the academic relationship is compounded by bereavement. Such disruptions are commoner than one might think. In our careers we have dealt with four people as replacement supervisor, line manager or examiner, whose theses were seriously damaged by the death of a supervisor.

Example 6.2: Intellectual bereavement

Professor Milo Kachigan was a towering intellect, and a much loved man, although, or because, his ideas were controversial. He died leaving Marten Cardenas only 18 months into a PhD. Dr Chris Kelly became Marten's supervisor. When Sara came to examine the thesis, there were three concatenating problems. Firstly, Marten was still grieving for Professor Kachigan, and could not be dispassionate about Kachigan's work. This meant the thesis was uncritical, and the viva difficult. Secondly, Dr Kelly's influence showed very clearly: the thesis was like a layer cake, with some early parts clearly showing Professor Kachigan's strong influence, and other parts, done later, showing Dr Kelly's equally clearly. The different ideas did not necessarily blend very well into a coherent research design, analytic strategy, or theoretical story. Thirdly, it appeared that Marten had adopted some of Kachigan's ideas without really internalizing them, and could not adequately explain them. Dr Kelly had not, apparently, forced Marten either to master the concepts adequately or to abandon them. Sara and the internal examiner referred the thesis for a substantial amount of further work, which Dr Kelly was rather angry about. Marten felt he had betrayed Kachigan's memory by his own inadequacies, and found the rewriting very painful.

There are four preventive strategies which can be used by individual supervisors and by departments to ensure against these disruptions: good handover procedures, supervision by teams, good documentation, and networks. It is quite common for departments to require arrangements to be made if a lecturer is going on sabbatical or research leave, or leaving for another post. However, these rarely involve a required checklist of issues, resolved and unresolved, discussed in a meeting of the outgoing and incoming, or caretaker, supervisor. The Nina Yeager saga, as seen by Dr Feste, reveals the lack of such a handover procedure at any of the five supervisory transitions she had experienced. Such an official handover, with formal checklist and a bureaucratic record, is excellent practice. It protects the incoming supervisor from accusations of neglect or redirection, and the institution from complaints. It also helps the student focus on what has been done and what remains to be done.

Supervisory teams or committees are used routinely in some universities. There is little research on what actually happens to the students who have such teams in terms of either practicalities, such as meetings and the reading of drafts, or intellectual relationships. Clearly, some teams are bureaucratic fictions, and exist only on paper, while others are intellectually engaged cooperatives. A supervisory team where several people are familiar with the student, the project and the intellectual agenda clearly protects the candidate against the upheavals experienced by Nina Yeager. We are, therefore, enthusiastic about teams that work together in the students' interests, and unenthusiastic about those which are intellectually or personally divided by disputes, or merely bureaucratic fictions.

Deaths are relatively rare, but other disruptions are not, and a good supervisor in a good department provides enough documentation to ease their impact. Good documentation is another way to prevent damage if a supervisor dies or leaves. If there are bullet points from the supervisions that record what was discussed, and what was agreed, then the incoming supervisor can grasp what the original person had in mind and the student can point to the sources of their actions and ideas. In several of the cases we have seen where the death of a supervisor led to a violent change of direction in the student's work, it was not clear whether the candidate had been too ready to take on the new ideas of the new supervisor, out of deference of whatever, or had not realized that a volte-face was underway. Making written records of supervisions or of decisions can seem a miserable chore, but they do protect the supervisor, and the student, if something goes wrong.

Our final preventive strategy is networks. If the current and past students supervised by a lecturer are known to each other, and new candidates read the successful theses of their predecessors, they can learn the supervisor's 'house style'. Then, if a disruption occurs the student can show the new supervisor the mental map that was guiding the thesis. In Cardiff we have a 25-year record of qualitative research on occupations and education, full of successful masters and doctoral theses (see Delamont, Atkinson, Coffey and Burgess 2001). A current student could discover a great deal about our priorities from that history, and from skimming a selection of the successful theses.

Data-collection problems

For many science PhD students the biggest academic problem is producing usable results, either in the laboratory or from the fieldwork outdoors in caves, mountains or riverbeds. We have presented in Chapter 5 a good deal of material from biochemistry doctoral students describing how they come to terms with the problems of producing usable results in their laboratory experiments, and have not recapitulated them here. The science supervisor has to help the students learn that 'real' science is not like undergraduate work where the results of experiments are normally known in advance. Our biochemistry respondents came to terms with failure by interpreting it as a fundamental component of scientific training which is ultimately resolvable. The immediate realization that initially nothing works is gradually replaced by a certainty that in the end it will work. Although coming to terms with initial failure is seen as a 'totally demoralizing process', it is nevertheless recognized as part of learning the ropes and therefore constitutes a crucial component of 'lab experience'. Coming to terms with uncertainty therefore constitutes an important benchmark for PhD students: 'You ... learn to accept that nine times out of ten things in the lab don't work; and if you can cope with that you'll be all right.'

Learning to cope when experiments do not work properly is an important survival skill for the science PhD student. Supervisors need to be alert for times when the failure of experimental work is demoralizing the student. In Chapter 5 we quoted accounts of the uncertainties faced by our respondents from biochemistry, physical geography and artificial intelligence, and their despondency when results were not forthcoming. Exactly the same points were made by the doctoral students in pharmaceutics interviewed by Whittlesea (1995). For example, one of Whittlesea's informants suggested that in 'med chem science' the sole criterion of success is the synthesis of a new compound, 'So they have to go on and get this product out and no matter how long it takes. So it is sometimes quite horrible for them' (pp. 68–9). Another respondent told of a friend who was 'starting something new at the end of the year. Some experimental work, which didn't go very well. He ended up spending ten months on it and getting nothing from it. That really disillusioned him' (p. 70).

We have already seen that when science students start to get their first results, they find the experience satisfying and even exhilarating. It is when PhD students first begin to produce results in the laboratory, that their previous worries and insecurities are overshadowed and despondency gives way to a growing conviction that ultimately their experiments will work.

The doctoral students we interviewed tended to locate their own work within the broader context of the scientific work in their area being carried out by all the researchers in their laboratory, and to keep up their motivation by looking at the wider picture of the overall research programme: 'In this department we tend to put everything into a wider perspective so we can see where everything fits in' (Geography postgraduate). Students tended to locate their research by specifically linking it with previous work:

> I've got a model . . . which was developed by a biologist, an ethnologist, and I've made a robot to simulate that model. I've found there are a number of problems with it, so I'm constantly trying to work out what are the best ways of adapting the model to try and make it work better.
> (Artificial intelligence postgraduate)

The majority of our science students described their projects as taking further or expanding upon the work of others: 'I think of my work as extending what other people have done, I think it has come out from a base and its pushed out from there' (Geography postgraduate).

In many cases respondents were able to cite the specific individual who had developed their work because they had been a postgraduate in, or were still a postdoctoral researcher in the department. This was often the supervisor:

> Once you identify a structure there's a lot you can do with it. I have the structure from her, and by looking at it and finding out what is important I take her work forward, using by own knowledge and methods.
> (Biochemistry postdoctoral researcher)

Equally, it might be a previous PhD student in the department:

> You can see the progress and how things are moving on. And results seem to have more of a major impact because I'm working with Pete's model and I'm extending it and seeing how it's application can be valuable. That means Pete (and John who worked on the model before Pete) are very interested in my results.
> (Geography postgraduate)

The number of people working on aspects of the same model at any one time can vary. The following postgraduate is also working on the model referred to above. 'Pete was here then, working on a computing model. He was just finishing his PhD as I started mine. Pete got John's job when he finished.' This pattern is not only retrospective but also provides a structure for individual research trajectories:

The idea is that she is doing a PhD and was going to take over from me when I finish. Also someone else is coming to be a PhD in October and by then I'll be the post-doc on the project.

(Geography postgraduate student)

Often individuals who have been working or are still working in the same project – whether it be the development of an enzyme or a modelling programme – have different funding sources:

Tim has got a joint SERC and industry grant and was funded to do his research on this enzyme. There was a person working on the enzyme before him. The first person tried to purify the enzyme and came quite close. Then a year later Tim started and actually purified the enzyme and started working on it. Now I shall be taking that work a little bit further.

(Biochemistry doctoral student)

The existence of this continuity is itself motivating for the student, but the supervisor may need to highlight the group's successes when the student is demoralized.

We found that PhD students in the early stages of their doctoral research were poorly prepared for the day-to-day uncertainty of scientific work in that they experience a qualitative difference between laboratory work at under-graduate and graduate level. Although all our biochemistry respondents had completed a practical project in their final year of undergraduate study this was often inadequate preparation for their later experiences as post-graduates. As noted by Delamont and Atkinson (1995), Collins (1985: 35) and others, experiments which are carried out as a routine component of education and training address questions to which the answers are already known and are constructed to produce only successful conclusions. The biochemistry supervisors recognized the difficulties experienced by post-graduates in coming to terms with this insecurity. Certainly the biochemistry postgraduates acknowledged their lack or preparation for laboratory work, and despondency and sometimes panic when their experiments constantly failed.

The realization that the outcomes of laboratory work are by no means certain, accompanies a growing concern among postgraduates that there is no guarantee that PhD requirement will be met. Day-to-day uncertainty encountered by doctoral students in the early stages of their research, can lead to doubts about the predictability of completing a PhD. An important aspect of the process of PhD work, particularly among our biochemistry respondents, was learning to cope with the insecurities associated with scien-tific work. There are a number of strategies or ways in which postgraduates learn to rationalize initial failure. One of these is by understanding that it is not personal; it happens to everybody. In reaching this understanding the role of 'significant others' (the supervisor and other members of the research group) is crucial.

Those of our respondents who relied upon the collection, collation or manipulation of data from natural phenomena, to a greater or lesser extent, described themselves at the mercy of natural elements over which they had no control. This applied equally to biochemistry PhD students waiting for rape seeds to germinate and geographers waiting for the rainy season: 'The reality is you get pushed and shoved, depending on the seasonality of the thing, that's very much a big problem with natural field conditions.' For the science students the biggest source of help with these problems was an active research group in a laboratory, with postdoctoral fellows around who could, *by their very existence*, show that there is hope: that theses do get done. For intellectual problems in science the intellectually vital laboratory is the best source of motivation. For the more individualized research characteristic of humanities and social sciences the supervisor may be the only source of help. If the social science or humanities project is going wrong, the supervisor should use his or her greater experience to help with the practical problems, or guide the student to refocus the research, or seek help with the technical problems, or get on with another aspect of their doctoral research until the difficulty is resolved.

Thus far we have focused on students being demoralized by their data collection. We now move on to deal with extrinsic sources of demotivation such as poverty. We discuss a set of problems than can beset all PhD students, leading to one, isolation, that is much commoner among non-scientists.

Problems and what the supervisor can do about them

The problems discussed here are: poverty; poor working habits; lack of motivation and depression; isolation. The major problems not discussed in detail in this chapter are those related to writing, because that is the focus of Chapter 9.

Poverty

Poverty is a crippling problem for many research students. They are living in poor quality housing, with inadequate food and clothing, and certainly cannot buy books, a PC, a decent workstation, a proper typing chair and so on. This has three consequences which impact upon their research.

1 A poor diet is likely to make them ill, spotty, tired, lethargic and so on.
2 Inadequate heat, light and facilities may make work at home difficult or even damaging to health.
3 Time may be eaten away by many hours spent on low-paid, possibly unpleasant work.

All these problems are multiplied if the student has dependent children and/or a dependent spouse, and may be multiplied even further if the student is from overseas. To be a poor 23-year-old single person is one thing; to be a poor 43-year-old woman with a disabled husband and two dependent teenagers, or a poor Tunisian with a wife and five children under 7, are different forms of poverty. The possible solutions the supervisor can offer will also vary. At its simplest, the older and more financially secure supervisor can invite a single 23-year-old to have a square meal every week, and ensure that they sometimes eat 'properly' by providing food in the supervision or a basket of fruit for the graduate room. Such 'solutions' are much less possible with a mature student who has a family home, or young professionals who are desperately poor themselves.

It may be possible in some universities to find paid work for the research student, ideally even paid work that could have some relevance to the thesis. Demonstrating in the lab has traditionally been available for some science and engineering students, but is rarely paid well enough to alleviate poverty. In some universities humanities and social science students get paid work taking tutorials or seminars for undergraduates. (Such work is rarely available for overseas students.) Some departments have no budget to pay for such help, however. These opportunities are usually beneficial to the student's higher degree: teaching something helps enormously with one's own understanding of it. However, the income is spasmodic: work for ten or twelve weeks, then nothing. It can also be a displacement activity: undergraduates can swamp the friendly postgraduate with demands, and it is often easier to spend time with a lonely or bewildered student than tackle the thesis task.

In these circumstances, the supervisor may be able to find demonstrating work, tutoring or the equivalent at another institution: in general our networks are better than theirs. Coaching local school children for GCSE or A level may also be a possibility – students with a family may even be able to do that in their own home. Again the supervisor may be able to advise a student to do such work, and help them find it. There may also be local colleges wanting A level lecturers, or a WEA/adult education set-up where the student would be able to teach. Recognizing that the student is broke, and will need to earn, and signalling that the supervisor would prefer the work to be subject-related, is more productive than the ostrich position.

If a student has dependants it may be worth checking that the family is getting all the available support: there may be local charities or scholarships, help from the students' union, or even work for the spouse which people in the university know about, but the student may not have been to see these welfare/union/pastoral offices. If the student has to take in other work it may be desirable to try and find some *in* the university such as proofreading or library assistance, rather than leaving them to stack shelves in a supermarket or clean offices.

The worst pressures of student poverty commonly occur when students are writing up the thesis after their full-time money has run out and they have not yet found proper employment, or, if from overseas, not been able to go home. The case of Heraclio Costa, Example 6.3, is not unusual.

Example 6.3: Heraclio Costa

Heraclio Costa was from Brazil. His grant had run out, but he knew that if he went back to Brazil he was unlikely ever to submit. He was reduced to selling his possessions: his watch, his PC, his car, and helping other overseas students with their written work.

Apart from the depressing effects of poverty and poor diet on health, it may be that poverty is impeding the student's thesis because they lack the basic facilities to do anything on their theses at home. A good supervisor needs to enquire whether students have got a warm room to work in. Clearly you cannot be expected to heat their homes, but you can, perhaps, heat a space in the university for them, *or* buy and lend them snuggle sacks. Have they got adequate lighting? Again, perhaps you can have ready a 'spare' desk lamp you could lend. Have they got a proper typing chair, foot rest, keyboard, a work table of the right height?

If the university does not provide the PhD students with adequate working conditions, and hardly any do for part-time students, even if their full-timers' spaces are lavishly equipped, a caring supervisor will check that the student is properly equipped to do the work. Getting the proper equipment, either owning it or borrowing it for the duration, can speed up completion considerably, as in the case of Caroline Sheppard.

Example 6.4: Caroline Sheppard

Teresa Rees and Sara discovered that Caroline Sheppard was transcribing her interviews using a Walkman to play back the tapes. She did not know that there are transcribing machines with a foot pedal and high quality 'pause' facility nor that our department owned several that research students could borrow. Once issued with a proper machine Caroline quickly finished her transcribing and moved on to analysis.

The case of Caroline Sheppard showed that we were not providing good enough induction and documentation for graduate students, so that they knew what was available.

Avoiding repetitive strain injury is also important, and students may need to be warned to give themselves breaks and not to spend too long at the keyboard. If the university has an occupational health expert who can give a precautionary talk on this, it could save much heartache (and other pains).

Poor or inappropriate working habits

Even when students have good physical conditions, they may be flagging because they are relying on academic working habits that were adequate or even successful when they were on taught courses with externally set deadlines and a timetable, but are woefully inadequate for a three-year stretch of self-directed research. If a supervisor suspects that this is a problem – deadlines missed, poorly presented work, an apparent lack of progress – it may be necessary to persuade, or even insist that the student takes stock of his or her working habits and becomes self-conscious about them. Students may not realize that they need to discover how they work best, perhaps by experimenting, and once they have decided what suits them, they must organize their lives to maximize the potential for achieving their best working conditions.

It may be helpful to confess to one's own problems. It can be liberating for a student if you describe how you cannot work before lunch or on Thursdays, or without a laptop, or whatever. This can be liberating for a student because it reveals that even successful academics have problems (they often think that they have problems we never have), and it can lead to a discussion of possible solutions. Clearly it is not helpful or fair to load all your problems onto the student, but some admission of fallibility is often a great lubricator.

Example 6.5: Unblocking Raymond Boynton and Margaret Rushbridger

We were giving a class on writing strategies – something we do regularly. Sara 'confessed' that she can work only on scrap paper: the backs of committee papers, previous drafts by others, spoilt sheets from the Xerox machine and circulars from publishers, shops or travel companies. Facing a clean pad of file paper paralyses her. One student in the room, Raymond Boynton, suddenly looked interested. A week later he came to find Sara and confessed that he'd been blocked for ages, but had gone home, abandoned his clean pad, and started drafting on some scrap paper. It had worked – he had written 3000 words of his thesis.

When Raymond told the rest of the doctoral students about his discovery, Margaret Rushbridger 'came out' as a person unblocked by the personal computer. She had discovered that she was paralysed by handwriting or typing, because her results seemed permanent, whereas words on the screen were infinitely malleable, and therefore she could fool herself that she was 'only drafting'.

Repeatedly, we have found students who have not thought about their biorhythms, their location, their posture, their preferred facilities. They have not experimented with silence versus noise, being alone versus being in company, the early morning versus the early evening, the clipboard in an armchair versus the laptop, the pen versus the typewriter, the desk versus the kitchen table. The supervisor can usefully explore with the student how to discover what their best working habits are, and then how to achieve them.

Example 6.6: Test Match Special versus Runrig or Zydeco

Sara's ideal working conditions occur during the cricket season or a simulation of it. She works best to noise rather than silence, and to speech rather than music. The *ideal* working condition is a test match – a long day of speech. She has the TV on, but silent, and the ball-by-ball commentary on the radio. If something happens, she looks up at the screen, but otherwise she lets the radio fill the room with 'burble'. If there is not a real test match, then a tape of one is the next best thing – cassettes of John Arlott and Brian Johnson burbling about Derek Underwood, Alan Knott, and chocolate cake. Paul, on the other hand, prefers music: not the serious music that demands attention but something that has bouncy rhythms. Companions to academic work include Country and Western and Zydeco, Runrig and compilations from the Stax and Atlantic labels.

We often share these predilections with our graduate classes – not to try to persuade them to share our particular tastes, but to encourage them to recognize that ideal working conditions vary from person to person, and the trick is to find what suits them best.

Some doctoral students may not have realized that they need to work steadily for 36 or 45 hours a week, because they were successful undergraduates by coasting and cramming in bursts. We know that students have very inaccurate ideas about what lecturers do all day (Startup 1979), and so they may not realize that the production of an 80,000-word thesis in three years needs to be a full-time job. Others may be 'overworking', because the task seems so overwhelming. A supervision can use the regular revisions of the timetable we advocated in Chapter 2 to introduce the discussion of the proper working day, week and year. It is often when investigating the student's working habits that the supervision uncovers the more disconcerting phenomenon: a lack or loss of motivation, and it is to this that we now turn.

Lack and loss of motivation

There are three separable aspects to this:

1   distaste for a specific aspect of the work (e.g. finding a site, doing analysis, writing, word-processing);

2   temporary loss of enthusiasm of the whole task;
3   serious, perhaps clinical, depression with a 'medical' origin or solution.

The supervisor's role in dealing with these is, of necessity, rather different. A student who is apparently suffering serious, even clinical depression needs to be urged towards counselling or the medical profession as soon as the supervisor is worried. Dealing with an underactive thyroid, SAD, ME or a mental illness is not within the scope of a supervisor's expertise or role. The other types of loss of motivation can be tackled by the supervisor.

If the student has distaste for a specific task, there are various things that can be done. Sometimes it is possible to find them help with it: perhaps they can arrange to work with another student and share the task, perhaps they can pay for some help with it, perhaps an undergraduate can be assigned to work with them, maybe there is a research assistant, associate or lecturer who likes that task and will help with it. Clearly the integrity of the thesis cannot be threatened, but help may be the answer. Another solution is to shelve that task and do something else for a while, or start some other parts of the whole project alongside the less preferred one. One reason students often stall at the writing-up stage is that they have left themselves with no other tasks but writing: if they had written while they did the other phases it would not be so all-or-nothing at the end. Learning to mix writing, data collection, analysis, and dull clerical tasks is an important part of learning how to be a productive researcher.

Sometimes distaste for the whole task is due to an intrinsic difficulty with the thesis, but it may be only a symptom of wider problems in the student's life, as in the cases of Jefferson Cope and Shannon Giroux.

Example 6.7: Jefferson Cope

Sara was supervising Jefferson Cope. He had done a Masters degree based on gathering oral histories from educational administrators in his native country. He wanted to do a larger study of educational administrators in the UK, again using oral history techniques. After a few months of supervision, Sara felt that he had not really understood the method, and that he needed to think much more deeply about it before conducting his doctoral fieldwork. She therefore set him to read 'classic' methods books and write about them while waiting for access to a research site. Jefferson baulked – it was too boring for words. After several months of stalemate, Jefferson went into the field. The data were not wonderful, and neither Jefferson nor Sara was satisfied with them. Jefferson withdrew. In retrospect, perhaps, Sara should have let him discover his own methodological inadequacies once it became clear that he would not or could not read the classics and face up to the issues in the abstract.

Example 6.8: Shannon Giroux

Shannon Giroux was at the thesis stage of her EdD. She was not making any progress, for reasons that were all too clear. She was deputy head of a school. Her head teacher was off sick so she was acting head, and her adult daughter's marriage had imploded, propelling daughter and three children home to mother. Clearly Shannon either had to give up, or devise a rescue strategy. Luckily the data were collected, but they lay, untouched in the loft. Luckily too, Shannon was not desperately hard up. We found a freelance audio typist, and another person to do the basic data entry for SPSS and the initial SPSS runs to kick-start the quantitative analysis. Shannon faced her daughter and renegotiated the household rules about noise, and housework. She got an extension, and eventually managed to complete.

If the distaste for the thesis seems serious, it is helpful to read Rudestam and Newton (2001: 134–7) who explore both emotional and task-related blocks that they have found among American graduate students. Broaching some of the problems Rudestam and Newton explore with the student may reveal whether their difficulties are emotional or task-related. Cryer (2000) has a chapter on 'flagging', which the student may find liberating. Leonard (2001) has an excellent chapter (7) on 'Keeping going and staying the course'. It is also worth pointing out to yourself and to the student that they should consider taking a break, registering for a lower category of degree, or even giving up altogether. There are always some students who will be well-advised to give up the unequal struggle and downgrade to a Masters degree or diploma or even withdraw altogether.

It is helpful if all the staff in the department are interested in the graduate students and enquire supportively about the work. Sometimes explicitly telling a colleague about a student's achievement and success – in a corridor or around the photocopier – can produce a spontaneous burst of pleasure which is more motivating than the routine encouragement of the thesis supervisor.

It may be possible to provide some motivational jolts to a student. If you can organize something to reinvigorate the student you will have done them the biggest favour or service of the whole relationship. Among the things you can try to organize are: a departmental seminar, presenting a paper at another department, a conference attendance, a conference paper, a summer school, a book review, an article (probably jointly with you), a book chapter (again, in collaboration), or organizing a small workshop. All these academic activities can help to refocus the student's energies on his or her thesis topic.

If the student has to prepare a departmental seminar paper for delivery, that can be a motivational jolt. If the department does not routinely request students to present their work, the supervisor may need to set up such a seminar: perhaps in a research group or with a small audience. Asking a colleague at another university to invite a flagging student to come and do a seminar can be motivating, especially if the invitation appears to come spontaneously, 'out of the blue'. (Good supervisors do not always reveal the strings they pull behind the scenes.) An intensive summer school is one excellent way of reinvigorating students, getting them specific skills and forcing them to meet new people.

Example 6.9: The intervention

Prescott Milholland had fallen behind the rest of his cohort: they had all submitted and he hadn't. He seemed to have lost all motivation and to be especially depressed about a major new book on his area which he felt might undermine his own ideas. Three of his friends approached a staff member, who organized a day conference on the topic of Prescott's research, with the author of the new book and Prescott as speakers. Prescott discovered that the new book did not make his work redundant, the day conference remotivated him, he quickly tidied up his draft, submitted and got his PhD.

Going to a conference, or better still, giving a conference paper, or helping to organize a conference, can all motivate a postgraduate. These things can be set up by a supervisor, who can couple a student's name with their own or that of a colleague. Learning to do a conference presentation, meeting new faces, and seeing how a conference is organized can all lift the student's eyes from their immediate problem, towards the longer-term goal of completing the research and submitting the thesis. Getting published is one of the most exciting things that happens to a young scholar, so setting up a publication opportunity for a flagging research student can work wonders.

In general, encourage the student to build in intrinsic rewards and extrinsic ones. Think about how you motivate yourself, and how you reward yourself, ask colleagues the same questions, and then get the student to focus on the rewards professionals use. We use stationery to motivate and reward ourselves. A new project is an excuse to choose a new set of folders and ring binders in an attractive pattern, new pencils, new pens, new disk boxes, new coloured disks, new ruler/eraser/pencil sharpener, or whatever. Then, starting the new project is a treat: using all the lovely new things.

Example 6.10: Extrinsic rewards

Desiree Shapiro is a shoe fanatic. When she was bogged down with her EdD thesis she designed herself a reward: she would invest in a pair of Patrick Cox boots when she handed in her dissertation. Whenever she found herself flagging she focused on the boots.

Isolation

All the research on PhD students has found that isolation, both social and intellectual, is a frequently mentioned problem. This was the worst problem for the students studied by Eggleston and Delamont (1981, 1983) and has been reported by many other researchers (Becher, Henkel and Kogan 1994; Brown 1982; Diamond and Zuber-Skerritt 1986; Hockey 1991, 1994a, 1994b; Katz and Hartnett 1976; Porter 1984; Rudd 1984, 1985; Scott 1985; Scott and Porter 1980, 1983, 1984; Vartuli 1982; Wright 1992; Young *et al.* 1987). It is less of a problem for scientists in a research group with a lab to work in but a particularly acute problem for many humanities and social science students, for part-timers of all disciplines and for those overseas students who are far from home, friends and family. It can be particularly acute for a graduate student who is 'different' from other research students in the department because of age, race, sex, religion or thesis topic.

Supervisors individually, and departments more generally, can do something to mitigate the isolation. First, it is vital to make it explicit that in one way isolation is essential. Once an original thesis project is well underway, the student has to be intellectually responsible for it and has to become the expert in the field. *Intellectual* isolation is necessary and desirable. However, there is no reason for this intellectual isolation to be accompanied by social or emotional loneliness. Indeed, students need to realize that the former is impeded by the latter. The supervisor can try to ensure that the graduate students in the department, or the whole faculty, have formal and informal opportunities to meet. Seminars on how to get published, build a CV, prepare for the viva, or apply for jobs, can be slotted regularly into the academic year, in addition to seminars at which students present their work to each other. If the research students do teaching, classes to help them teach better, or workshops on teaching, assessment or pastoral care can be useful occasions to bring them together. Access to a staff common room, a buffet lunch with staff, or drinks after work can also reduce isolation, as long as the students are encouraged to mix and not left in a corner. However, 'social' occasions, especially if alcohol is involved, may be alienating or even 'out of bounds', unthinkable, for overseas students from Islamic cultures, for women from cultures with strict chaperonage, and for those with child-care responsibilities (for whom after-hours social activities may be difficult). A good department tries a variety of ways to encourage students to mix and make friends.

Example 6.11: Shared solution

A group of EdD students found the isolation of the thesis stage demotivating, and missed the camaraderie of the taught modules. They formed two subgroups. Some men all met in the library on a Monday evening, did three hours' work and then went to a pub. Some women formed a Saturday lunch club, and met once a month to enjoy a good meal and urge each other on. Both subgroups found this motivating.

The importance of the social life attached to a research group in science was made clear to David Pearson (2002). As for team mentality, one scientist illustrated the need for social fluency in a very literal sense:

> What I'm looking for are people who will fit in with the group, who are very sociable, basically, because I like to run a group which is a happy group. We get on well, not just that they do good research but they also interact socially and basically have a good time. I mean, I look back and that was one of the happiest times of my life as a PhD student and I want them to leave having enjoyed themselves but also done good research. But I say, more often than not, we have to take who we can get. But having said that, I mean, there are people who come and you think, 'Well, will they really fit into the group?' You often take a gamble but you're not that bothered if they don't come and you may delay a little bit and maybe put them off. Obviously, you have to be a bit careful. So, as I say, it's not so much an academic ability these days. [He clarified what kind of ability he was searching for when he discussed sport later in the interview]: Our criterion for research students before they come is: 'Do you play football and are you good?' If they're good, that's no good. I mean we play sort of social football – five-a-side, including women, and I think it's good – creates the right sort of atmosphere in the group.

Pearson comments wryly: 'As someone who values solitude and has no interest or ability in sport whatsoever, I wondered how easy it would be to survive in such a group, even if I was a brilliant scientist!'

Overseas students may find vital support from a university or locally-based 'national' or religious society: an Indian in an Indian Society, or a Chilean in a Chilean Society, a Greek Cypriot in a link to a Greek Orthodox church, a Muslim in a local mosque. If there do not seem to be enough students from a country to make up a society, meeting undergraduates who can speak the language can help. We had a Brazilian PhD student in the 1980s who we introduced to an undergraduate reading Portuguese and taking a course on contemporary Brazilian film. They met for coffee occasionally and discussed current Brazilian fiction in Portuguese. Both benefited. The PhD student was able to speak in his own language and about his own culture, the undergraduate got 'free' conversation classes from a native speaker. One important source of support for postgraduates can be a learned society, particularly if there is a postgraduate section (and if there is not, your postgraduates might start one). Such a forum can provide students with a network, a disciplinary identity, administrative experience, an entry on a CV, and mitigate intellectual and social isolation. Beyond the department, or the faculty, there may be scholarly communities to be joined by e-mail, on the Internet, by newsletter and so on.

Our research on geography found very good practice with regard to postgraduate involvement in a learned society. Many of the geography PhD students belonged to the learned society for geographers, the Institute for

British Geographers (IBG). The IBG has a strong postgraduate section, as Patsy Schroeder from Wellferry explained, 'To me the IBG is great!' but she felt this was partly because 'I've been involved.' She had been an active IBG postgraduate since her first year as a PhD student, and spoke highly of the newsletter, the conferences and also the networking functions. Patsy and her friends believe that 'if you want to be a professional geographer you have to get into the circuit early'.

Most of the students had not joined what were in the early 1990s the other two geographical organizations, the Royal Geographical Society (RGS) and the Geographical Association (GA). The RGS (which has since merged with the IBG) then had a rather old-fashioned image among the doctoral students. As Brian Faul explained:

> my own perception of it is that it seems to have gone very much towards exploration, hacking through the jungles and showing slides about it. The IBG seems more academic, it organizes a postgraduate forum which is quite useful.

Similarly, Julian Perini described joining the IBG as 'the natural choice . . . and it's cheap to join and it's meant to be very good'. Those who had not joined the IBG were likely to have been to the IBG conference or the IBG postgraduate forum or an associated conference. Of all our student groups, they were the most clearly attached to a professional learned society. This was particularly because of the IBG's inclusive policies on doctoral students. The social anthropologists we studied had no opportunity to join the anthropological equivalent of the IBG, the Association of Social Anthropologists. In the past it only allowed established lecturers with doctorates to join, and had no section or division for PhD students. Our anthropological respondents felt isolated from their peers and their superiors in other institutions, and detached from their discipline in a way the human geographers did not. The ASA and the Royal Anthropological Institute introduced a new membership scheme for graduates in the new century.

If your discipline/learned society has a postgraduate section, pushing your students towards it is a good insurance against isolation. The specific value of postgraduate student membership of a professional association is but a particular solution to a very general set of issues. As we have indicated throughout this chapter, and indeed throughout the book, postgraduate research can be wonderfully rewarding for all concerned. But it can be problematic in all sorts of ways, personal and intellectual. While the experienced and successful supervisor will always hope for the best, he or she might do well at least to be prepared for the worst. In the face of problems, whether financial, personal, or intellectual the research student can easily flag. Motivation and self-belief can be damaged by setbacks. Academics who have successfully completed a higher degree by research will know that it is possible to overcome those personal and academic obstacles and to succeed. Likewise, experienced supervisors can point to their own graduate students and hold them up as positive role models. They and their students will need reminding from time to time of the successes, and how pleasurable those successes are. Supervisors need to be aware of the kinds of problems that students might well be facing. They certainly need to take on board the recurrent finding that research students feel some degree of isolation. To some extent, as we have acknowledged, intellectual isolation is inherent in the role of the graduate student: the long-term pursuit of an individual research project for which – ultimately – the student has sole authority is, almost inevitably, a lonely and risky business. The student who is not aware of those risks and the consequent loneliness at some point in their career is probably insufficiently reflective. On the other hand, undue social isolation can be detrimental. Supervisors need to beware of the research student who loses his or her way and starts to drift aimlessly, or whose work becomes such alienated labour that the savour of research fades. By the same token, the research student whose research is not 'working' for whatever reason is by no means rare. As we have seen, scientists' experiments do not always run smoothly; social science students may have difficulty obtaining access, or usable samples of respondents, or interpretable results; humanities students may find themselves adrift in a sea of texts or archives, and cannot see the wood for the trees. Whatever the reason, ennui and disillusionment are real dangers. Good supervisors look out for the signs, and try to work out with the student where the problems seem to lie, what kinds of solutions will be most fruitful, and practical action-plans to tackle them. Avoidance of these issues, through misplaced tact, embarrassment or guilt on either side, will only perpetuate and exacerbate them.

7

Contorted corkscrew: the getting and giving of judgement

> accentuated by the presence, on the chest of drawers, of a curious statu-
> ette or three-dimensional diagram carried out in aluminium, which
> resembled a gigantic and contorted corkscrew, and was labelled upon its
> base: ASPIRATION.
>
> (Sayers 1972: 12)

Introduction

When Dorothy Sayers wrote that paragraph she was contrasting an undergraduate's lack of aesthetic 'taste' with the sophisticated judgements of good
and bad art made by the older woman looking at the statuette. The focus of
this chapter is on how the supervisor can guide the student towards developing the academic equivalent of 'good taste' (Bourdieu and Passeron 1977,
1979). The research student has to develop the skill to judge when an
experiment has worked and when it has not, when an analysis is 'correct',
when a reading is plausible, when the null hypothesis has been falsified, and
so on. The issues in this chapter are fundamental ones, and this is the chapter
we are proudest of and value most.

Such judgement is a vital part of being a fully accredited professional. As
the Nobel Laureate Biochemist 'Spencer', in an interview with Gilbert and
Mulkay (1984), makes clear: 'If you are an experimenter you know what is
important and what is not important.' Similarly a physicist interviewed by
Gumport (1993: 265–6) said

> I try to teach them a set of skills. The biggest one is to know when you're
> right and when you're wrong. It's common for them to miss it when
> they're wrong. After a while they can see it. It's intuitive partially.

Some of these issues have been foreshadowed in Chapter 5, but we have
returned to them here because judgement is such a crucial issue in doctoral
supervision. Both parties have to develop judgement. The student has to
learn, over the three years, to judge his or her own work by standards
appropriate to fully independent research, rather than undergraduate student standards. The supervisor has to learn how to judge not only the student's current work, but also the potential for further improvement, while at
the same time helping the student develop his or her own skills.

This is a complex area, particularly so because it deals with the indeterminate, tacit and implicit aspects of a particular academic discipline (see Atkinson,
Reid and Sheldrake 1977 for a discussion of this terminology). It is much easier
to teach technical, explicit things than the indeterminate, implicit ones. This
is very clear from the literature on occupational – especially professional –
socialization, particularly that on medicine (Becker *et al.* 1961; Atkinson 1981,
1984, 1996), nurses (Olesen and Whittaker 1968), lawyers (Granfield 1992;
Phillips 1982), schoolteachers (Atkinson and Delamont 1985) and even
apprentice musicians (Kadushin 1969). However, we do not know very much
either about how apprentice scholars learn the necessary discriminations in
their discipline or subspecialization, or about how established scholars exercise discrimination in their own work. The literature on academics (e.g. Ashmore *et al.* 1994; Becher 1989, 1990; Bourdieu 1988; Evans 1988, 1993; Latour
and Woolgar 1986; Lynch 1985) has not produced an easily transferable
'model' of how academic judgement is exercised: because, of course, such a
model is inconceivable. Experienced academics learn how to judge research
and publications in their field over the course of their career, without explicit
instruction for the most part, as the physicist already quoted has stated.

In this chapter we discuss how to cultivate your judgement of the student's
work, and how to help the students develop their own 'taste' and discrimination. Before we move on into detailed discussion of how judgement and
discrimination can be developed, two contrasting stories will make concrete
the type of issue that is central to this chapter. Two of the respondents to the
Eggleston and Delamont (1983) survey had had problems with deciding
which statistical techniques were appropriate for their data:

> The analysis of data was not a problem until the thesis, submitted on the
> advice of the internal supervisor, and presented for examination, was
> returned on the ground that the methods of analysis were not suitable.
> A new external tutor was appointed to take a fresh look at the data. Work
> has since progressed in a very satisfactory way but this problem has taken
> one academic year to resolve. It has also involved me in much extra
> expense.
>
> (Len Clement)

> A crucial problem arose in the statistical evaluation of my experimental
> data. Having completed a number of experiments I read a paper by an
> American Psychologist criticising the sort of statistics traditionally used
> in that type of experiment. I had succeeded in doing the original stat-
> istics only through the guidance of Violet Willet and the convenient
> provision of a ready-made computer programme. It took me a long time
> to realise that the criticisms actually applied to my statistics, and even
> longer to understand exactly what the objection was. For some reason I
> felt disinclined to broach this question with my supervisor until I could
> at least explain sensibly what the problem was. When I did raise the
> matter my supervisor (Prof. Burnaby) was so helpful and understanding
> about it I regretted not seeing him earlier. He immediately set to work

helping me to find a method of re-analysing my data in response to the more rigorous requirements outlined by the American.

(Joseph Trevelyn)

In the case of Len Clement, the problem was not spotted by him or his supervisor until the external examiner referred the thesis. Len's recognition of the judgement came too late. One aim of this chapter is help supervisors and students avoid scenarios like Len's. Our second respondent – Joseph Trevelyn – is a more positive example, because it is clear that he has learned how to make his own professional judgement. Joseph's story, in which he read a paper, realized that the criticisms applied to his own work, and decided to reanalyse his own data, is an excellent example of a research student becoming a mature scholar exercising judgement. Joseph Trevelyan had clearly learned a great deal about standards of statistical rigour in Psychology, and had realized that he had learned it. Len Clement is less explicit, and it is not clear whether he accepted the judgement of his external examiner or not. The good supervisor wants the student to learn, before submission, as Joseph did.

Statistical techniques are only one possible area where judgement has to be exercised, but these two contrasting stories show one aspect of the wider issues we raise in this chapter. We have divided the argument into three major sections: how supervisors can develop their judgement of work in progress; how supervisors can train students so their judgement develops; and examining: an issue we raise here before returning to it in Chapter 9. This area is largely absent from the literature on doctoral supervision (see Phillips 1994) and is addressed in an unsophisticated way in Phillips and Pugh (2000), and Cryer (2000). We regard it as a fundamental part of doctoral studies, during which successful students will become discriminating scholars as well as finishing their own theses. Several of David Pearson's (2002) respondents talked about this issue, such as:

> Dr Phillips (chemist): They have to know . . . the judgement of knowing when they can do something off their own bat without talking to their supervisor about it and when it's appropriate to come and ask. And that's a balance that has to be learned and for each student it will be different. Some are very capable and have an instinct as to what is safe and what can be done. Others are not.

Developing your judgement

New supervisors are frequently unsure about their own abilities to judge the work of supervisees during the registration period and, most crucially, when deciding if it is 'good enough' to be submitted for examination. One useful way to develop your judgement of doctoral work is to read some successful theses supervised by colleagues, and then talk to the colleagues who supervised and/or examined them.

It is especially difficult for younger academics to feel that they have sufficient confidence in their own judgement to advise advanced students appropriately. Given the nature of academic life, it is always hard to do something for the very first time, given the general lack of explicit instruction. It is now widespread practice for such scholars at the beginning of their career to undertake higher-degree supervision jointly with a more experienced colleague. The value of sharing the supervisory task are several. In particular, the more senior partner can be relied on to provide general advice and support concerning strategic planning, and to advise both the candidate and the fellow supervisor on general requirements, and that elusive but crucial aspect – the appropriate scope and standards expected of the research and the relevant degree aimed for. Likewise, younger supervisors can often gain the necessary experience through the supervision of part-requirement dissertations associated with taught Masters degree schemes. Informed confidence is crucial. We have been at pains to emphasize at various points that 'confidence' is of fundamental importance in the entire supervisory process. The supervisor needs to feel confident in the student, and the student needs to feel confident in the overall judgement of the supervisor. Such confidence has to be 'informed', not blind faith. To a considerable extent, confidence comes from experience. It comes, more crucially, from the supervisor's own research activity. For the kind of reasons we shall explore below, the assured supervisor needs to be an active researcher who can provide and encourage a broad view of the discipline, and can help the candidate keep a strategic perspective on the whole research enterprise. The confident supervisor can help to develop many of the indeterminate skills that the fledgling graduate student will need to acquire.

In addition to learning through joint supervision, learning from being an examiner is invaluable. It is now standard practice for higher-degree theses to be examined by an internal examiner who has not been involved in the supervision, in addition to the external examiner. Acting as an internal examiner is an excellent way of gaining experience in judging theses; discussion with the external examiner and participation at the viva voce examination (if there is one) will provide excellent experience in evaluating the final product, and insight into how academic judgement is brought to bear. Equally, of course, the experience of external examining is directly transferable to that of supervising. It is extremely useful to see how other people's students have tackled things, and how they and their supervisor talk about the research process. It is usually reassuring to discover that other university departments do *not* have very different experiences, and that good theses from elsewhere have the same sort of strengths and weaknesses as your own.

Being an examiner, of course, forces you to read the thesis in question. By and large most of us read only those theses that we supervise or examine. But if you feel you lack confidence and experience as a supervisor, then reading other theses can be a very valuable experience. Indeed, this is a good way of acquainting oneself with some of the best and most recent work in your field – by borrowing some of the doctoral theses from good research groups, that are by young scholars who are making a mark in the field. In many disciplines – especially those in the humanities and social sciences – it will take a long while for the best doctoral work to appear and make its full impact: monographs appear years later, and journals often have long lead times. Reading the original thesis will have several advantages: you will read the whole thing long before the monograph appears; you will get a very good sense of the standard and overall style of doctoral work in your field; you will start to identify the good new researchers in your field which may be useful in sponsoring them and in building your own research group (Atkinson and Delamont 2004).

There is also a danger of treating supervision as a largely private matter (even when conducted in pairs as a joint exercise). As a professional activity it is often much less visible than undergraduate teaching (given that lecture courses appear in timetables, undergraduate results are discussed at departmental examination boards, and taught courses occupy the greater part of most academics' teaching loads). There is no reason why graduate students' work and progress should not be regarded as a collective, shared interest. Supervisors should feel free to discuss their graduate students' work, as a matter of their own professional commitment.

More generally, there is no reason why issues of graduate thesis supervision should not feature in a university-wide or departmental staff development programme. While the bases of judgement and 'good taste' are usually tacit, and are highly specific to particular disciplines, general discussion about how to approach the relationship between supervisor and supervised, and how to promote an appreciation of academic culture, norms and judgement is beneficial to all parties.

The getting of judgement by graduate students depends in large measure on how supervisors and their academic colleagues sponsor graduate students into the full range of the academic culture. One needs to remember that the majority of new graduate students will have a very limited exposure to academic life. Undergraduate degrees introduce one to a very restricted version of academic knowledge, and – understandably – inculcate 'textbook' knowledge (Fleck 1979). Taught Masters courses provide few opportunities for students to become incorporated into the complexities of academic life and work. They have relatively little insight into the *processes* of knowledge-production, as opposed to consuming the products. Students enrolled on professional doctorates may be knowledgeable about academic life, but it would be a mistake to assume that they are. Myths and misapprehensions about academia are widespread in the other occupations from which most students on professional doctorates originate. It is important to help the students gain insight into the diffuse, personal and practical issues and contingencies that permeate the academy. A recognition of those aspects of academic life will help the graduate students in various related ways: they will start to gain a mature perspective on their own work; they will start to see their own work in relation to that of others in the discipline; and they will start to understand and to put into practice the everyday, local knowledge of the discipline; and they will more readily become colleagues and members of the research group and/or department – as we shall elaborate further.

Training the student's own judgement

There are two aspects to this: things you can (and should) do during their period as a student, to show them, as explicitly as possible, how the scholarly community exercises its judgements, and the more implicit aspects of scholarly activity. Graduate students need to be introduced to the ways in which the academic community functions: how 'peer review' works in your discipline and your speciality. As Deem and Brehony (2000) have pointed out, graduate students in the arts and the social sciences have little chance to observe or join their supervisors and other staff actually doing research. You also need to be able to set up contexts and occasions in which students can learn how to discriminate, without explicit instruction in the more mechanical procedures. The more the student is cue-deaf, the more explicit you need to be in teaching them about judgement.

This is an area of supervision where the more professional contexts the supervisor is active in, the better. If the supervisor is editing a journal, refereeing journal articles, refereeing conference proposals, writing book reviews, going to conferences and examining theses, then there are many opportunities for the supervisor to practise academic judgements, and to explain and share them with graduate students. The less the supervisor is active in the discipline, the less chance the student has to learn about judgement. So, one important way to help your students is to be active yourself.

Let us take some concrete examples. When relevant visiting speakers come to the department or the university, you should attend yourself with your graduate students, encourage them to ask questions (if appropriate) and afterwards discuss with them what was good and bad about the session, and why. If you are unable to attend, get them to tell you about the talk and the discussion, drawing out the criticisms made. When a relevant conference comes along, this process can be repeated in an expanded form: discuss explicitly what you do at conferences and why, go to papers together and then discuss your responses and theirs. If they go to a conference alone, encourage them to debrief you about what you missed – and if you can compare their reports with those of colleagues, share those comparisons. This only works, of course, if they learn to respond honestly: if they are unimpressed by a great name, they need to learn to justify their criticisms.

A second way to help students develop judgement is for them to read work in progress. You can encourage them to read each other's work, but it is even more helpful for them to see and comment on the work of established scholars. You can share your draft papers with them, encourage colleagues to do the same, and discuss why you are preparing your work for publication in the way that you are. If you get a paper back from a journal with referees' comments, and can face sharing them with students, that is a priceless experience for them. It has value for the development of their own career (a theme we return to in Chapter 10) and for helping them to learn how peer evaluation works.

If you are involved in refereeing other scholars' work (for a journal, a conference or an edited book) and you can allow your graduate students to help, this will show them peer review in action. This must be done within the ethical constraints of confidentiality, of course, and if the refereeing process is not being undertaken anonymously you will need to exercise discretion. But where work is read anonymously, then it is often useful on both sides to solicit the advice of graduate students – especially if the subject matter falls within their specialist area. They may discover that they are more knowledgeable than you are!

It is easy for experienced academics to assume that aspects of academic work like peer review are self-evident. It is so pervasive in the approval of material for publication, the award of research grants, and recognition exercises, that we all become thoroughly involved in it, and – however irksome we find it on occasion – most of us participate in the general process. We get used to the fact that it is part of the general give-and-take of the profession, and how important these human judgements are in promoting academic disciplines, approving or rejecting scholarly work, and so on. It is easy to overlook the fact that more junior students see little if anything of that. We have occasionally been surprised to discover that in the course of classes for graduate students, they have welcomed the opportunity to discuss peer review and its implications – in particular how it will impinge on their work, and in more general terms about its place in the exercise of academic decision-making.

Students can thus be introduced to a range of specific issues that will inform many, if not all, such decisions. The kinds of checklists that journal editors, commissioning editors, and grant-awarding bodies often use can form the basis of a workshop discussion. The group will be able to see the range of criteria that are commonly brought to bear. Commercial publishers ask things like: Is the material clearly organized? Is it an important addition to the existing literature? Who will be the audience? Is the coverage comprehensive? Research councils ask: Will this make a significant theoretical/ methodological advance? Is the research timely? Is it original? How does it relate to prior work in the area? Will it make a significant contribution to the discipline? Will it have important policy implications? How does it relate to current research priorities? Is the research feasible? Are the research methods appropriate? Is the timescale realistic? and so on. Journal editors need to know: Are the research methods described adequately? Is the research ethical? Is the analysis correct, using relevant methods? Is the discussion clear? Is knowledge of the relevant literature demonstrated adequately? It does graduate students no harm to be introduced to the constraints and opportunities of policy frameworks like the Technology Foresight Initiative, or European Union directives. These are intrinsically valuable aspects of academic socialization in general. Moreover, students can start to appreciate the range of criteria that are brought to bear on scholarly work, and how particular interests and audiences are implicated in the different kinds of decisions that are made. Some of the specific criteria are not directly relevant to their own thesis work, of course, and higher-degree students are fortunate in having some degree of licence in pursuing curiosity-driven research. Nevertheless, they can start to think about their own research and that of others using the same kinds of interpretative frameworks.

However much graduate students are free to pursue 'blue skies' research, they still need to be aware of the fact that evaluative criteria will be brought to bear on their work. Immediately, of course, they need to think about their own project and the ultimate evaluation of their thesis. It does no harm to share with them the kinds of criteria that external examiners are asked to consider by universities. The actual lists differ from institution to institution, but judicious use of your own institution's criteria, and those from elsewhere, can help to develop an informed awareness of the assessment process. Of course, the application of those criteria is what is important. The requirement that doctoral research is an 'original' contribution is key – as in other contexts – but what 'counts' as originality is diffuse. Seminar or workshop discussion about degrees of originality, and how the notion is typically interpreted in the discipline, can help illuminate general features of academic judgement, as well as helping students become aware of how it might apply to their own work. Likewise the criterion of whether aspects of the work are 'publishable' can help students reflect on the significance of their work, and also their plans for publication in the short to medium term. An appraisal of these and related issues can help students formulate realistic reviews of their progress and aspirations. In the absence of such perspectives, then graduate students can all too easily arrive at quite unrealistic views of themselves and their work.

If graduate students can start to gain an informed impression of these kinds of issues, then they can start to build their self-confidence. They will begin to appreciate how their own work compares with that of their peers and with more established members of the profession. It may help them put their own work into scholarly frameworks and perspectives. By thinking critically and pragmatically about the research of others, they will be able to locate their own work. They will have the kinds of analytic tools to place their own contribution within the intellectual traditions of the discipline, and relate it to other research that is going on in an informed way. They will not start to handicap themselves by harbouring over-ambitious plans, and thinking they have to satisfy evaluative criteria that are unrealistically demanding. If they can begin to think reflectively about these kinds of issues, then they will start to gain a sense of many of the less tangible aspects of academic judgement. In recognizing that issues like 'originality' are not absolute criteria, and are not subject to formulaic prescription, then they are in a better position to develop the kind of 'feel' for their own and others' work that comes with growing experience and confidence.

It is notoriously difficult to pin down the more tacit aspects of the culture. We aim to help graduate students to become 'reflective practitioners' who are able to internalize skills and criteria, in order to exercise judgement, and reflect on their own work in progress. The discussion of formal, explicit formalities and contexts can at least provide the kind of framework within which more personal, tacit knowledge can be gained and deployed. It is on the basis of such awareness that students can start to appreciate those intangible things that external examiners find themselves looking for. (We shall return to how external examiners express the issues themselves below.) Reading others' work, discussing formal and informal requirements together, supervisors and students can start to share a sense of the overall style and 'shape' of successful research. Depending on the discipline, they can start to appreciate the balance between data, findings, analysis and interpretation; how references to previous research can be woven into discussions of their own research; how to discuss and develop theoretical ideas; how to construct a thesis that 'hangs together' as a coherent piece of work; how to master the particular stylistic requirements of scholarly writing. They can thus be helped to grasp – often knowing at the same intuitive level as their more seasoned peers – the features of their work that will help to establish them as accomplished and self-assured practitioners of their craft.

Another source of coaching in judgement is the reading of PhD theses: as well as reading some good local ones, it can be useful for students to get on inter-library loan theses from other universities – perhaps including theses that you externalled, or that relevant colleagues examined, or were supervised by potential external examiners of their own work. The student can then usefully read publications that came from those theses, to see how they differ and how the work has been developed for that purpose. Again, these tasks will work better if you can encourage explicit discussion.

If your students do undergraduate teaching, and especially if they mark work, this can also help them develop a sense of discrimination and judgement. As they learn to tell first-class work from more run-of-the-mill student efforts, and start to gain experience in providing constructive feedback to more junior students about their work, so they can be encouraged to develop a more discriminating approach to their own work, and to respond to your own feedback on their working papers, draft chapters and so on. Supervising laboratory practicals, if discussed with more experienced colleagues, can help graduates in laboratory subjects to think about good and bad experimental work.

The acquisition and exercise of academic judgement becomes pressing for postgraduate students when it comes to shaping their work into a thesis that is ready for submission, and they need to be able to stand back from the detail of their work, and to learn to see the big picture as well. Too often, students cannot see the proverbial wood for the trees. Understandably enough, they become absorbed in the minutiae of their particular study, often becoming bogged down. They can become obsessive about small issues, and lose sight of the greater ones.

The supervisor's task is not always about resolving the details. It is often about helping the student to gain a sensible perspective on the overall project. A good deal of this work hinges on realistic aspirations for what a postgraduate thesis is meant to be. Too often, students become obsessed with impossible aspirations. The PhD is the highest earned degree that most people aspire to: the higher doctorate is awarded to relatively few academics, and only when they are very well established in their own right. The PhD is, in one sense, therefore, the pinnacle of academic training. In a sense, therefore, the PhD thesis is a 'masterpiece' of academic work. In saying that, however, it is useful to recall the original sense of 'masterpiece'. That is, a piece of work that confirmed the status of the 'master' craft worker, and the transition from apprenticehood. Too often, the notion of the 'masterpiece' dominates doctoral work in its more romantic sense – the great *chef d'oeuvre*. Many graduate students need to be disabused of the latter notion, and have their sights firmly set on the more realistic and more appropriate kind of aspiration. In many disciplines the implicit requirements for a doctoral thesis seem to have grown to the extent that experienced academics come to harbour unrealistic expectations for their own students, and to pass them on to succeeding generations. In recent years, there has been a trend towards more realistic goals. The external pressures on funding and completion rates, while not always welcome in themselves, have provided a useful impetus towards collective and individual appraisal of what is realistic. Students and supervisors need repeatedly to ask themselves: What can realistically be achieved in the registration period? They need to keep before them the appreciation that this thesis itself is not the be-all and end-all of the research enterprise, nor of the graduate student's career. The thesis itself is just one of a number of outcomes of the research work. Depending on the discipline, the PhD project should result in a monograph or a series of journal articles, form the basis of further research, applications for external research funding for postdoctoral work, and so on. If student and supervisor become obsessively focused on making the thesis alone the ultimate goal, then they can both all too easily lose sight of the more general issues of academic progress and achievement.

Losing sight of the overall goals can occur at any stage of the doctorate, but analysing the results of empirical work often provides this loss of vision. Many students pursuing empirical projects flag when faced with their own data. Many research students are either paralysed when faced with data, or become so engrossed in the technicalities of analysis they lose track of time and 'drown'. Here we consider how the supervisor can help the students master analytic techniques with confidence and prevent them drowning in technicalities. Many experienced supervisors will be familiar with the phenomenon that graduate students just collect 'too much' information. This is not always a major problem – if one recognizes that the thesis itself will not be the only outcome, then having more data than actually are used in it can provide a useful resource for future research activities, future publications and so on. The period of initial registration for full-time students will be a rare period in an academic career when research can be pursued with few other distractions, and can result in a 'camel's hump' of research material that can be used in the future. On the other hand, an over-enthusiasm for detailed work can prove a waste of time and effort. An example from sociology is given as 7.1.

Example 7.1: Over-elaborated

Clovis Hobden was doing a study of British soccer fans on the net. He was himself a passionate supporter of Glasgow Celtic, and found it very difficult to separate time online arguing with other Celtic fans from his research which was meant to be a comparison of three different chatrooms where supporters of three 'Protestant' clubs: Rangers, Hearts and Dundee interacted. He found it hard to be dispassionate about the virulent anti-Catholic and Ulster Unionist sentiments he found in his chatrooms, and kept retreating into writing excessively long, arcane working papers about the ethics of online research. Analysing the data and drafting the thesis kept being put off.

Such wasted time and effort reflect a lack of judgement. The supervisor's main task here is to help the student recognize the overall purpose of the task of information gathering. Students often recognize that they are in danger of becoming like Clovis Hobden. As some respondents to the BERA survey wrote, when asked to describe a problem they faced:

> With 40 per cent of the data collected, what to do with it. It includes transcripts of two rather different sets of interviews, and two different sets of pencil and paper exercises. There just seems to be so much of it. I must learn new methods of analysis and at the same time see each piece as a part of a whole.
>
> (Gerald Wade)

> One problem which was critical for my study was the use of a computer for the analysis of my results. I did not have any experience in the use of computing when I started my research work . . . After about six months of struggle I am now able to use the computer with some confidence.
>
> (Bill Eversleigh)

> Attempts to use factor analysis on the data – on this I spent quite a lot of time, and it was to no avail for it just seemed to complicate the picture. This should have been spotted at an earlier stage than was the case. It was a pity, for with different guidance I might have been able to make something of it, in the end it was abandoned.
>
> (Ada Mason)

> Analysis of over two years data from classroom observation, teacher reports, case study notes and transcripts present a problem.
>
> (Lawrence Redding)

The biggest problem I faced was a lack of knowledge of statistics. I was not prepared to solve this problem, never having studied this area, and having done no mathematics since O Levels. This problem was solved by the fact that my second supervisor within the polytechnic was able to give me sufficient help to understand the use of SPSS [Statistical Package for the Social Sciences] and to help me in my initial problems in using the computer. I was able to pick up sufficient knowledge to cope with my own programmes. Following this my difficulties continued when I wrote up the chapter and my thesis dealing with the statistical findings, as I worried about the correct use of statistical terms. Both my supervisors guided me to useful references in the literature, and I was able to read around the subject.

(Nick Buckley)

There are several ways in which the supervisor can prestructure the student's analytic work which might help prevent data handling from becoming a problem. First, the supervisor needs to be ruthlessly honest about his or her own shortcomings. Analytic techniques may be moving faster than a supervisor has been able to keep up with, especially software packages for humanities and social science. It is vital that a supervisor with weaknesses explicitly sends the student elsewhere for expert help: to a colleague, a summer school, a special training course. All meetings of students produce stories of supervisors who have fallen behind in their field, but are too insecure, jealous or even ignorant to recognize that their students need help from someone more au fait with current analytic techniques, or theories, or developments in their field.

Example 7.2: Outdated supervisor

Mirinda Clively came to a summer school we were teaching in 2003. When she presented her work in a small group we heard her talk about a project that would have seemed passé in 1983. She was making tape recordings of therapeutic talk, and planning to analyse them using ideas from Basil Bernstein's work of the 1970s not because she had made a rational decision to return to that thirty-year-old work, but because she did not know that Bernstein's ideas had developed and changed markedly since the seventies. After the summer school she wrote to us that when she had discussed with her supervisor why he was advising her to use only the very old work, she had discovered that he had not read any of Bernstein's work from the 1980s or 1990s, nor any of the critical and laudatory reappraisals since his death.

Second, the supervisor needs to focus the students on the big picture – on the whole thesis – and keep them from drowning in analytic detail.

Third, the supervisor can work on the analysis alongside the student, which gives the supervisor first-hand experience of the analytic technique, the students' competencies, *and* any snags with the techniques in question.

Our last theme in this chapter is that of the 'final' judgement: the recognition of doctoral quality.

Recognizing doctoral quality

In the course of our own research on academic socialization we interviewed experienced supervisors about a range of issues, and included questions about their experience as external examiners of PhD theses. Their responses are illuminating, and may help to illustrate several of the issues we have raised in this chapter. It is, incidentally, worth noting that even among well-established academics, the spread of experience is broad. Some have accumulated a good deal of relevant experience, others may have examined very few theses in the course of their career. This no doubt reflects various factors, including the nature of their particular specialism, and the character of their academic network. One should not assume, however, that there is a large cadre of experienced external examiners who are totally confident about what they are doing, and 'know' how to apply the right criteria in precise ways. The comments of these experienced academics show a range of responses.

These experienced academics all want to identify in successful doctoral theses work that 'makes a contribution'. This general description, in a number of variants, recurs throughout the interview data. There is some degree of consensus about how a 'contribution' is to be described and recognized and a view about 'competent work'. Professor Paget (town planning) described his extensive experience ('I've examined an awful lot of PhDs') in terms of topics, scope and competence:

> A whole variety of things. Substance again I think is important. I do think it needs to be a fairly meaty document. I don't mean tomes and tomes. I've had some two-volume eight hundred page jobs, and frankly I think they're nightmarish. So topic is important. The conduct of the thesis – an understanding of literature, of method and its limitations and strengths, an application of general research methods . . . The best PhD I've ever read: it was beautifully presented, rigorously argued, delightfully researched, the literature was bang on, theoretically very competent, methodologically very competent – in essence it seemed to me to be honest.

Here, then, is a fairly recognizable listing of elements of the successful PhD, expressed in terms of a range of competencies. As Professor Woodrose (development studies) expressed it, a contribution has to do with the candidate's grasp of the literature, the adequacy of the methodology, and the likely opportunities for publication:

I guess there's a minimum level. At a minimum level I'm looking for a good understanding of the state of the literature. I'm looking for total confidence in the application of research methodology. And I'm looking for anything that allows me to say 'This is a contribution to knowledge.' I guess if I'm going beyond that, I'm looking for the kind of PhD that one hope produces papers or a book. I'd like to see something that looks original – a true contribution to knowledge. It's something about the scope of the exercise, that they've really bitten off something – either to apply a set of methods to a new country, or to a new sector, or that they've applied them in a rather distinctive way.

Some of the academics we interviewed expressed the criteria for success in terms of the achievement of 'objectives', such as Professor Portland (urban studies):

Clear specification of objectives of research, careful design of research, good literature review – well structured, not rambling – fair amount of precision in thought, good strong use of theory, picking out appropriate propositions which are being tested ... Good ability to manage data handling. Good writing style and good conclusions.

For the most part, however, merely meeting the objectives of the research is insufficient without additional value. As Professor Pethwick, a political scientist told us:

Fundamentally, whether the aims of the student, that they've set, have been accomplished. And whether the research is sufficiently original in terms of sourcing material, the ways it's been executed, the way it's written.

A number of supervisors emphasise that same sense of going beyond mere competence. Making a contribution means something more than satisfying the formal, mechanistic requirements. That extra something is, as Dr Ridgeway (urban studies) expressed it, 'something that grabs you':

Looking for originality and excitement, critically ... A PhD has to have something about it that's theoretically exciting, and original, without being world-shattering ... But I think originality is the critical thing. And excitement. Something that grabs you. It's not just a competent pragmatic piece of work. There's something behind it that shows the person is engaged in the debates.

'Originality' is clearly a key issue in evaluating whether a PhD thesis has gone beyond the minimum basis of competence and starts to 'grab you':

A coherent argument. I look to see what they are setting out to do. I look to see whether they've done it. I look for a decent chunk of empirical work which relates to the argument and supports it. And I look to see whether there's a spark of something original which makes something more of it than just putting together a literature review and empirical material – not something desperately new, but evidence of original thought. I weigh it as well. If it's more than eighty thousand words – brevity is something I look for, economy, let's say not brevity – there isn't more there than there needs to be.

Dr Rowlandson (geography)

First of all I'm looking for the originality of the work – is it just a very competent piece of work with clear presentation of ideas, or is it really going to be a new contribution to knowledge? And underlying all that is the rigorous approach of the candidate – the independent approach to the work and how testable that particular work is – so I know that what the person proposes is valid both theoretically and practically.

Dr Savanake (town planning)

Then, for some of the academics we interviewed, all this needs to be organized and presented with coherence and style, and needs to engage with theoretical development:

How clear is the analytical framework that is being used, and is it being used to illuminate a particular theme or thesis, or is the substantive area being investigated being used to test the robustness of the theory? I clearly feel more comfortable if I see theory testing going on and some contribution to theory . . . I'm very pleased when I find it.

Professor Borringer (urban studies)

In addition, a recognition of the limitations of the research may be looked for. Confidence should, from this perspective, be mingled with a proper degree of reticence:

I guess I look for, increasingly, a sense of intellectual modesty about the contribution of their particular research to knowledge. An understanding of the fragility of understanding anything through social science, and therefore a willingness to make tentative claims, to be very explicit about the way to approach different alternative answers, weaknesses with the data – that approach is more than any other thing what impresses me . . . I tend to look for fluency in writing, presentation and argument . . . definite linkage to an existing body of theory.

Dr Huntingforest (geology)

I see the PhD as incorporating a number of skills. You've got your research skills, your analytical skills that are brought together, then you've got the pure administrative skills of actually writing, ensuring that the references are correct, making sure your section heads are appropriate – the actual putting together of the thesis itself: . . . critical perspective; . . . thoroughness . . . coherence – a picture being built up – a systematic progress through the thesis.

Dr Wishart (development studies)

I guess coherence to start with ... is there a definite topic, a defined problem, have they been able to cut that problem up into a set of hypotheses and have they been able to operationalize those hypotheses – are they testable? Have they been able to relate that to the literature on the field ... Next, fieldwork ... Have they been able to conduct fieldwork, have they used their methodology as planned, have they been able to cope with problems in the field which inevitably arise? Can they present the data clearly and can they tie their data into their actual hypotheses?

Dr Wynyard (development studies)

In a PhD you are looking for a development of ideas, methods, concepts beyond the current literature, into a new area which excites the examiner and the supervisor and in which the student feels perfectly assured. Just that ... if it extends me in some way. If there has been a good coverage of the previous literature, theoretical and substantive, and there has been some well-conducted fieldwork that further illuminates the theory, then if that is well done, written well, organized well – that for me is a PhD.

Professor Sherring (biochemistry)

Mullins and Kiley (2002) summarize the earlier research on how examiners judge higher-degree theses, and interviewed 30 experienced examiners in Australia about the assessment of the traditional PhD. These respondents made very similar comments to those reported here.

This chapter has covered what is, in the great scheme of things, the heart of doctoral supervision: how to help students become scholars who can exercise the judgements appropriate to their discipline. We move on to other topics: writing, the examination, and career building. These are relatively straightforward for the supervisor whose students have developed appropriate judgement.

8

An emotional excitement: writing up the thesis

'Isn't the writing of good prose an emotional excitement?'
'Yes of course it is. At least when you get the thing dead right and know its dead right, there's no excitement like it. It's marvellous. It makes you feel like God on the Seventh Day – for a bit, anyhow.'

(Sayers 1972: 171)

Introduction

We have already referred to the need to get students writing from the earliest days of their registration – persuading them to 'write early and write often'. Students' attitudes to writing are highly variable, as are the skills they bring to the tasks involved. Sometimes, as in our vignette, the problem is writer's block, and a reluctance or inability to draft thesis material. Sometimes the problem is more about the structure and style of the writing that students engage in. We saw from the remarks we quoted from experienced academics in Chapter 7 – talking about the criteria they use as external examiners – that the capacity to organize the material into a coherent text is crucial if the student is to succeed. Most, if not all, graduate students need advice about their writing. Indeed, such a need is not confined to students. All academics can benefit from a critical and reflective perspective on their writing, and many of the things we discuss in this chapter apply to one's own writing as well as students' efforts.

This chapter is focused on how to help the research student to write. It is a mixture of data, of tips based on courses we have run, and some reflections on the nature of academic writing in the social sciences and the natural sciences. We start with a quote from a woman doing a PhD in geography, asked about her 'writing up': 'It has been a lonely process. There are ups and downs. There are times when I'm sick and tired of reading my own prose, I don't want to do it any more' (Eunice Lester).

Similar points were made by two respondents to the BERA survey:

The major problem was in getting used to the 'academic' style of writing expected. The nature of the project, whose leader is also my supervisor, has given me daily contact in working with and writing with him and another colleague. This has been invaluable, and I would, I suspect, have faced an almost insurmountable problem had I not had this advantage.

(Emily Trefusis)

The most critical problem in my view was that of actually getting down to writing. It is so much easier to keep collecting material from the primary sources, making notes, sorting them, filing them, reading them, rereading them – anything rather than organizing the material into a coherent piece of writing. I have seen this happen to my daughter and my son-in-law, both of whom started working for PhDs but have not completed the projects. Both have mountains of notes, etc. but only a few slender pages of their own written work. Now here I believe I was very fortunate because within a few months of my embarking on reading, my supervisor started asking for written work and refused to be put off by my pleas that I wasn't ready to write yet. So, just to satisfy him I started writing – a piece of work which in the end was only of limited use for my thesis but that didn't matter: I had passed the great psychological barrier of starting the writing and, from then onwards, I carried out my supervisor's recommendation to work at research and writing simultaneously even if it meant that some of the earlier pieces of writing had to be partially rewritten later.

My thesis is finished but at least two problems remain, and if anything are worse than before. One is the domestic problem of finding uninterrupted time in which to write and the other is the increasing sense of isolation, particularly as I no longer have contact with the university. This can only partly be offset by reading appropriate journals. Possibly later I may be able to attend conferences and join in the discussion groups with other people working in my field.

(Mary Pearson)

These problems are not new. Dorothy Smith (1994: 50) recalls her PhD in sociology at Berkeley in the 1960s, when she found it hard to produce her thesis: 'The nightmare writing in which you know not who you write for, what it is you might be saying . . . And what it would be proper, correct, sociological, to say. Round and round . . .'

Many of the PhD students Odette Parry interviewed had problems with writing up their thesis. Not only that, the supervisors interviewed were eloquent about how the students' writing successes and failure were central to the supervisory process. One very famous respondent even admitted that he was frequently tempted to draft the PhD thesis for the student. This man, Professor Brande (a social scientist at Hernchester) recognized that he was in danger of being too interventionist a supervisor. He told us:

I think also I'm too anxious to do the work for them or with them. I can't bear to see them do something which I could do slightly better . . . I tend to be too closely involved . . . it gets to be my dissertation rather than their dissertation and that's not fair on them. It's even worse with word-processors because they bring in their text on a disk and you sit at the keyboard together.

In this quote from Professor Brande he raises the whole topic of the supervisors' appropriate role in the production of the text of the thesis which was a problem for many of our supervisor respondents. A social scientist, Professor Woodrose of Latchendon, told us that: 'You can't drive them any faster than they can write – the papers, the literature reviews, the definitional papers which take them on to the next stage.' Dr Godlee, from Gossingham, was eloquent about the supervisor's role in text production.

> you get a first draft which consists of probably some interesting sets of ideas, but not very effectively linked together. And most students I've supervised seem to have a lot of difficulty in establishing a clear line of argument which runs through the thesis as a whole. My job as a supervisor is to try to discuss with the student the different stories that can be told with the material that has been assembled and then to execute the option which is selected as professionally as possible.

The experienced supervisors we interviewed tackled the writing issues early. As Dr Jelf says: 'I try to get them writing very early on. I insist on that. It's essential. They don't solve half the problems they come across until they try to write them down.'

Not all supervisors expect the early writing to end up in the thesis, as one of David Pearson's (2002) informants explained to him.

> But in the first year of the PhD, lots of reading – reading around, rather than doing lots of writing, because anything you write in the first year of your PhD is probably gonna strike you after a couple of years as being, you know, sort of unformed and naïve or just off the point, so, a bit of writing just to keep their hand in. I think you need to do that: produce a bit of work every month, but not anything directly thesis-related really. It's a good thing nowadays – again with the RAE – for them to produce a couple of reviews for a journal.
>
> (Professor Olbrick, philosophy)

This chapter is about helping the students like Eunice Lester by offering some strategies to them: strategies to avoid taking over their text, as Professor Brande reported, and fulfilling Dr Godlee's and Dr Jelf's aims. The chapter makes some very concrete proposals, and then steps back with a consideration of the ways in which it is possible to supervise the text.

Practical advice

Harry Wolcott (1990) advises researchers to plan the eventual text at the very outset of the project. This is certainly an excellent piece of advice for a PhD student, and so, at a very early stage, we recommend getting the student to take Step 1.

Step 1: The plan

At an early stage, do a thesis plan with the words divided up across the chapters, and a timetable for writing them: For instance:

Introduction	5000 words	May 2006–July 2006
Literature	5000 words	August 2004–October 2004
Methods	6000 words	November 2004–January 2005

The other main elements of the thesis can be blocked in a similar fashion. Here we are assuming – in this hypothetical example – that the introduction will be drafted last.

Once this is done, and agreed with the supervisor, it can be pinned up above the desk, and also turned into a progress tracing chart, such as the following.

Figure 8.1: Specimen progress tracing chart

Chapter	Draft 1	Draft 2	Draft 3
Introduction			
Part 1 500	x		
Part 2 1000	x		
Part 3 500	x	x	
Part 4 100	x		
Part 5 2000	x	x	x
Literature review			
Introduction 500	x	x	x
Material up to 1970			
Key psychological studies			
Critique of key studies			
Methods			
Pilot study	x		
Questionnaire design			
Response rate			
Analytic strategies			
and so on			

It is useful to encourage students to break the task down into very small steps, and to mark their progress in small stages, so that the crosses march across the paper and they can see themselves making progress. A 'progress' chart on yellowing paper that only moves when 20,000 words are written will not help anyone. If there is a visible mark for each small piece of writing, the student can build in rewards (such as having an evening off) and also safeguards (such as backing up each piece and putting the disk somewhere secure). The precise form and content of such a chart needs to be devised so it is informative and motivating for the student, and the supervisor can help explore a form that works for each student. It may be sensible to have one chart for the whole thesis, and a much more detailed one for each chapter, so progress can be made on one chapter and traced, while the overall chart is not showing much movement. Getting students to do a thesis plan, time-table, and progress tracing chart early on is the first step in getting them to write. It not only sets the tone – that the writing is part of the deal, can be done and will be done – it also encourages students to start writing from Day One.

Step 2: The two golden rules

These two rules are so important that it would be worth having them on T-shirts or lapel badges. They are: (1) Write early and write often; (2) Don't get it right, get it written. Students may not realize how vital these rules are, or why you are advocating them. Offer the following explanations. Take the two golden rules seriously. The 'Write early and write often' rule works because:

1 The more you write, the easier it gets.
2 If you write every day, it becomes a habit.
3 Tiny bits of writing add up to a lot of writing. Break the writing up into small bits. Write 100 words on X, 200 words on Y, and file them safely. It all mounts up.
4 The longer you leave it unwritten the worse the task becomes.

The 'Don't get it right, get it written' rule works because

1 Until it is on paper no one can help you get it right. Draft, show the draft to people, redraft.
2 Drafting is a vital stage in clarifying thought (see Torrance and Thomas 1994).
3 Start writing the bit that is clearest in your head. *Not* the Introduction, but Chapter 4, or the appendices, or the conclusions, or the methods. As you draft, other bits become clear.
4 Drafting reveals the places where 'it' isn't right (yet) in ways that nothing else does.

As we were gathering materials to prepare this new edition of this book *The Guardian* reprinted a short essay on writing from the *New York Times* by Walter Mosley (2000), the author of a series of detective stories set in Los Angeles after the Second World War. Mosley writes about writing: 'If you want to be a writer, you have to write every day. . . . You don't skip a child's breakfast or forget to wake up in the morning. Sleep comes to you each day, and so does the muse.' Later in the piece he describes writing a novel as 'gathering smoke', and also as 'a kind of guerrilla warfare' because 'there is no vac-ation'. Academic writing is a little easier because we have data to start from: the image of 'gathering smoke' is harsher than academic authors need. 'Guerrilla warfare' and the idea that we should write as regularly as we feed our children or wake up or sleep, are as appropriate for academic production as for novels.

Step 3: The safeguards

Students never believe that their work can get lost, stolen or destroyed. Do say to them that it is not paranoid but sensible to have several copies of what they have written. Hard disks crash, floppy disks get lost, laptops are wiped by the airport X-ray and so on. So just as it is vital for them to keep writing, it is especially vital to back up the disks, keep a spare set in a safe place, keep a hard copy at their family home, put a set of disks in a place a thief will not steal them. They need to keep back-up disks and keep photocopies of any key bits of writing.

The best way to ram this message home is to steal the work of one of the current cohort, but assuming you are too moral to do that, a dramatic story is one way of getting the message across. The following are possible:

1 Screen the episode of *Blackadder* (from the series in which he is butler to the Prince Regent) in which Dr Johnson's dictionary and Blackadder's bonkbuster novel are destroyed by Baldrick.
2 Tell the best 'lost manuscript' story in your discipline. In History, Carlyle's maid lighting the fire with the manuscript of Gibbon's *Decline and Fall*; in the social sciences, Franz Steiner's leaving the only copy of *Taboo* on the Underground.
3 Tell one of your own disaster stories about losing a disk or manuscript.
4 Tell your best 'lost manuscript' story about a fellow PhD student or one of your previous students. The three that follow are all true, but we have changed the names because all the postgraduates are still alive and well – and might even read this book.

Example 8.1: The clot

David Middleton-Brown was in the last couple of months of writing up his thesis. His main supervisor, Professor Daviot, was about to leave for a semester's attachment to a Finnish university. David gave Professor Daviot a set of floppy discs with the thesis draft on them. Disaster struck. David's hard drive collapsed, losing all that was on it. Professor Daviot's luggage was lost en route to Finland. Suddenly there was no current version of seven chapters of the thesis. David had no back-up copy of the floppies or another hard drive. There were some drafts of earlier versions of some chapters in hard copy, but much of his last 2–3 months work was gone. For the price of a box or two of floppies, and about half an hour's work, David could, and should have had back-ups stored in the department and in Professor Daviot's office, or at his mother's, or somewhere.

Example 8.2: The thief

Meg Larminie's project involved a particularly expensive computer which could handle digital images, because she was studying the iconography of holiday videos. A thief stole her machine from the university, with a consequent loss of data and analysis.

Example 8.3: 'The miracle'

Eustace Pedler had been destined for the Catholic priesthood, but had decided he lacked a true vocation, and was doing a PhD instead. He had, however, remained a communicant, and was, therefore, well known in the university's Catholic chaplaincy. One day he left an advanced draft of his thesis – in the days before microcomputers when the text was produced on a manual typewriter with carbon paper copies – in a telephone box in a suburb. It was in a folder which did not have his name and address on it, but did bear the telephone number of the Catholic chaplaincy. The next person to use the phone box dialled that number, and told the chaplain that she or he had 'found something that looks important'. The chaplain got on his motorbike and drove to the phone box to retrieve the folder, recognized that it was Eustace's work, and was able to return it to him.

The moral of this story is that God clearly forgave Eustace for not becoming a priest, but most students cannot rely on God, a Good Samaritan or a chaplain with a motorbike.

Once you have alerted students to the need to write regularly from the earliest days of their enrolment, and convinced them to keep back-up disks and keep them safe, you have helped your students more than most of us older academics were ever helped. However, there are several other ways in which the supervisor can encourage students to see writing as an integral part of the whole doctoral process, and even learn to enjoy it. When Paul and Sara were doctoral students, Liam Hudson offered us a set of guidelines which we have shared with graduate students ever after, modified in the light of our experience. We have reproduced it here as Figure 8.2.

Figure 8.2: Some practical suggestions for thesis writing

Technical writing does not come easily – as the contents of the university library testify. There is no recipe for success, but there are rules of thumb:

1 Allow yourself time. No one will believe in advance how long analysis, writing-up and checking take.
2 Set yourself deadlines, and hit them with zeal. (And beware the typist who lets you down at the last moment.)
3 Give shape to what you write. There are all sorts of usable models: the hypothetico-deductive (theory, prediction, verification); the ritualistic (introduction, review of literature, method, results, discussion); the 'auto-biographic' narrative and so on. The choice is largely a matter of taste. Pick the one that gives the least sense of artificiality.
4 Use sub-headings, at the side and/or in the centre of the page, to structure your text, and include lots of sentences that tell the reader where he or she has been and where they are going next.
5 Method: just say what you did, in words that a child would understand. Keep your discussion of methodology, the pros and cons of the various possible methods, to a minimum. Don't feel compelled to report in detail everything you do.
6 Avoid clichés. 'Situation', 'at this moment in time', 'in this regard' and anything else said frequently on television should be avoided.
7 Decide which of your results are the important ones, and give them prominent place.
8 Don't allow technicalities to clog up the main text. Put them in appendices.
9 Expect to suffer over the presentation of statistics. Raw data belong at the back, next to the references. The right way of summarizing them in the main text may only come to you after weeks of trial and error.
10 Tables should speak for themselves. Don't force your reader to grope around in the main text to discover what your tables mean.
11 Don't pad out your references with works you haven't read.
12 Hack and hack at your own prose. Sentence by sentence, the simplest form is usually the best. At the level of paragraphs and chapters, aim for the sequence which gives the smoothest flow.
13 Most examiners dislike the first person singular, so use it sparingly.
14 Don't circumlocute: 'It will be seen that the above tables are not without significance . . .'
15 Re-examine any piece of jargon. As often as not you will find it disguises sloppiness. Bear in mind, too, that the educational sciences are inter-disciplinary. What you write should make sense to any intelligent person, irrespective of his or her particular technical skills.
16 Proof-reading your typed version is essential. Ideally work with a partner and read it aloud, punctuation and all.

A set of guidelines like this can be quickly produced for any discipline. Despite the supervisor and the golden rules, many PhD students need help to make the transition from undergraduate to professional writing. The supervisor can lead them to sources of help, and create a climate in which students realize that it is a technical skill that can be learned, not a 'natural' talent given only to a few. Some students are helped by reading books on writing, and we discuss these later in this chapter. Others are helped by practical activities, and others by making the process collegial; for instance by writing circles. The most important role for the supervisor is to force the students to discover what will help them, and then cajole them into using that help.

Dispelling the myths

Probably the biggest favour a supervisor can do for a PhD student is stop them developing a belief that 'writing' is a separate kind of activity that can or should be left until 'the end', an activity that is somehow different from everyday life as a researcher and teacher. Nothing is more inimical to productive writing than the romantic image of the lone author, searching for inspiration, and struggling for expression. Writing is not a special kind of experience, and – as we have emphasized already – it is not a natural talent. While it seems to be true that some people find it easier than others, it does not come naturally to anybody. It is something that all authors have to work at. Books, theses, journal articles and all the other 'products' of academic life do not 'just happen'. Students need to be encouraged to recognize that their scholarly writing is simply a part – albeit a very important part – of their everyday work. They need to lose any idea they might have had previously that 'writing up' is something they can always leave until the end of everything else, or that can be done at the last minute.

This is, indeed, one area in which the transition from successful under-graduate student, or Masters student, or even professional doing the course-work of a professional doctorate, to research student may prove tricky. Even very good undergraduates may be able to manage their university career by treating writing as a relatively unproblematic activity. Many essays and pro-jects are indeed written in a short timespan, and any experienced internal or external examiner will recognize that much work is submitted in more-or-less first draft. Students carry forward such behaviours into research work at their peril. Many have come to grief – or at least have come to a grinding halt – when they recognize that writing the equivalent of a complete book cannot safely be left to the last minute.

Inappropriate expectations and patterns of behaviour about writing need to be tackled if students are to develop sound and productive work habits. Many academics suffer from myths about writing and supervisors themselves need to reflect on whether they themselves may inadvertently encourage them in their students. Experienced academics sometimes cling to the myth of 'getting down to it during the summer'. This is an extension of the understandable desire to devote coherent stretches of time to writing tasks – such as drafting the next book or writing up the current research project. It is perfectly reasonable, and the rationale for relatively short undergraduate terms is to release academic time for scholarly tasks. On the other hand, the long summer 'vacation' often is not all that long, sandwiched between assessment periods at each end, and with many other academic tasks to complete. If any real holiday is to be taken, and family or other social obligations fulfilled, then the summer suddenly seems very pressured. The mirage of the empty summer can prevent busy academics from looking for ways to fit their writing commitments into regular schedules. A similar, equally handicapping, myth is to wait until 'the desk is clear'. Again, this is based on the desire to write only when other pressing commitments have been got out of the way. The problem with this belief is that an empty desk is a very rare privilege. Again, the solution is to schedule writing as a regular commitment like any other. A third mistake arises from the desire to delay writing until 'all the data are collected and finally analysed', or the equivalent. As we have suggested already, leaving writing to the end, and treating it as a final 'big bang' is a risky attitude. It can leave a huge, new task to be tackled after a great many other activities have been completed. While some people can cope successfully with this strategy, a good many find it daunting, and paralysingly so. Such 'myths', then, are based on need to see writing as a separate and special activity; needing different time and concentration from routine activity. This is damaging for most people: summer is very short, desks are *never* clear, the data are never all collected and finally analysed. Established academics need to review their own work habits, and think whether they base their own work on unhelpful assumptions. They also need to consider whether they may inadvertently promote such behaviours in their graduate students.

If writing the thesis is not seen as a separate kind of activity, then it is not necessary to harbour these sustaining myths. So the wise person does not rely on periods of time totally free of other commitments to 'write up'. Even if the student does have a clear desk or a period of leave it is not a good idea to wait for such things to do a thesis: it may be useful to finish and revise the thesis but not to start it from cold. In addition, we have to recognize that major writing undertakings may need commitment of time and effort over and above nine-to-five working hours. There is no great need, in our experience, to work all the hours or to forgo everything else. Most of Paul Atkinson's productive writing is done in the evening – usually between about 8.30 and 10.00 p.m. Some people manage an hour early in the day. Since Paul does not function particularly well in the morning, that does not work for him. So, part of the task seems to involve the *management* of time and effort as well as freeing oneself from myths that actually hinder productivity. The other side of the equation would seem to be the management of the task. We need to free ourselves from any disabling myths about theses as process or product.

Theses are only a type of routine, craft work like any other. They are divisible into entirely manageable sets of small tasks.

Students should be encouraged to think about writing projects, including the entire thesis, in terms of sensible and manageable chunks of effort, time and other resources. Sensible planning and regular work habits can help transform writing into perfectly manageable everyday activities. The agreed thesis plan should exist – and there is no point in writing without one – then the synopsis or outline will already have been constructed and will already define the structure. While plans and structures should always be subject to review, and should not be a straitjacket, provided they are realistic, students should always be able to write productively on identifiable aspects of the thesis. This in turn means that students need encouragement to break the tasks down into bite-sized chunks. Whole theses and whole chapters are major undertakings: sensible, robust structures and plans will help the student and his or her supervisor to identify manageable stretches of writing.

Equally, one needs to work flexibly within the thesis plan. Students often need to be encouraged *not* to think they have to 'start at the beginning', or turn the thesis plan into a temporal work-plan. Starting at page 1 is rarely a sensible approach. Students should be encouraged to feel able to write what they feel like writing at the time. There should always be something about which they feel relatively confident, or about which they have ideas that need drafting out, or where they feel they have a 'finding', or a significant story to tell. If so, then why not encourage them to write about *that* aspect of the work. In other words, students should not be tied to their structure, but encouraged to use it as a framework to keep control over the emerging whole.

Advice on writing, then, needs to concentrate on helping the graduate students to approach their work pragmatically. It is not a huge task to write a PhD thesis, provided they do not *make* it look that way. We encourage our own students to try to write as part of their normal academic work, and to mingle writing with other research activities. Equally, therefore, we urge them never to approach writing 'cold'. Sitting down at the desk, with a blank computer screen, or a blank sheet of paper can be paralysing. It is all too easy to suck the pen or fiddle with the mouse without getting words down. Students should be helped to recognize how helpful it is to have some ideas about what to write and how to start before they begin the mechanical work. Thinking about how to start, an apposite quote to get them going, a striking bit of data, a concrete instance, a striking analogy – all these things can be thought about creatively before actually settling down to 'write' – on the way to and from work, in the shower, or wherever. They do not need to have everything mapped out beforehand – just a starting-point.

In the same vein, one needs repeatedly to counsel most graduate students against yet another paralysing belief: that they have to know exactly what they think before they dare start to write. Many experienced academics know that what they think emerges partly out of the act of writing. Waiting until everything is perfectly understood and perfectly planned out is a sure recipe for yet another displacement activity. Students should be encouraged to realize that early drafts are just that. Supervisors therefore need to establish the kind of trust that allows students to share preliminary draft material with them. The supervisory relationship needs to give students 'permission' to produce material in a preliminary form, in the knowledge that they will be redrafting. Equally, supervisors need to be able to comment constructively on draft writing without undermining the student's confidence by being unduly critical of early efforts. As with so many aspects of that working relationship, this is based on the establishment of mutual trust and confidence.

Research students may also be encouraged by the thought that, in many ways, writing a thesis is more liberating than trying to produce the equivalent output in terms of research reports and journal articles. A thesis is much less restrictive in terms of formats, style, internal structure and length than articles or research reports: the author of a thesis can be more idiosyncratic, can set the agenda, can control the process much more. While there are many requirements and obligations in terms of structure and content, the author of a research thesis is able to exert more individual control than he or she will be able to in many other academic contexts. Not only is the research the student's own, original work, the thesis is something they themselves can 'own'. For that reason, writing a thesis should be exhilarating, not a crushing obligation.

Many graduate students need to be reminded that reading is the thief of writing. It can easily become another kind of displacement activity, that rivals waiting for the uninterrupted period free of other tasks. Graduate students have to read, of course, and they must make sure that they are 'up' with the research literature. But obsessive reading can severely interfere with getting the work written. Since 'the literature' can be virtually infinite, then the belief that one should *read first* can put the thesis off indefinitely. Likewise, students can put off writing intermediate and final drafts by persuading themselves that they cannot embark on those tasks until they have tracked down and read yet one more vital text, or chased further elusive references. One does not produce manageable draft writing out of the activity of reading and taking notes from sources. Students need to be encouraged not to confuse reading and writing (it is obvious, but a lot of people in fact do so). Indeed, they often need to be persuaded to *stop* reading the work of others, in order to step back from other people's writing, and their own information, in order to start marshalling their own work into their own texts.

Help with writing

Apart from establishing early on that the student should write regularly right from the beginning of their higher degree, a supportive supervisor will want to provide a context in which learning how to write, and seeking help with writing problems, is part of the PhD experience. We will discuss a number of ideas here, starting with building a library of books on writing, and then writing circles, writing clinics, dealing with writer's block; and then we, briefly, address students' word-processing needs.

One of the ways in which the life of a PhD student or young scholar has improved in the past decade is the explosion of helpful books on academic writing and publication. We have separated four kinds of books on writing. First there are style manuals – to help people write clearly and/or in the style of a particular journal, such as the American Psychological Association's style manual. This category would include old favourites such as: Turabian, *A Manual for Writers of Theses* (1937, 1982, 1995) with its British editions prepared since 1982. As a library resource there is *The Oxford Guide to Style* (Ritter 2002) or *The Chicago Manual of Style* (2003) too big and expensive for students, but essential in the library and on their book list. Bloomsbury Press have produced a dictionary designed to help contemporary students avoid their most common mistakes: *The Encarta Concise Dictionary Student Edition* (2001) which is so cheap you can insist they all own it. Oxford University Press have a new series of tiny books on common problems such as Allen (2002a, 2002b) on *Spelling* and *Punctuation* and Seely (2002a) on *Words*. Every higher-degree student we have ever had would have benefitted from these. An earlier book in this genre is Dummett, *Grammar and Style* (1993). We have provided a list of such books in the Further Reading section.

The second category of books contains advice provided for people in one discipline, or a group of closely allied disciplines. Social scientists are particularly lucky in that there are three outstanding books about how to settle down and actually produce something. They are: Becker, *Writing for Social Scientists* (1986), which is marvellous – helpful *and* funny; Wolcott, *How to Write Up Qualitative Research*, which is similar, though less funny; and Richardson, *Writing Strategies* (1990), which demonstrates how to redraft the same material for different types of audience – such as for a thesis and for an article in the *Guardian*. This last text is especially good in that it helps students think about how to present their ideas to particular types of reader. Such books for sciences and humanities students are less common. Supervisors might find that their students could benefit from them anyway, and they might even help a science student think about the contrast between the conventions of natural science and other disciplines. For scientists there are the following: Day, *How to Write and Publish a Scientific Paper* (1995), which covers all aspects of scientific publication, not just journal papers. There is a useful section on thesis writing, as well as preparing for all forms of public presentation, oral and written. Pechenik and Lamb, *How to Write about Biology* (1995) lacks jokes, or any sense of excitement and buzz, but has good biological examples. For humanities students Barzun, *On Writing, Editing and Publishing* (1986) remains a classic. We have again provided a list of such subject-specific books in the Further Reading section.

The rapidly growing literature specifically for higher-degree students includes books on writing the thesis such as Murray (2002), Brause (2000), Glatthorn (1998), Bolker (1998) and Dunleavy (2003). The students we teach seem to find Becker (1986) more helpful than the thesis-specific books, but yours may not. We found the Dunleavy rather dry, but that tone could, in itself, be reassuring for some candidates. The Brause, Bolker and Glatthorn are American, which makes them useful as a basis for discussion about how the thesis differs in America, and, perhaps, helpful for those writing theses for the professional doctorate.

Fourthly, there is a large literature analysing the appropriate rhetorical styles of different disciplines, to which Paul Atkinson (1990, 1992, 1996) has contributed. We have put a select list of titles on the rhetoric of inquiry into the Further Reading.

What unites these four types of book is the belief that writing is a technical, or craft skill which can be improved with self-conscious practice. Books of advice are invaluable resources. Students should be encouraged to think positively about them – that there is nothing intrinsically stigmatizing or 'naff' about using them, and thinking in a critical way about one's writing. It will often help if students can recognize that their supervisors also need to think carefully about their writing: that it does not come naturally to them either; that it is hard work for everyone; and that everyone needs to work at writing in order to improve.

Books of advice are, as we have suggested an invaluable resource. Students and supervisors alike need to build up a systematic acquaintance with such resources, and get into the habit of consulting them and using them. But one cannot learn and improve only from the use of handbooks. There is a great deal to be said for running some collegial seminars and workshops on writing. This, incidentally, is where Becker's *Writing For Social Scientists* is especially valuable, even for colleagues in other disciplines, as it reports on experiences of such a seminar group on writing. Fox (1985) contains an autobiographical account of how a writing circle helped some young American scholars to become productive authors, which can be recommended for emulation by graduate students. Such occasions can be part of a training programme for graduate students in the faculty or department; they can also become part of a regular 'writing circle' that draws together graduate students, research workers and more experienced academics.

However the membership is drawn together for such groups, there is always a need for mutual trust. We all know that having our writing evaluated by critics, however sympathetic, can be traumatic. It is difficult to distance oneself from one's writing, and anything that smacks of adverse criticism can hurt. Participants have to commit themselves to working constructively with one another, to agree to share equally in the group's activities, and to maintain mutual respect. Sometimes it may help things along to have a shared writing exercise. This helps everyone to focus on the same task, and is an easier introduction to sharing processes, problems and products that are more personal.

One set of classes we have run in Cardiff is based on the strategy outlined in Chapter 12 of Spradley's two parallel books *The Ethnographic Interview* (1979) and *Participant Observation* (1980). Spradley himself breaks writing down into nine steps, as follows.

Spradley's writing stages

Step 1 Select an audience
 2 Select your major argument/theme/thesis
 3 Make a list of topics and create an outline
 4 Write a rough draft of each section
 5 Revise the outline and create subheadings
 6 Edit the rough draft
 7 Write the Introduction and Conclusion
 8 Reread the manuscript to check that there are enough examples
 9 Write the final draft

We had a group of eight or nine higher-degree candidates and colleagues, and we all worked together through Spradley's early steps, in a weekly class. After the first meeting of the group, everyone agreed to carry out the first two steps: choosing an audience, and stating their main argument. Each member of the group wrote a paragraph or two about their current work under these two headings, and handed it in a day before the next class. We photocopied all the examples and in class circulated and discussed them. We have included here the contributions as tabled by two of the authors of this book and one MPhil student who was a regular member of the circle.

Examples of Spradley's first two steps

1 *Sara Delamont: A chapter on sex/gender in middle/secondary schools*

 a Audience: Educational Researchers, with some teachers.
 b Thesis: That pupils' taken-for-granted gender roles are re-inforced, rather than challenged, by teachers in everyday inter-action, by curriculum content, and by the organization of the school.

2 *Chris Stevens: An MSc Econ Thesis on gay women*

 a Audience: External examiner.
 b Thesis: To show how some gay women – especially those 'off the scene' – manage their homosexual identity. In particular: what the identity 'homosexual' means to them, how they came to identify as such, how far they see it as important in explaining their behaviour and affecting their daily lives, and the social areas where being 'homosexual' is thought relevant. A con-sideration of what this may reveal about the taken-for-granted notions about sex and gender.

3   *Odette Parry: An MSc Econ thesis on naturists*

a   Audience: External examiner whom I will assume for my own convenience to be an audience not unsimilar to that of my supervisor – Sara (because the substance of the material is naturism, I will be presuming that my audience will be largely in the dark concern the basics of the activity).

b   Thesis: Naturists are often reticent about declaring their activities because of expected social reprisal. Because information about naturist clubs is far less available than information about other social clubs, views of naturism tend to be limited only by the polite or otherwise imaginations of the non-naturist public. This paper looks at the ways in which naturists present themselves in a club environment in accordance with naturist beliefs about what constitutes proper and respectable nudist behaviour.

Spradley also argues that there are *levels* of writing, and that good writing comes from combining statements at the different levels. We have tried out these 'levels' on our own students. While they may appear to impose a somewhat mechanistic framework on the work of authoring, they can be invaluable in helping participants concentrate on issues of audience and style. Spradley himself gives examples from his ethnographic monograph, *The Cocktail Waitress* (Spradley and Mann 1975). Here we have used a mixture of examples from Spradley and Mann as well as Cardiff theses to illustrate work produced in the group.

Examples of Spradley's levels of writing

Level 1   Every society takes the biological difference between female and male to create a special kind of reality: feminine and masculine identities (1975: 145).

Level 2   Cross-cultural descriptive statements
e.g. In Boston schools for 5-year-olds are . . .
In Goa schools for young children . . .

Level 3   General statements about a society or cultural group
e.g. Police stations in Wales are places in which . . .

Level 4   General statements about a specific cultural scene
e.g. Teachers in Goan schools experience high levels of stress when . . .

Level 5   Specific statements about a cultural domain
e.g. Many doctors in the Sudan have to treat infectious diseases. These include . . .

Level 6   Specific examples of incidents
e.g. In a French lesson on a wet Tuesday Miss Phillips was explaining tense to 2C when . . .

Colin Rees

1   Universal statements. Records are a general feature of many people processing organizations.
2   Cross-cultural statements. Records made by social workers may contain more personal statements by the writer than those made by medical staff. Patient records tend to contain entries which appear to have been made by 'any doctor'.
3   General statements about a society or cultural group. Ward routine on the paediatric ward was punctuated by the use of the medical record.
4   General statements about a specific cultural scene. When it comes to the 'dirty work' of looking after records on ward rounds it is usually the house officer who takes the appropriate record out of the trolley and delegated the job of recording the consultant's 'pearls of wisdom'.
5   Although the house officer makes almost daily entries in the notes, an examination of those comments reveals that they say very little about the patient. 'No change' say little about the patient but it does tell the reader that the patient was seen by the house officer X on that day.
6   We came to a cot of one child and the consultant said, 'What's she got?' David, the house officer, already had the notes in his hand and said, 'Diarrhoea and vomiting. It says here she'd had it for 12 hours before coming in.' The consultant took the notes and flicked through the pages himself.

Sara Delamont

1   All human societies have a division of labour of sex, and therefore a sex-role, or gender-role system.
2   Whereas in many tribal societies there is consensus about the gender-role system – to be inculcated in children, modern Britain is divided about 'correct' sex-role socialization.
3   Schools are places where sex/gender-role socialization takes place, but generally as a by-product of other activities.
4   Pupils own sex-role stereotypes were reinforced by many aspects of their school lives.
5   Schools officially separate boys and girls in many ways. For example, all six schools list of boys and girls separately on the registers, have separate lavatories and changing rooms, and teach them different sports and games.
6   In the woodwork room at Melin Court School (on 4 September 1978) the new pupils are being allocated places at the benches, in alphabetical order, with boys first. When Mr Beech found he had 23 in the group it was girls left without bench places – about 3 girls (were) left to work where someone was absent (i.e. changing seats every week or starting each lesson by trying to find a space).

Our Cardiff group used Spradley's (1979) ideas on writing to provide a syllabus for its work for an eight week period.

Writing clinics, in which the participants become self-conscious about their writing practices and experiment with other ways of writing, can be beneficial for doctoral students. It may be helpful to get an 'outside expert' in to run such a clinic, but a trusted friendly member of staff from the department may be equally able to run such a clinic. Torrance and Thomas (1994) report on three different ways of running such clinics, all of which were found to be helpful by doctoral students. Torrance and Thomas argue that, at doctoral level, it is particularly important to focus on the production of text in the clinics (not on strategies for planning text) and to allow for individual variations in approach. Torrance and Thomas are also convinced, on the basis of extensive empirical research on academic writing, that PhD students should be encouraged to abandon the 'think then write' or 'plan then draft' approach, and replace it with a model of 'As I draft I clarify my thinking' or 'I draft therefore I think'.

Part-time students with full-time jobs may genuinely find it hard to clear time to write. For such students 'little but often' is a vital rule: they need to learn to write small bits whever they can. For part-timers particularly, encourage them to recognize that the 'patchwork quilt' principle applies to theses. If they break the task up into small chunks – five hundred words on this, a thousand on that, two hundred on the other – then they can write the two hundred on Monday, half the five hundred on Tuesday, the rest on Thursday, do the thousand on Friday and so on. Encourage them to realize that *it mounts up.*

Encourage students to travel by train, and never to get on the train without a task that can be done on it. They can learn to write on the train (using a laptop or a dictating machine), or make notes while the train is moving, summarizing at stations. The literature review can be completed on train journeys if the student reads and writes on trains in a cold-blooded and disciplined way. For *Fieldwork in Educational Settings* (Delamont 2002) Sara needed to 'gut' journal articles: it was done on trains. The student can read and reread the piece that he or she is criticizing and make the notes to write from.

If the graduate student is teaching others, it may be possible to organize that teaching so that bits of the thesis are coming from their lecture or tutorial preparation. As the classes have to be given, chunks of thesis-relevant work will have to get written. Fixing up a course on a topic forces all of us to prepare coherent ideas on it. However, the students on the course may pester the graduate for help and take too much of their time.

Finally, the most important thing is to ensure your PhD students learn to engage in tough-minded self-examination. Could they get up an hour earlier each day for a year? If they are routinely disturbed by undergraduates coming to the postgraduate room or asking for help with experiments, can they establish clearly specified and limited office hours for such consultations? Could they stay home one day a week and not do the housework? Do they *need* a new computer? a new printer? a dictaphone? new folders and pens? a new desk? a decent working chair? Train them to examine where they can write, when they can write, and how they can write (on their lap? in bed? in the bath? in the pub?), and then to go there, at that time, with the tools, and do it.

In general, encouraging and helping students to write is always one of the most rewarding aspects of the supervisor's role. Writing is a set of craft skills, and once a graduate student has begun to learn and apply them, then he or she will be able to write for the rest of their academic or professional career. Seeing the draft material take shape and pile up over the weeks and months is as gratifying for the supervisor as it is for the student. When they have worked collaboratively on writing as an activity, they can share the pleasure equally.

Dealing with writer's block

If the worst comes to the worst, and despite your best efforts the student does get blocked with their writing, you need to act quickly. It is easy to miss the onset of a writing block because students may avoid supervision appointments and/or fail to mention the problem. Once you realize that there is a difficulty, you need to act. We have already suggested ways to remotivate a demoralized candidate in Chapter 6, and all these ploys can help with writer's block. There are some other strategies that you can try specifically to jolt the student into producing draft text. First, you may have to change your role from 'good cop' to 'bad cop'. We have advocated throughout this book an approach based on supportive cajoling, but it is always worth thinking about a tactical change. It may be time to get tough: to set a series of deadlines quite close together and demand small bits of text before each. If the student fails to produce, then the pair of you need to examine very closely and seriously what is holding the student up – a fear of failure, a misguided perfectionism, unhelpful working habits, apprehension about your response to the work, or whatever it may turn out to be. In some cases, you may judge that getting tough will work. In all cases, positive reinforcement will be in order. If you can coax some text out of a blocked student, then a display of enthusiasm may lead to further writing. Your response to the draft material will need careful handling. Students who are anxious about their writing can easily be discouraged. They can easily interpret an enthusiastic and energetic engagement with their draft (lots of marginal comments, questions, lots of red ink) as damningly critical, and lose all confidence. If you do have a great deal to say and write about draft material, then you need to persuade the student that you are doing so because you believe in them and the work. The occasional treat and reward may work too – a drink or a shared meal, a book or some similar token.

Apart from emotional work, the supervisor may need to engage in writing *with* the blocked student. You and your student can try sitting side by side at the desk or at the PC, drafting or redrafting in concert. Get the student to decide what needs to be in a paragraph and start working on it. With luck, the student will start out by dictating to you, and you can let him or her take over. If not, then you may need to meet the student regularly and frequently to help get through the block with such joint sessions – until the student takes off on their own, or until you decide that the tactic is not paying off.

It may be helpful to get the student to try dictating onto tape rather than writing (although dictating needs its own skills). Sometimes it may help to tape a supervision, during which you get the student to talk through the issues he or she is struggling to express. A transcript of the discussion may be a surrogate first draft. More prosaically, a deadline for a seminar paper in the department, or a conference paper, may exert external pressure, and produce useful material. (Again, the presentation itself can always be taped and form the basis of a written version.)

Sometimes the problem is less drastic than a complete block, and the student can leave a particular chapter on one side and work on some other part of the thesis. Occasionally their problem may arise because they are trying to write the 'wrong' section anyway. Some students seem to be convinced that they must start at the beginning of the Introduction, or get their literature review sorted out first, or describe the methods before they can write about their results. A temporary block can often be overcome by persuading a student to write something that comes more easily, rather than getting stuck at one particular point.

If a student is blocked in a slightly different sense – with a chapter or section that the supervisor thinks is unacceptably weak and that the student cannot seem to improve – we would recommend putting that section aside and writing something else. The student is less likely to become demoralized, the supervisor can take a rest, and the student may learn how to rework the weak part while pushing on with another. At least the student will have a break, and may be able to see the weaknesses in their own work when they revisit it. This certainly happened to Annabel Pierce.

Example 8.4: Annabel Pierce

Annabel Pierce had done a Masters degree which included a 20,000-word thesis, supervised by Sara. She then registered at Lymstock University to do a PhD, supervised by Megan Hunter. Eighteen months into the PhD, Megan told Sara that Annabel was having enormous difficulty producing an acceptable 'theory' chapter. That same week Sara met Annabel at Sainsbury's and Annabel told Sara the same sad story. Sara suggested to both parties, separately and without disclosing it to the other, that it was perfectly sensible to put the unsatisfactory draft aside, and to push on with a draft of the rest of the thesis. This would restore Annabel's confidence, give Megan a respite, and get the rest of the thesis drafted. Six months later when Sara next met Annabel she was much more optimistic about finishing: she had realized how weak her original theory chapter was in comparison with the more sophisticated material she had succeeded in writing since. We reported Annabel's story in 1997. She got her PhD in 1999 and became a university lecturer.

In general, we have found that getting a first draft of the whole thesis, and then redrafting it, moves the student on faster than trying to get each chapter 'right' in isolation. The refrain of the *Startrek* song about 'always going forward' is a good motto for writing a thesis.

Word-processing

It is very easy to assume that all today's graduate students are computer literate and skilled at using word processors, spreadsheets, graphics packages, and so on. Such assumptions are not usually made about overseas students from developing countries, or mature students (unless they have been office workers in a previous career). But it is all too easy to make such an assumption about graduate students in their twenties. Equally, one may well assume that the sort of research training that is now available in most departments will ensure that students acquire the relevant skills.

The wise supervisor will not, however, take such skills for granted. Research on doctoral students in pharmaceutics in schools of pharmacy in 1994 (Whittlesea 1995) revealed that many of them were hampered by a lack of word-processing skills. These respondents were all first-language English speakers with a recent UK degree in pharmacy. However, many of them reported that the word-processing skills that they had picked up as undergraduates were inadequate for doctoral work. Many needed formal courses, or tuition packages, or extensive personal help. The supervisor needs to ask students how good their skills are, steer them towards relevant courses, or ensure that they use the tuition software that the university has available. In doing so, one should be aware that not all students are able to diagnose their needs and abilities accurately, or may not be able to gauge what range of skills and software they will need. Rudestam and Newton (2001, chapter 10) has an excellent discussion of how graduate students can learn to maximize their information technology skills.

Part of the supervisor's task is to ensure that students learn to word-process well enough to be able to prepare drafts of their work. They should discuss with their students the initial and final word-processing of the thesis itself. There are some key questions that need to be addressed. When the student is full time, access to an adequate workstation should be routine. For part-time students it may not be straightforward. One cannot take access to a machine

for granted. Part-time students in well-paid jobs will probably have a computer at home, but those who are unemployed, in low-paid work, retired or
in a low-income household may not have one at all, or may be stuck with an
obsolete machine incompatible with those in the university. It is important to
establish in the early stages of the part-timer's research how he or she is to
maintain access to the necessary computers – at work, at home, or in the
university's facilities in the evenings and at weekends. If the part-timer is
dependent on home or work, then it is important for them to ensure that
they keep up to date with changing software, and remain adequately compatible with the university department. (A well-resourced university or department can alleviate these problems by lending or hiring out laptop computers
to graduate students who cannot otherwise be guaranteed access.)

Example 8.5: PC problems

Lily Wu and Claudia Seferius both had severe problems with finishing
their theses because of PC access problems. Lily and her husband
shared one machine, and it was clear that her use of it was entirely
dependent on his whim: we tried to persuade her to write in the
department on a university machine, but they came from a country
where Macs were used, owned a Mac and she felt it was impossible to
work on a strange PC. It is not usually wise to interfere in the marriages
of graduate students, so we felt unable to do more. Claudia had a job
which involved her in a great deal of writing and word-processing: she
found it refreshing to read or gather data for her thesis, but very hard
to put in more hours at a PC. In the end she decided to pay an audio
typist to type her first draft from her dictated tapes, because she felt
unable to do her own word-processing. As a director of research in
local government with grown-up children, she decided to spend money
to get past her writing impasse.

It is useful to discuss with the student from early on how much of their
final thesis text they will prepare themselves. They may decide to prepare
their own drafts, but pay a professional to complete the final editing, format-
ting and printing; or they may elect to do the whole thing themselves. If they
want to do the whole thing, you can discuss with them where they can get
access to a good quality printer. The student needs to cultivate the skills of a
careful proofreader, as well as learning to use a spellchecker. He or she will
also need to learn how to format the page correctly, in accordance with the
university's regulations, lay out tables, prepare graphics, and so on. Software
for the management of references and bibliographies is almost always useful
for graduate students, and rarely introduced as part of basic word-processing
courses. Training and practice need to be planned: it is a bad idea to try to do
all these things in a rush at the end of the research.

Access to word-processing can handicap some students because they keep fiddling with their texts in ways that were never possible in the days of typescript. Likewise, they can waste precious weeks perfecting the appearance of the thesis, as if it were an exercise in desktop publishing. Others, on the other hand, are liberated by writing and editing directly with the word processor. Here again, an explicit discussion of how word-processing has affected academic writing, and how the particular student prefers to work, can be beneficial. Discussion of the intersection between the medium and the process is usually helpful for students. The autobiographical reflections of scholars can help. Peter Woods (1986) describes how he wrote in the days of pen and paper. In his 1996 book he explores how he moved from writing by hand and giving it to a typist to working onto a word processor. He explores his shift, and illustrates his exploration with a wonderful range of quotes from academic, creative writers such as the late Iris Murdoch, and popular novelists such a Joanna Trollope. He argues persuasively for keeping the pen, as an alternative to the keyboard.

Lastly, the supervisor may also need to help the student to *stop* writing. The most able of students can sometimes find it hard to let the thesis go. Writing and rewriting can sometimes become almost obsessional. The cultivation of a certain perfectionism in polishing the text can become a kind of displacement activity. Supervisors can find themselves in a kind of double-bind. Having encouraged the able graduate student to draft, redraft and respond to critical appraisal of their work, they can finally find themselves telling a student *not* to write any more: not to add that further chapter; not to incorporate yet more recent or obscure literature; not be influenced by yet another fashionable theorist, but to call it a day and recognize that it really is done. Again, this depends to a considerable extent on mutual trust between student and supervisor. The student needs to have sufficient faith in the supervisor's own academic judgement, and ultimately in her or his own, to recognize that the writing has reached its end – at least as far as the thesis is concerned. Once the thesis draft is advancing towards completion, the supervisor can focus on preparing the student for the examination, which is the subject of Chapter 9.

9

A lack of genuine interest: choosing the right external and preparing the student for the examination

> Fundamental mistakes arise out of lack of genuine interest.
>
> (Sayers 1972: 171)

Introduction

A good supervisor does not lose interest in the student when the thesis is written up. The student needs continued help until the viva is over, and that help has to be grounded in a genuine interest in the choice of examiner, the preparations for the examination, and the final presentation of the text.

In some universities the supervisor is not empowered to choose the internal or external examiners, and may not be involved in the viva voce examination in any way. This can lead a supervisor to forget his or her most important task: that is, preparing the students for their submission, examination and viva. This chapter is written for supervisors who have some role in choosing the external(s), some role in the viva voce, and, most important, a major role in preparing the student for the examination. We cover the choice of external, preparing the thesis for submission, preparing the student for examination, the conduct of viva voce sessions, and the role(s) of examiners. We hope that it will be useful for lecturers who have not yet examined a thesis themselves, as well as those with students coming up for submission. We start by recommending that you read the fictional viva voce from Cross (1970). This is a viva in the Graduate School of English Literature at Columbia, taking place at the height of the anti-Vietnam movement, during a year of campus unrest. The heroine, Professor Kate Fansler, is presenting Mr Cornford for a PhD, and his thesis is on W.H. Auden. American universities do not use external examiners, but do make up panels with professors from other departments in the same university. Cross's account takes eight pages, and is *extremely* funny: among other problems the panel is supposed to include Professor Chang from the Department of Asian Civilization (because Auden had been to China and had written about it), but in fact another Professor Chang, an expert in limestone landscapes from the School of Engineering is there instead. This Chang opens up his contribution to the viva by asking,' "Tell me please", Professor Chang said, turning courteously in his chair, "in China your Mr Auden found limestone landscapes? And what, please, is dildo?" ' Although there are a great many campus novels (see Carter 1990) there are very few doctoral vivas depicted in them, and this is certainly the funniest. But no one would want their own students to be exposed to anything like it.

Preparing for the examination of the thesis

Background work

Few students realize why there are external and internal examiners, and what they are supposed to do. Nor are they aware who is eligible to be an external or internal, how the external and internal get chosen, who appoints the external and internal examiners, or how long the whole process from submission to viva may take. Supervisors have a duty to explain the procedures that operate in their institution – first ensuring that they actually understand them themselves.

One of the first things to find out about is submission dates and how these relate to degree ceremonies, funding-council deadlines, local rules about continuation fees, and other timetabling constraints that may affect students. Many lecturers do not need to have such dates in their heads, and most students are blissfully unaware of how bureaucracies work. It is a shame if a good relationship, and the processing of a sound thesis, are spoiled by discord over the technicalities of submission, examination and graduation. That happened to us in the case of Guy Pagett, a lecturer in the School of Modern Languages, who, it transpired, had never been involved with any higher-degree submissions and did not know the timetable governing submission and degree day at Cardiff.

Example 9.1: Mrs Pagett's hat

Guy Pagett was a lecturer in the Department of Russian, who was registered for his PhD in sociology. Sara was director of graduate studies. In Cardiff, staff have to have two external examiners, and no internal. We had some trouble finding two appropriate externals free on the same day to viva Guy. One of our original choices was in Canada on sabbatical, and we only got the panel fixed up as Guy was getting his thesis bound. Guy handed in his thesis in May, thinking he could graduate at the 10 July ceremony, for which his mother had already bought a new hat. In fact in the University of Wales, 15 April is the last date on which a thesis can be submitted if the candidate is to graduate in July, and the viva has to happen before 15 June so the paperwork can be completed. Sara took it for granted that Guy knew these things because he was a lecturer and they were all in the university calendar. She had not explained to Guy that as he had missed 15 April *and* as his panel had been problematic he would not be able to graduate at a ceremony that year. She fixed the viva for 3 July, it took place, and Guy passed. He was then hurt and angry to find he could not graduate for 12 months, and his mother was mortified. What should have been an unalloyed pleasure for Guy – the thesis had been a long time coming to fruition and he received lots of praise from his examiners – was soured by this lapse of Sara's.

It is always wise to spell out to students how the institution works and what consequences that will have. Students also need to understand how the pressure on institutions to improve their completion rates, and the impact of the Reynolds Report (CVCP 1985) on examination procedures, have changed the pattern of submission and examination respectively over the past decade. The paragraphs we issue at Cardiff read:

> Since the Reynolds Report (prepared for the CVCP in the 1980s) there have been changes in the way theses are examined. For Masters degrees by thesis (MPhil) and PhDs, there will be an external examiner (from outside the University of Wales) and an internal examiner (from UWCC – but not your supervisor). The head of the department is legally responsible for choosing the external – but the supervisor's suggestions are normally followed. The external examiner should be interested in the topic, an expert on it, and an established scholar. For PhDs a professor is ideal – but there may not be a suitable professor around.

Such a paragraph begins the education of the graduate student. It is usually illuminating for graduate students to talk through the criteria used in the department to choose an external and the internal. Among the points to discuss will probably be: how poorly paid examining is, the motivation of examiners, the balancing of specialist knowledge and 'fairness', and the longer-term consequences of the choice. We discuss these all briefly below.

Students are very unlikely to know what sort of fee external examiners get (and that internal examiners are not paid at all). It is illuminating to explain that being the external examiner of a thesis pays considerably below the hourly rate of the UK national minimum wage. (The actual hourly rate depends on how good or bad the thesis actually is, and therefore how much effort must be put into reading and annotating.) This reason for choosing an external with an intrinsic interest in the topic is probably hidden from candidates. It helps to explain to them that there are no worthwhile extrinsic rewards for being an external examiner. Rather, the intrinsic interest is the 'bait' we all dangle to persuade colleagues to act. While on this topic it is useful to mention that externalling a thesis can be stressful for the examiner too: candidates are rarely good enough at 'taking the role of the other' to realize that until they become an examiner themselves. Paul always warns his students – undergraduate as well as graduate – that they might as well assume that their examiner for any examination or piece of course work is tired, over-committed and stressed. They should therefore write with a view to seizing his or her attention, making their work as clear and accessible as possible. If they can do that, then they can make their work accessible and memorable for other readers as well, now or in the future.

In the UK there are marked differences between universities in the arrangements for the examination of higher-degree theses. Some places have a chair, usually a senior staff member, who knows the rules and ensures that the procedures are fairly followed. Others ask the external to be the chair, or use the supervisor, or the internal, or are silent on the issue. If the thesis is a clear pass the lack of a chair hardly matters, but if the thesis and/or the viva are remotely problematic a chair is a good idea.

Most places insist on two externals if the candidate is a staff member, some require a good deal of previous experience before anyone can act as the sole internal or external. Some institutions insist the supervisor is present, some allow the students to choose whether to have them or not, others forbid their attendance. In London University the internal examiner is from a different college (so if the candidate is at Queen Mary's, the internal will be from UCL, or King's, or Royal Holloway, or another London college). In Edinburgh the internal is from a different department, so if the candidate is from the theology department the internal will be from classics or ancient history or oriental studies or philosophy, as appropriate.

The question usually arises: why does anyone agree to be an external? Among the reasons that motivate externals we know are altruism and 'duty': it is part of the generalized reciprocity all academics owe to the continuation of the system and their particular discipline. That explains the general predisposition and willingness to serve. As far as agreeing to act for specific candidates, the main motivations are probably interest in the topic, friendship or reciprocity with the supervisor or head of department, level of work commitments at the time of year, including other externalling tasks, and perhaps some personal reasons. This last category can include combining the viva with a visit to family, friends or collaborators, or the proximity of a sporting venue, or access to some other treat.

There is one other extreme reason for agreeing to be an external, which is a principal reason for agreeing to be an internal examiner, and that is gaining the experience. Like many tasks, the more often one has examined a thesis the more confident one becomes, and therefore the easier both supervision and examination are. The more examining you have done, the better supervisor you may be.

From the supervisor's viewpoint, the choice of external involves judging how far the potential external should be *the* specialist expert on the topic, how far a generalist in the area, and how far that expertise has to be balanced against their reputation as a fair, judicious, rational examiner. An expert on the topic who is horrendously severe on students, or obsessively 'picky' is probably a bad choice; a more generalist, less specialized, external who is fair and makes balanced judgements will be better. The supervisor needs to decide whether or not to discuss that judgement call (but not, of course, discussing specific individuals) with students. However, we all have a duty to protect our candidates from externals who behave unfairly, and that means, brutally, 'gossip'. If you and your close colleagues do not know how Professor X behaves as an external, then it is necessary to ask around and find out.

Students often ask if they can have someone 'soft' or 'easy' as their external. (Though often not in so many words.) That is a good enquiry because it allows you to discuss explicitly the importance of having the right external, not just for the viva, but for their longer-term future. The animal welfare slogan about pets and Christmas can be modified as: 'An external isn't just for the examination – he or she can be a patron, referee and gatekeeper for life.' You know that it is important to have an external; one who is not just about to retire but will be active for a decade or so, so that he or she can write references, open opportunities and make recommendations for the candidate for years to come. The following examples, 9.2 and 9.3 set out some pitfalls surrounding the choice of external. Example 9.2 reflects successful choices, while 9.3 was a disaster.

Example 9.2: Long-term benefits for Margaret Rushbridger

When Margaret Rushbridger finished her thesis we chose Professor William Purvis. We had rejected using the leading theorist at the centre of Margaret's argument because we felt he would find it difficult to judge objectively a thesis which was very largely critical of his work. Professor Purvis liked the thesis and Margaret's work. The PhD was awarded and praise bestowed liberally. Professor Purvis subsequently sponsored Margaret's career so that she got a trip to Australia, became reviews editor of Purvis's journal, and he commissioned from her two chapters for edited collections. The leading theorist only read the ideas once they were published, by which time he could debate with Margaret as an equal. We were pleased with our choice.

It is a good idea to find out both what the formal rules are in your own institution and what the local/departmental customs are. The rule book may very well say that the Head of Department or Dean of the Graduate School chooses the examiners, but you probably need to find out what advice they take. If the decisions do not formally include the supervisor, it may be normal for someone to take 'soundings' from him or her. There may be many informal ways to influence the choices: by having good ideas, by squashing bad ones, by asking colleagues to drop hints, and so on.

There is also the thorny question of the candidate's own views on the prospective external(s) and internal. Many places have rules against the student being consulted, but it is very hard, and can be very risky, not to have at least a general discussion about the issue. Whoever makes the final choice, he or she needs to know if the potential examiners have any pre-existing links with the candidate, formal or informal, licit or illicit, good or bad. It would be very easy if the student were not at least consulted in general terms, to appoint a candidate's godmother, aunt by marriage, discarded or current lover, former landlord, or squash partner. More realistically, and less facetiously, it is necessary to ensure that sensible choices of external examiner are made, in order to avoid unnecessary disputes about fundamental disagreements over research philosophy, methodology and the like. There are appropriate arenas for vigorous disputes to be conducted among academic equals. They have their own entertainment value for the spectators and their own rules of engagement. The exchange of vituperative recriminations through correspondence pages of academic journals or the public press is good blood sport, perhaps, and the academy would not be the same environment without it. But a graduate student's examination is not the right place to practise the academic equivalent of the martial arts.

Students often think that they need to know who their external is before they finalize their text so they can include positive citations and/or remove negative ones. That is, of course, not necessary in itself, but if an external is relevant enough to the thesis to examine it, then his or her work should probably be cited somewhere in any case. Students need to be reminded that they need to think, if at all, not so much about who their external will be (as an individual) so much as what he or she will be (in terms of interests, experience, skills and interests). Preparing for a more generalized audience than just the one ideal external – who may not be available, and may not be appointed anyway – is a more productive way of approaching things, and is a more fruitful way of constructing an 'implied reader' for the thesis anyway. Discussing a small short-list of examiners may well be a tactic to force a student to check the comprehensiveness of their coverage of the field. The crucial issue is whether the external examiner is going to be an *appropriate* one. As we have implied already, there are various ways in which one might usefully think about what appropriateness means in this context. A supervisor, or a director or dean of graduate studies, will normally do well to think constructively about at least some of those criteria when proposing or approving the nomination of an external for a particular student.

This brings us to the academic criteria that should be used in choosing external and internal examiners. There are several criteria to be borne in mind. First, does the potential examiner suffer from the 'drawbridge' mentality? This is a common disease. The examiner, having achieved a higher degree himself believes that he should be the last person to enter the ivory tower before the drawbridge is raised, and unworthy unwashed multitudes lay siege to the castle. In practice that means all attempts by higher-degree candidates to join the elite are repulsed as below standard. This is what the late Erving Goffman meant when he advised candidates and supervisors, 'Don't get anyone sociologically young' (Wiseman 1994: 192).

The second issue relates to broadmindedness or matching. The good examiner needs either to be a user of the same broad theory and methods of data collection and analysis as the candidate, together with an interest in the empirical subject matter, *or* to be broadminded enough to appreciate the merits of approaches other than his/her own. It is reasonable to expect students to have a reasoned defence of their theories, methods and topic choices both in the thesis and orally in the viva. However, it is not reasonable to ask the student to defend a school of thought against blind prejudice. If the external examiner is implacably and irrationally hostile to a position, they will in all likelihood not prove a fair examiner.

Example 9.3: The wrong external

Sinclair Dolan had been a PhD student for several years in a Department of Classics that was closed down. His supervisor, furious at the closure, took a post in New Zealand and severed all contact with Sinclair and the university. The School of Mediterranean Studies took him in and did their best. The thesis was submitted, and the Director of Graduate Studies did his best to find and appropriate external, and an 'internal' from the History Department. These examiners found the thesis inadequate, and referred it. Sinclair felt that the substitute supervisor had let him down, and that the wrong external had been appointed. Sinclair's thesis was an application of Queer Theory to nineteenth-century German writing on Horace, and the external turned out to be virulently opposed to Queer Theory, and to any scholarship on classical scholars of the past rather than on the classical texts themselves.

The department decided to fund Sinclair for a year while he rewrote, to pay a supervisor from the classics department of another university who could supervise Sinclair on the videolink and by e-mail, and to ensure the resubmission viva was chaired by the Head of Department. Sinclair rewrote the thesis, carefully dealing with every point raised by the external, and with the help of the new supervisor, defending the Queer Theory and the re-scrutiny of the nineteenth-century German classics much more explicitly. The revised thesis was passed, although the external still disapproved of it, because it met the written criteria and made explicit the areas where it was controversial.

The examiner's reputation in the discipline may be very relevant. If the student is at all likely to have an academic career, then it is wise to find an examiner who can help with that career: someone whose sponsorship will be seen as a bonus. The examples of Rosalie Otterbourne and Luke Fitzwilliam (9.4) illustrate this.

Example 9.4: Rosalie Otterbourne and Luke Fitzwilliam

Sara was Rosalie Otterbourne's external examiner, Anthony Cade was Luke Fitzwilliam's. Sara became one of Rosalie's referees and was able to recommend her to Anthony Cade when he needed a research assistant. In turn Anthony, who had been impressed by Luke's PhD, recommended Luke to Sara as a strong candidate for tutoring at a summer school she was running. Rosalie and Luke both got their careers boosted by recommendations from their externals.

Sometimes the choice of an academically appropriate external can have social consequences. For example, the best external may involve the candidate travelling to the external, or possibly chaperonage, as in the following example.

Example 9.5: The chaperoned viva

Fatima Ibn Battuta was from an Islamic country with very strict sex segregation. She had been supervised by Dr Cecily Sinclair. When Fatima was ready to submit there was discussion of how to organize her viva. We chose a female external, and Sara as chair, with a male internal. We assured Fatima that she would never be alone with the male internal. She remained veiled throughout the main proceedings. After the formal examination, Dr Sinclair and the man withdrew, leaving Fatima with her external and Sara, at which point Fatima could unveil to meet her famous external.

By contrast to the bad experiences of examinations and inappropriate selection of external examiners, one must emphasize that when an external examiner is the right sort of person, and when things are handled well, then the entire process can be a thoroughly rewarding one for all concerned. When a thesis is a competent one or better, and when it satisfies the normal criterion – that is an original contribution to knowledge in the candidate's field – then reading it and examining it should be interesting and indeed pleasurable for the examiner(s). Likewise, when there is little or no chance of the degree being withheld, the viva voce examination itself may prove to be a worthwhile experience. Under such circumstances, the occasion becomes much more collegial than might otherwise be the case. The candidate can talk about her or his plans for future research, plans for publication, ideas for further research funding and so on. On such occasions, the external examiner can prove to be a genuine adviser, and help can often be promised for the future. The occasion of the examination becomes a two-way exchange of views and ideas. When the thesis is sound and the external examiner is the right person, then, the 'examination' becomes something altogether more egalitarian and less confrontational than that term normally conveys.

On the receiving end

The higher-degree student may well fear and dread the examination. Even when the student is outstandingly competent, and however excellent the thesis itself may be, the process of examination can be a stressful one. Indeed, given that the assessment of the thesis is indeed an examination, conducted primarily by one or more examiners not well known to the candidate, one can argue that the process is necessarily so. We know from a survey of higher-degree students (Eggleston and Delamont 1983) that most feel worried by the indeterminacy of thesis examination, and that supervisors with relatively little experience of examining theses in other universities are common. Consider the account of an examination by Dr Nancy Enright, who was regarded by Kingford as one of their most successful alumnae, and is now a lecturer at Latchendon University. Her story of her viva was not the recollection of a happy experience:

> I had the most horrible viva anybody could ever have, I think. I did the most deplorable thing, I got upset and burst into tears, and that was awful, so I have a very bad memory of my viva. Looking back at the one I assisted with, I realized that with mine it was a question of human rights. It was appallingly badly examined. It was probably partly my fault, because you're not meant to know who your external is going to be, but usually there's an unofficial discussion about it. And I was not entirely happy about my external . . . I was examined by a historian from Reddingdale. There were things like he didn't know the conventions for the bibliography in anthropology – we have a convention where you don't capitalize every single word in a book title – and I had a twenty-five page bibliography and he went through and put a circle through every single letter he thought should have been capitalized. There were a lot of typing errors, but I got the cheapest typist I could, who typed a lot of things wrong, so that he said things like 'This sentence hasn't got a verb in it.' And the examiner missed the train, so I was waiting for two hours with the other examiner and the supervisor, so in terms of nervous stress it was awful . . . And they didn't say, 'Well done' or anything, it was just 'We want the typing mistakes corrected in three weeks.'

Rereading the interview with Dr Enright for this edition it is clear that she was generally very poorly prepared for the assessment of her work, because she says at one point, 'I didn't know a thesis could be referred.'

Ruth Wallace (1994: 104–5) recalled her oral examination at Berkeley: 'Glazer's strategy on the orals was to interrupt any student as soon as he was satisfied that the student was headed towards a correct answer. No one had warned me, however, that his interruptions meant success, not failure.'

Supervisors can, and should reduce the fear and the pain. A great deal can be done to reduce anxiety, both by demystifying the processes, and by helping the student reduce the likelihood of a referral by impeccable presentation.

De-mystifying the examination

There are a least eight ways to demystify the examination of the thesis.

• First, there are two books by Murray (2003) and by Tinkler and Jackson (2004), which all students (and colleagues) can usefully read.
• Second, there is a video prepared by Rowena Murray at Strathclyde which can be purchased for use with students, perhaps by a consortium of departments.
• Third, it is possible to organize classes with handouts and worksheets for group discussion.
• Fourth, the procedure of a viva before the upgrade from MPhil to PhD, or as part of annual progress reviews, can be used to open discussions about the final examination. Such regular reviews are likely to become part of the system of quality management for all postgraduates in the UK during the next decade.
• Fifth, an individual mock viva to prepare for the real one when the thesis is nearing completion.
• Sixth, it is helpful for students to give each other vivas as part of a course.
• Seventh, it is salutary for students read a mock thesis and design a set of questions, to ask its authors.
• Eighth, a simulated public mock viva with staff playing the roles is invaluable.

There is little or no research on the efficacy of these different ways to prepare students except the work of Hartley on graduate students in psychology (Hartley and Jory 2000; Hartley and Fox 2004). His research suggests that most universities do not provide systematic preparation for vivas. There is some research on PhD students' experience of their vivas (Tinkler and Jackson 2000; Morley, Leonard and David 2002), but not yet on vivas for the professional doctorate. The research is overwhelmingly based on the horror stories of volunteers, and we are somewhat sceptical about the generalizability of the experiences of the minority of narrators of such horror stories, as we have written elsewhere (Delamont and Atkinson, nd). We have some experience of some of the strategies, and have discussed those in more detail below. In preparing our own students, and in the attempt to dispel some of their anxieties, we include sessions on the viva examination in our series of graduate classes. We have a handout on some of the procedures, and then we provide two types of mock viva. These are introduced in the next section.

Reducing the fear

In Scandinavia, the Netherlands and Belgium the doctoral viva is a public event, so a candidate can watch other people defending their theses. In the UK vivas are private, so the supervisor and departments need to think about ways of simulating the viva. There are two ways to do this: an individual mock viva, and a public mock viva. Each has its merits. Students can also be helped by handouts and classes about what happens in a typical viva, and about the criteria that externals use to evaluate theses. We have reproduced our handout on external examiners' criteria in Figure 9.1, and our handout on what happens in a typical viva and how students should present themselves in Figure 9.2. We then discuss how to simulate vivas.

Figure 9.1: What does an external do?

The external's job is to judge whether the work is of the correct standard, compared to other UK universities. If she or he is not satisfied the thesis can be referred for further work, or failed altogether. The current categories available for a PhD are:

1   That the candidate be approved for the degree of PhD.
   (NB: examining boards may require a candidate to make typographical or minor corrections in a thesis that has been approved, before deposit in the libraries.)
2   That the candidate be approved for the degree of PhD, *subject to the completion of such minor corrections as may be required by the examining board.* (In such circumstances the examining board may stipulate that the external examiner(s) should be satisfied that minor corrections have been completed prior to the award process being initiated.)
3   That the candidate be not approved for the degree of PhD but that, the thesis being satisfactory in substance but defective in presentation or in detail, the candidate be allowed to modify the thesis and resubmit it for the degree of PhD on payment of a reduced fee.
4   That the candidate be not approved for the degree of PhD but be allowed to modify the thesis and resubmit it for the degree of PhD on payment of a re-presentation fee.
5   That the candidate be not approved for the degrees of PhD
6   That the candidate be not approved for the degree of PhD, but having satisfied the requirements for the award of MPhil be approved for that degree.

7　That the candidate be not approved for the degree of PhD, but be approved for the degree of MPhil, *subject to completion of such minor corrections as may be required by the Examining Board.* (In such circumstances the examining board may stipulate that the external examiner(s) should be satisfied that minor corrections have been completed prior to the award process being initiated.)

The viva is to check that the thesis is the student's own work, that she or he understands what was done and why, and can explain or justify any features that the examiners want to raise.

How does the examiner reach a judgement?

1　Typing/word-processing: Are there lots of mistakes? Does it need to be referred for retyping, or can it be hand corrected?
2　Is the bibliography complete? (Is every reference in the text listed at the back?)
3　Is the bibliography correctly prepared?
4　Is the literature review comprehensive and up to date? If not, how much more work does the student need to do?
5　What sort of thesis is it? If it is empirical, the following questions arise?

    (a) Is the problem worth studying?
    (b) Were the right (or at least relevant) methods chosen?
    (c) Were the methods used properly?
    (d) Are the relevant methods text books cited?
    (e) Was the sample big enough and chosen well?
    (f) Are the data presented clearly?
    (g) Has the author a realistic understanding of where his/her data fit into the literature?
    (h) Does the discussion illuminate the results?
    (i) Do the conclusions follow from the results?

6　If it is theoretical, the main criterion is whether the theoretical argument is coherent, well expressed and develops logically.
7　If it is an account of a practical project (such as a new curriculum in the student's own school), the main criterion has to be: Has the author achieved some distance from his or her own work?

If you want to read about examining, pages 141–6 in Brown and Atkins (1988) *Effective Teaching in Higher Education* are about being an examiner.

This is accompanied by the following handout on the viva itself.

Figure 9.2: What happens in a viva

Be prepared

Attend the mock vivas whenever you can, and watch what happens carefully, so you are clear what will happen in yours. Take notes, and discuss any queries with your supervisor.

The viva will take at least one hour, and can last for 4–5 hours. Make sure that you are wearing clothes that enable you to sit comfortably, and that you won't need to go out to the lavatory too often. Don't have garlic, curry or alcohol for lunch!

Don't wear a strong cologne/perfume/after shave: Vivas are hot sweaty occasions.

You should have with you:

(a)   a copy of your thesis;
(b)   a pencil, a pen with *black* ink, a note pad;
(c)   a clean handkerchief;
(d)   a list of typing mistakes you've already spotted in your own thesis since you handed it in!

Dress respectably – but as long as you are clean and tidy it isn't essential to put on a suit. Wear something you feel relaxed in – so not a new shirt that's rubbing your neck raw, or a skirt too tight to sit down in, or shoes that are crushing your feet! Don't smoke without asking if you can.

What will probably happen

Your external, internal, chairperson and supervisor will probably have been out to lunch. (Most vivas happen at 2.00 p.m. or 2.15 p.m.) They will certainly have met, and discussed what they think of your work and how to organize the viva. So they will have prepared questions, statements, etc.

You will be invited in, and you should be introduced to the external (and the internal if a stranger). The chairperson, who will be a senior member of the department's staff, will tell you what's going to happen. 'Dr X will start the questioning ...' or 'Both Professor Z and Dr P have some questions, but I'd like to start by asking ...'

The chairperson has not read the thesis. Their job is to ensure the rules are followed and the viva is fair.

In Cardiff examiners are not allowed to tell you the result until the viva is over – so answer the questions carefully.

When they have finished questioning you, you will be asked to leave while they decide on the verdict. Then you will be invited back in to hear it.

It is a good idea to ask your supervisor to make notes during the viva so that you can discuss them together afterwards.

Likely viva questions

You can expect to be asked – and should prepare to answer:

1 Why did you select this particular topic?
2 Tell us how you came to be interested in this particular area of [education].
3 What have you discovered as a result of your research?
4 Tell us about the theoretical framework that underpins your research.
5 What theories inform your work? Why this particular one?
6 What other theoretical approaches did you consider but reject?
7 Outline your research design.
8 What are the relative advantages of the methods of enquiry you employed?
9 What research instruments did you use?
10 Take us through the main features of your sample. Were there any differences in the planned and achieved samples?
11 Are you satisfied with the sample you achieved?
12 Questions about the research process

   (a) There is likely to be an extensive discussion of the evidence you have presented (interview data, tables etc.) and your interpretation of this material and a discussion of other possible interpretations.
   (b) There will also be an extensive discussion of whether the conclusions you have presented are justifiable
   (c) What is the (professional) relevance of your findings/what advice would you give to policy makers?
   (d) Would you do anything differently?

If the examiner says 'On page 692 you say', don't look surprised – s/he should have read it that carefully. Just turn to page 692 and take time to reread what you *did* say! However idiotic the question, be polite.

If you didn't understand the question, *say so.* Ask politely to hear it again.

Defend your work firmly but calmly –

'Yes – that is a good criticism. At the time I didn't realize X so I did Y. There are benefits from doing Y – as I show in Chapter 7.'

'I'm sorry I haven't read Delamont. My supervisor and I agreed to use literature by good scholars, and Delamont isn't a good scholar.'

'I'm afraid I don't agree. Atkinson's work is interesting – but it really isn't relevant to my argument in Chapter 7, as I explained on page 10.'

Sound modest, but not grovellingly wet. Try not to waffle, and answer concisely with reference to the thesis.

If you are asked to leave the room and wait, don't panic, and don't vanish. If you have to go and phone someone, tell the secretary where you've gone and be quick.

The individual mock viva is particularly useful for students whose first language is not English. The ideal format is to have a couple of staff who are relative strangers to the student, who have read the thesis abstract, introduction and conclusion. They should take about forty minutes, and grill the student in a shortened version of a real viva. Ideally this should be taped, or even videotaped, so that the student can be taken through his or her performance by the supervisor, and helped to think about how to frame answers to questions and defend the thesis.

The public mock viva is a parallel way to demystify the viva. We have organized at least one every year since 1987. This is how we do it. First a staff member who has a PhD 'volunteers' to be the candidate. She chooses a published article she has written, held in the university library, and it is designated as 'the thesis'. Other staff are chosen to act as external examiner, internal examiner, supervisor and chair. A date is set, invitations issued to postgraduates, and posters put up. For example, the one shown in Figure 9.3, is a recent example. On the appointed day, the cast assemble in the lecture room, and the chairperson explains what is going to happen. The 'candidate' waits outside the room, while the chair introduces the panel to the audience explaining their roles. Then the viva begins. The chair reminds the panel of their duties – quoting the university's rules, and then asks to have the candidate brought in. We then have a viva, lasting forty minutes or so, with the candidate trying to answer the panel's questions as well as possible, and the panel asking supportive questions. That is, the first performance is a successful viva: the thesis is a pass and the candidate is trying hard to be a 'good' student.

Figure 9.3: Poster for mock viva

MOCK VIVA 2003

Research and Graduate School in the Social Science (RGS) Mock Viva
5.15 p.m. Monday 12 May 2003, Room 1.61, Bute Building

The candidate:	Dr Aditya Bharadwaj, SOCSI
The chair:	Professor Roger Mansfield, CARBS
The external:	Dr Evelyn Parsons, UWCM
The internal:	Dr Sara Delamont, SOCSI
The supervisor:	Dr William Housley, SOCSI

(for further details and to request a copy of the thesis, please e-mail rgs@cardiff.ac.uk)

After the first enactment of a viva, we stop and send the candidate out. The lecturer alters his or her appearance – swapping the smart suit for a t-shirt and jeans – and is again brought in. This time the candidate acts bad student, and the panel are forced to fail the thesis. Different staff play 'bad' student in different styles – weeping, monosyllabic, depressed, aggressive, drunk, elaborately flippant. One year Dr Ian Shaw played 'bad' student as an increasingly depressed person, who shrank into a foetal curl, and developed a maddening sniff. Paul Atkinson has played it as a 60s communard, accusing the panel of middle-class prejudice against working-class candidates whenever he did not like a criticism.

We get an audience of 75–150 doctoral students with a few staff who are about to be an internal or external examiner for the first time. The audience watch the successful performance with interest, but when the student is 'failing' they become completely absorbed in the drama. They groan, squirm with embarrassment, wince and giggle nervously as the lecturer messes up her/his chances of getting a PhD. When a question is mishandled, the audience reaction is clearly audible. A few people find the mock viva frightening, but most respond that it is both entertaining and informative. It takes a good deal of organizing, but the benefits are worth it. The event is demystified.

The supervisor can choose the examiners carefully, and set up all the mock vivas in the world, but it is also important to ensure that the student has done all the basic presentational work on the thesis properly so the ideas are examined not the typing.

Preparing the student for submission

Students rarely appreciate how long it takes to proofread a text, especially if they have typed it themselves. They need to be told, repeatedly, that they must find a friend and read the whole thing *aloud*, punctuation and all, especially checking all the tables, figures and data against the original lab books, computer print-out or hand-drawn versions. It is helpful if the supervisor can pay the student to proofread something the supervisor has written early on in the registration period, so the student learns how to do it professionally. Postgraduates can, and should, be encouraged to work together, helping each other to proofread each other's theses. The story of Ariel and Texana, coupled with that of the worst case from your own experience should encourage your students to aim for an immaculate presentation.

Example 9.6: Give the examiners an inch

Ariel Gold and Texana Jones were both racing to submit their theses by 14 April – the final date for them, unless they got extensions. Ariel's had clearly not been spell-checked or grammar-checked at all: there were 'sentences' without verbs, singular verbs with plural nouns, and several typing errors on every page. Texana's photocopier or printer had obviously been having a bad day: one bound copy had 4 page 9s and then page 16, the other bound copy had no page 9 at all, and so on throughout the 272 pages. Texana's external refused to read the copy sent, demanded a fresh manuscript, and that meant her viva did not take place till the following September.

Ariel's external examiner, because every page of the thesis had to be corrected anyway, demanded large numbers of revisions, additional literature reviewed, and different statistical tests done.

In both cases the students were forced to do not only the work they should have done properly in the first place, but also found themselves under stress (in Texana's case), and having to do extra work (in Ariel's), plus having extra costs to bear.

Students may need advice on whether to submit in temporary or permanent binding (depending on the university's regulations), help with the paperwork required by the university (such as notification of intention to submit, if such a procedure exists), or a loan to pay the immediate costs of submission (if required). They may be shy about asking for help. Again, do not underestimate the extent to which some students are 'cue deaf' and fail to register what other students take for granted. One student we heard about submitted his thesis on bright blue paper, having failed to read the university's rules.

Once the thesis is handed in, and the candidate is waiting for the viva, the supervisor can do little more, except 'rehearse' him or her for the event. However, one way to help them prepare for their submission and examination is to encourage them to work through the relevant chapters of Cryer (2000) and Phillips and Pugh (2000). They have a number of good ideas for how students can usefully occupy the time. But supervisors should be very wary about recommending them all uncritically. Phillips and Pugh, for instance, advise students to compile a detailed (obsessively detailed) condensation of their thesis by way of revision and preparation. For many theses that would be inappropriate, while for some students, such an exercise would provoke anxiety and do little or nothing to improve their performance. On the other hand, all students can probably benefit from thinking of a few good questions to ask the examiners – advice about publication being a recurrent topic for such enquiries. Likewise, some general homework about the external examiner may be useful. Equally, however, one should not make a fetish of it, nor expect the candidate to come over as fawning by focusing too much on the external's interests and achievements.

Finally, it is vital to ensure that the student realizes that submission leads to an examination. Your role is to decide the thesis is ready to be submitted and examined, not to guarantee that it passes. Irrespective of whether they have followed your advice to the letter or not, candidates do need to take responsibility for their own work. It is they who will be awarded the degree if they are successful, not their supervisor.

The examination and its outcomes

Before your student actually walks into the viva, there are three tasks you need to have performed. First, you need to be aware of the regulations governing the degree the student is being examined for, and especially what the possible outcomes of the viva can be. These are different in different universities, and are subject to change, so it is easy to think one knows the ropes when in fact one's knowledge is out of date. Second, it is useful to know what happens in vivas in your department or institution: who attends and what roles they have. (Some, for instance, have a chairperson, others do not.) In particular, you need to be clear about whether you are expected to attend or not, and if you are, what role you are supposed to play. (In some universities the supervisor is clearly expected to be present, although not as an examiner; in others the presence of the supervisor is explicitly proscribed.) Third, you need to ensure that your student is clear on these points. The candidate especially needs to know whether you will be present or not, and if so in what capacity: one cannot assume that they fully understand the niceties of having a supervisor present, but not as a full participant in the examining process, for instance.

In Cardiff there are eight possible outcomes from a PhD examination as we showed in Figure 9.1. We use them here as the basis for a brief consideration of what the supervisor can do once the verdict is arrived at and announced to the candidate. The outcome where a PhD candidate is given an MPhil instead is likely to disappear in the UK, as the QAA (2001) view is that it violates a key principle of fair assessment.

Universities have different regulations and wordings: supervisors and students must make absolutely sure they know and understand the regulations that apply to them. Looking at the University of Wales rules we have reproduced, you can see that the possible outcomes of a PhD examination are varied. They are not perfectly straightforward either. It sometimes takes judgement on the part of the examiners and the chair of the board to determine precisely which category to apply. The differences between outcome 2 and outcome 3 are not clear-cut, for instance. It is, therefore, important that the examiners and the chair know and understand the categories and their normal interpretation. External examiners cannot be expected to have a feel for all different universities' practices. It is, therefore, especially important that the chair of the exam board, or the director of graduate studies (or whoever is responsible) ensures that the external examiner does understand what decisions the examiners are empowered to come to.

If the version is either of the first two, then the supervisor's role is to join in the celebrations, and after the excitement has settled down, then to get on with helping the newly elevated Dr So-and-So progress their career still further. (We discuss this in the next chapter.) If the thesis is referred for revisions, then the supervisor can usefully do several things. First, discuss with the director of graduate studies, the head of department, or whoever is responsible, and the candidate whether a different staff member could better oversee the revisions. Often a fresh perspective helps everyone. Second, the supervisor can ensure that the examiners have provided a clear rationale for the referral, so that he or she *and the student* understand the reasons for the outcome, and that clear guidance has been provided as to what revisions are being required. If the supervisor is to retain responsibility for the candidate, and is charged with supervising the revision process, then it is imperative that he or she should understand thoroughly what is being asked of the student, the timeframe within which the revisions may (and must) be completed, and the regulations governing resubmission and examination. Supervisors can be very disappointed by any outcome that is not an outright pass and award of the degree. A referral for a moderate amount of revision is not a disgrace for a student or the supervisor, however. If everyone passed first time, then it would not be much of an examination, and it certainly would not carry the cachet that a doctorate does. That does not preclude some degree of self-examination on the supervisor's part. It is worth reviewing whether the weaknesses in the thesis could and should have been spotted and corrected at an earlier stage; whether one's advice was always for the best; indeed, whether the student has followed advice adequately. One can always learn something from the examination of one's own students' work, whether they pass or are referred, and in the latter case one does need to think whether there are lessons for the future. Of course, you may feel that the examiners were purblind idiots to refer your student. But if they both had the same problems with the thesis, then perhaps you and your student need to accept the fact that the argument was not quite as convincing as you thought, or the evidence not quite as strong, or the conclusions not quite as self-evident.

Outright failure is uncommon, but not unknown. We shall not go into lengthy discussion of that outcome here. It rarely comes as a shock to supervisors and internal examiners. It normally reflects a major weakness or problem that will be known to you already. Unless something is sadly amiss, it often reflects a student's failure to perform tasks that the supervisor has proposed and agreed, a failure to accept advice, an omission of major parts of the research literature to which the supervisor has directed them. In these cases, it is especially important to ensure that your role is properly understood and documented. If it comes to complaints and appeals at a later stage, you do not want to stand accused of incompetent supervision because the student has not followed it. The actual process of appeal is very different in different universities and we do not need to dwell on it here. But if you have had problems with a weak, lazy or headstrong student, and the thesis is failed as a result, then you do need to be prepared. It needs to be clearly understood, as we have said already, that in supervising the work you are not implicitly guaranteeing that the thesis will be successful.

Sometimes the student who has written a reasonable text can behave foolishly in the viva, as in the case of Ellis Pargeter.

Example 9.7: Poor viva performance

Paul was chairing the viva of Ellis Pargeter. The external and internal asked perfectly sensible questions, but Ellis was so paralysed with terror and so nervous that the viva was almost entirely pointless. After the formal proceedings, Paul asked Ellis if he had had an individual mock viva, and how many of the department's annual public mock vivas he had attended. Ellis said his supervisor had told him not to bother. The moral of this is that we all have colleagues who give their students bad advice.

Such cases are mercifully rare.

Example 9.8: Good viva performance

Sara chaired Lillian Udvary's EdD viva. Although Lillian was nervous, she performed well. Afterwards, when her external said to her that she had defended her thesis well, Lillian pulled out the departmental handout, and said: 'I did what we were taught to do: and I learned a lot from the people role-playing the candidate in the mock vivas!'

Given that all kinds of mock viva are quite time consuming to organize, and quite stressful for the participant, every Lillian is very rewarding and makes up for the occasional Ellis.

Once the examination or re-examination is over, the supervisor has one remaining responsibility to discharge: launching the student's career. This is the focus of the next chapter.

10

The brave pretence at confidence: launching the student's career

> The brave pretence at confidence had been given up . . . They were no longer angry and suspicious. They were afraid.
>
> (Sayers 1972: 248)

Introduction

Sayers was describing a group of women threatened by anonymous letters and malicious damage. Many graduate students who want to stay in academic research and teaching are equally suspicious, afraid and even angry with the scholarly world. Many supervisors may feel that their job ends at the viva, and what happens thereafter is none of their business: it is the PhD students' careers, let them build up a CV and find a post. We do not take that position, and believe instead that a good supervisor should help doctoral candidates to build good strong foundations for their careers.

We believe that supervisors should see the doctoral period as an important part of the career, and help the student to develop the beginnings of a well-rounded CV, a list of useful contacts and a set of strategies for advancement. Once the viva is over, the former student can usefully be helped into single-handed publication and a first job. This chapter is divided into three main sections: career building while a PhD student is still a student, job-seeking after the viva, and publication matters. Clearly much of this chapter applies primarily to the full-time student who wants an 'academic' or research job, rather than the person who is heading for a career in commerce or industry, or the part-time student who enjoys their current career. For both stages of career building, the supervisor may find it helpful to consult the literature. Blaxter, Hughes and Tight (1998) have a useful volume on all aspects of career building, and on establishing a research career there is Atkinson and Delamont (2004).

There is good evidence that students are not knowledgeable about the job market, and it is clear that understanding of the workings of academic careers is not great in the student body (e.g. Startup 1979). The most recent research also suggests strongly that recent graduates are ill-prepared for the contemporary labour market. Brown and Scase's (1994) study is a case in point. Their empirical material at the heart of that volume is drawn from a questionnaire issued in 1990 to students in three English universities: 'Inner City' (a former polytechnic), 'Home Counties' and 'Oxbridge': and

120 interviews with students at the same three universities done in 1991 and 1992. These data were supplemented with employer interviews – thirty 'graduate recruiters' (p. 50) from sixteen organizations – and with follow-up interviews with twenty of the students a year into employment. The authors were investigating 'the changing relationship between higher education and the intergenerational reproduction of class inequalities' (p. 165) in England. They wanted to use data to test the two competing theories which explain the relationships between occupational stratification and educational stratification. The first of these, social exclusion theory, emphasizes how elite groups are offered differentiated credentials to exclude certain social groups from top jobs, and is associated with Randall Collins's conflict theory. The second theory, a technocratic one, associated with Burton Clark, sees mass higher education as a necessary correlate of an increasingly complex post-industrial society in which the credentials are used to sort qualified people into specialized jobs.

Brown and Scase (1994: 173) conclude that in Britain:

> the recent increase in graduate numbers will simply mean that differences between the institutions of higher learning will increase . . . and the labour market for graduates will come polarised between the 'fast-track' leading to senior managerial positions, and a mass of other jobs which offer little in the way of career prospects.

They are pessimistic about the prospects of talent-led economic innovation in Britain because 'traditional processes of cultural and social reproduction are able to sustain themselves' (p. 175). Brown and Scase found that the twenty graduates they reinterviewed were disillusioned 'with the realities of working life' (p. 147), partly because they were 'unprepared for the realities of life in the 1990s: namely the more uncertain career prospects of the adaptive organisation' (p. 147). The middle-class and Oxbridge-educated graduates were 'better-prepared for the transition to work' (p. 147). This was related to the findings from the employer/recruiter interviews, which led Brown and Scase to conclude that: 'the demand placed on employers to ensure a personal fit between existing employees and new recruits led to a search for "safe bets" ' (p. 144).

There is no reason to believe that the PhD student will be any better prepared for career building than these respondents of Brown and Scase's. While few doctoral candidates today come out of their period as a research student as naive about, for example, publishing as many of their supervisors were in the past, it is easy to overestimate their sophistication. Deem and Brehony (2000) point out that in the social sciences and humanities graduate students have little chance to see or experience the intellectual work of their supervisors. Roberts (2002) and the four higher-education funding councils (HEFCE 2003) have strongly recommended career guidance and mentoring for higher-degree students, although it is hard to see how this can be delivered efficiently for the many part-timers with careers outside academia.

Career building during the PhD registration

In this section we focus on using the doctoral registration period to set the foundations of a career in place. We start with teaching the courtesies, and move on to building a well-rounded CV, networking, conferences, and become aware of fundraising. Publication issues are covered in the third section of the chapter.

Teaching the courtesies

One of the important tasks that might fall to the supervisor is training the student in academic courtesies. This can begin very early in the registration period. Some students do not seem to realize why academic work requires acknowledgements, and need to be trained to thank the funding body, their mentors, technical, secretarial and library staff, the head of the department or research group, and their supervisor. In the early days a supervisor can discuss why there is an acknowledgements page in the thesis, and suggest the student opens a file, or keeps a notebook in which the names of helpful individuals are recorded so they get remembered. If it is possible to acknowledge the student in a publication of yours, this will be motivating for them and a part of their training. Much later on, checking the acknowledgements section of the thesis, and ideally the footnote in which they put their acknowledgements in their early publications, enables you to train them so they do not offend others for much of their lives. Students may need to be told that readers will check their acknowledgements to see where they 'fit' into the discipline, that sponsors and funding bodies *require* acknowledgement, and that a nice acknowledgement creates loyalty and renewed enthusiasm in clerical, technical and library staff. It may be necessary to explain explicitly that scholars who do not acknowledge help are likely to lose out in career opportunities, as in the case of Candace Pert (1997). The dispute she started caused her former supervisor to lose the Lasker Prize and probably all chance of the Nobel Prize, and displays her ignorance about the taken-for-granted courtesies of academic science.

Example 10.1: Academic courtesies

In the 1970s Paul supervised Judd Springfield for an MEd. Years later he got a PhD, in another university. He wrote to Paul, with a copy of the graduation picture and the abstract and acknowledgements of the PhD thesis in which Paul was mentioned as an earlier influence. Paul has always written Judd good references, and will continue to do so. In contrast, he put many hours into helping Aurora Teagarden get her thesis finished when her supervisor was off sick after an operation, but Aurora did not acknowledge him in her thesis, or in her publications, and Paul never puts her name forward when opportunities arise.

Building the curriculum vitae

The successful graduate student will need to think about a bit more than just completing their research and submitting the thesis (though for much of the time even that may seem quite demanding enough). It is worth thinking more broadly about career development. The ambitious student may want to think constructively and strategically about how to acquire useful skills and experience that will give him or her an edge in the career stakes. They include the acquisition of teaching skills and experience; the projection of future research; identifying funding sources and research sites. The precise mix of experience will depend on the discipline and on practical circumstances, but some broad issues will be generic.

Most graduate students and research assistants are permitted to undertake specified amounts of teaching. Indeed, some varieties of institutionally funded studentships and tutorial posts specifically require a commitment to teaching as well as to doctoral research. Research council studentships explicitly permit a small number of hours per week. If the department has a teaching programme (and in exclusively research centres and institutes things are different) then graduate students should be encouraged to acquire teaching experience. This is normally acquired through provision of tutorials/seminars and, in the laboratory sciences, demonstrating (supervising practical classes). Teaching experience is valuable in its own right. Many academics find that the necessity of preparing their thoughts in order to teach undergraduates helps them organize their material in a way they otherwise would not. Teaching – even if only demonstrating and conducting tutorials – thus has intrinsic value for the younger academic. The ability to organize one's thoughts in order to help the average undergraduate may also help to articulate hitherto implicit ideas. Equally, and even more importantly for the longer term, the would-be academic needs to be thinking about how to build some teaching experience into the curriculum vitae. Few academic departments these days can afford to overlook the potential contribution to a teaching programme in making appointments to their regular staff.

The role of the research supervisor may be fairly remote from the allocation of basic teaching duties in the department. Her or his relationship with the graduate student, on the other hand, means that input on general career planning may be appropriate – possibly in discussion with the director of graduate studies, the dean of the graduate school, or whoever has overall responsibility. Even though graduate students' teaching is not a major part of their commitment, they should not be used as 'dogsbodies' without having their efforts recognized, and without proper supervision and training. It is increasingly recognized, indeed, that some initial training and mentoring in introductory teaching should be provided as part of the staff development offered to graduate students, research assistants and the like. They should not be thrown in at the deep end, with no guidance, back-up or advice. The overview taken by the supervisor might well include general advice on how to manage the allocation of time between research, teaching and other activities. Equally, it should probably involve supervisory discussions on what skills and experiences the candidate wants to accumulate for career-building purposes. If there is access to a certificate in teaching, which many places now offer part-time to postgraduate tutors and demonstrators, then it is worth discussing with the postgraduate student whether they can and should obtain the credential. The benefits of teacher training for Chemistry postgraduates was made clear in the evaluation of an experimental PhD/PGCE programme conducted by Galton and Delamont (1976). Students, supervisors and the heads of chemistry departments all saw benefits for the chemistry PhD stemming from the PGCE element.

As well as formal credentials, students need to build networks.

Networking in general and conferences in particular

Academic life is dependent on networking: keeping up with the field, judging the merits of others' work and one's own, discovering the status of journals, looking for externals, finding publication outlets, hearing about conferences, jobs and gossip, and making life tolerable. These are all vital parts of academic life that rely on networking. Students have to learn this, and the best way to help them into networks is via yours. Some students seem 'naturally' to be able to develop their own networks, both with people of their own generation and with more senior colleagues. Others need to be encouraged and sponsored, and some may even need to have the significance of networking pointed out to them explicitly. Students may not realize that they need to build up a network of contacts in their discipline, and that it is never too soon to start. Summer schools attended by graduate students from a number of universities are a good start, followed up by conferences.

Academic conferences are, of course, one mechanism for promoting students' professional networks. If you enjoy going to conferences, then it is straightforward to encourage your doctoral students to come with you, so that you can introduce them to your friends, enemies, and the publishers' representatives. The main obstacle is money, and it is important to find out what funds are available for them in the department, the university and beyond, and encourage them to apply for financial support. Some students may be unwilling to go to the professional meetings, and if so you need to find out the cause of their reluctance. If their reluctance is due to ignorance of the importance of conferences, or to shyness or feelings of inferiority about mixing with 'big names', then the supervisor needs to explain why serious scholars have to overcome those barriers. If the problems are financial or domestic (children who cannot be left overnight, or a sick spouse who needs nursing) then a long-term plan to find solutions to the problems will be necessary – to help enable the student to get away.

If there do not seem to be any opportunities for your graduate students to attend conferences elsewhere, it may be necessary for you to organize one, or help your students to do so in your own university. Involving graduate students in conference organization is excellent professional training for them: there is nothing like discovering that an FRS cannot complete a simple form indicating if he wants a vegetarian meal or not to prepare the novice for university life. More importantly, the practical experience of conference organization – especially gained in the relative security of one's home department – represents a set of transferable skills that can be deployed most usefully in later years. Conference organization, together with conference attendance, is part of the network-building strategy that many younger academics will need to start cultivating.

It is also important for students to start presenting their results at the right conferences. Again, the precise range of opportunities vary from discipline to discipline, and our general observations must remain general. Some professional associations have regional conferences intended specifically for postgraduate students and other junior staff to present the results of research in progress. These are very useful occasions for one's students to learn the basics of conference presentation, as well as presenting their materials before a wider professional audience.

Larger national and international conferences may also offer the opportunity for graduate students to present their work. In many disciplines, the poster presentation is an appropriate method for graduate students to get their results out to a professional audience. There may also be opportunities for research students to participate in roundtables, symposia and the like. The major international conference is rather like 'the season' of a former era. You can 'bring out' your graduate students, your research assistants and other junior colleagues. Successful presentations can have a significant impact on research students' reputations, and can also have a very positive effect on that of the department and the research group.

If conference presentations are to be successful, then preparation and training will be in order. Enough of our readers will have suffered the excruciating pain of sitting through conference papers that have been prepared inadequately – that typically overrun the allotted time, are delivered inaudibly, have illegible overheads and so on – to appreciate the value of preparation. The conference presentation is an unnatural mode of communication. There are very severe constraints on time and format. Members of the audience may not be especially interested. Supervisors and members of the graduate committee or school should ensure that research students and others have every opportunity to practise their presentation skills.

Regular presentations by graduate students need to be given about their current research. Allot the students exactly twenty minutes, and allow them to choose what aspect of the work to present. Full-time students should be required to make such a research presentation each year. Explain to them that while twenty minutes may sound like a niggardly allocation, that is the longest time they will get at a major conference, and in many cases they will get less. Explain that an audience of friends and colleagues is a useful one so students should get used to presenting their work before they venture onto the conference circuit. Comment on the content of the students' presenta-tions, offer advice on 'artistic impression'. Comment on how to get the key ideas over to the audience, for instance: experience shows that too many presenters (of all ages and statuses) take too much time going over inessen-tial preliminaries rather than getting to the heart of their work immediately. Encourage students to have punchy papers, with a small number of bullet-points to get over. Help them to avoid the dreadful pitfalls of the poor presenter – such as reading the paper without looking at the audience! Doing handouts and using the OHP and PowerPoint should be encouraged. The chair must behave very strictly, stopping the presentation dead on time.

Supervisors should make every effort to attend whenever their graduates present, and should apologize officially if they cannot be there. Ideally senior staff, up to and including the head of department, should attend. Ian Cook (2000) states that one of this supervisors 'had never been to a single presen-tation that I'd given'. The Department where he did his PhD required him to remove that statement from the autobiographical account in his thesis. It is often a good idea to ensure that new students do not go to conferences alone. Experienced academics can sometimes forget that academic confer-ences can be quite daunting and lonely occasions. Cook states that the first paper he ever gave, as a third-year PhD student, in the UK was at the IBG annual conference when he planned to read from a 3,500-word paper. He did not even get half way through before the chair stopped him. Because he was nervous he made jokes that led to him being accused of racism and sexism. He had not been prepared to present his work in public.

A group of students and younger researchers can be a valuable source of mutual support. Sponsoring and mentoring does not necessarily end with helping a student get an abstract or poster accepted. If a student is to get out of a conference all that she or he might, then the supervisor or other senior colleague should be alert for opportunities to effect introductions to useful contacts, advice as to which sessions will be worth attending (if any!). Since our own discipline is heavily dependent on books, we believe that it is an important function of conferences that our students and colleagues get to meet the publishers and their representatives at the publishers' exhibition. They will not necessarily start to negotiate with the publishers when they first meet them, but it may be valuable in the medium term to establish friendly professional relationships with representatives of key publishing houses. In some disciplines, meeting the equipment sales staff may be just as important. Students should learn to do what politically astute professors and lecturers do at conferences.

Before your students are launched into the conference scene they might enjoy, and learn from, reading some of the novels in which wise and foolish academic conference behaviour is featured. David Lodge's *Small World* (1984) is the most famous, but there are many others. Emma Lathen's *Green Grow the Dollars* (1982) features an American Plant Science meeting, while D.J.H. Jones's *Murder at the MLA* (1993), set at the Modern Language Associ-ation) compares and contrasts different people's trajectories through the meeting. Taking a few minutes to discuss the novel(s) with the student is, of course, necessary if the message is going to be understood.

General networking can be extremely valuable for the graduate student's immediate and mid-term career. The typical career trajectory differs from discipline to discipline. But personal knowledge and professional relationships are almost invariably important. Career development in the laboratory sciences is often dependent not just on the research degree itself, but on postdoctoral positions, and postdoctoral research development. Sometimes that can be pursued in the same department, sometimes the research student can move to another lab for a period of postdoctoral work. The supervisor and student will need to discuss and think about how to manage such career contingencies, recognizing that the PhD is not the be-all and end-all: it is an important stepping-stone towards a more general career. The development of professional networks can be a significant part of career planning – helping to identify laboratories and research groups in which further research can be pursued.

Postdoctoral research in the laboratory sciences reflects the funding and relative stability of successful research groups. Labs and groups that are able to attract external research funding at a sufficient level expect to maintain a population of post-docs. They often take on day-to-day tasks of supervising and looking after the graduate students. They are crucial to the continued well-being of the research group, and postdoctoral research in a laboratory with the right kind of reputation can be a most valuable credential on a young scientist's career. Networks and collaborations that are established at this stage can have significance for the rest of one's career.

In other disciplines, external funding may not provide a regular supply of postdoctoral positions. That does not preclude planning for future research after the completion of the thesis. Supervisors and their students can always think constructively about obtaining external funding to develop good research through a new project, and in order to secure a short-term continuation of the student's career. This is possible in disciplines in which external research funding is possible. It is hit-and-miss career planning, in that the odds are usually against any particular proposal actually being funded by a research council, charity, or other agency. Nevertheless, a joint research proposal between a supervisor and research student can be a useful avenue to explore. Indeed, drafting a plausible and fundable research proposal is a research skill that can be included in any programme of research student training and academic staff development. Involving students in discussions about how to raise funds for an archaeological dig, for a foreign trip, for equipment, for CD-ROM resources, or whatever, should figure in their development.

Publication is the one aspect of career-building during the registration period that needs attention. We have, however, devoted a separate section to that topic, after the next section, which deals with job seeking.

The job seeker's dilemmas

In this section we deal mainly with references, where the role of the supervisor is crucial for the student's future career.

References and referees

The working relationship between the graduate student and the supervisor may well continue for years after the thesis is submitted and the degree awarded. The supervisor can often be a useful sponsor in the years ahead. The external examiner can come to fulfil a similar function, which is one reason for thinking strategically about the choice of external, as we stressed in Chapter 9. Here we concentrate on some of the continuing obligations of the supervisor.

The supervisor can expect to be a professional referee for his or her graduate students. The provision of references – mainly for academic and other posts – is an important and recurrent duty for virtually all academics. Like refereeing journal articles and grant applications, writing book reviews and the like, it is a task that contributes directly to the reproduction of the discipline. Like those other tasks too, it impinges directly on the career prospects and interests of individuals. We all have a dual set of obligations. We have an obligation to our colleagues, to ensure that the right things get published, the right research gets funded, and the right people get appointed. Equally, we have an obligation to our students and former students to ensure that we help them to make the best of themselves, and have reasonable career prospects.

Academic references are an interesting genre in their own right, and one could easily devote a small volume about the conventions of writing and reading them. We shall not do so here. Suffice it to say that the inexperienced academic would do well to seek and take advice on how to support their own students in this way. There are many ways of expressing positive support and enthusiasm, and there are many ways of expressing reservations. Referees often damn candidates with faint praise rather than with outright criticism, for instance. An inexperienced referee might well benefit from showing a draft to a more experienced colleague, in order to see if she or he is achieving the desired effect. If a reference is too tentative and low-key, for instance, it may come across as an unsupportive one, even if the author really intends it to be positive. Equally, one needs to get some sense of the appropriate style for the expression of enthusiasm. There are undoubtedly cultural differences in this regard. Referees in the USA seem to be expected to be positive in a way that British academics might regard as 'over-the-top'. Academics from the USA seem much more inclined than their UK counterparts to claim that a particular candidate is the most outstanding graduate student they have ever taught; UK academics may be less overtly enthusiastic. Indeed, too many superlatives in a reference for a

British appointing committee may do the candidate a disservice. (Equally, of course, a reference written for an American institution may need to comply with their cultural conventions and expectations.)

Novice academics need to learn something of the genre of references, if their former students are to get the best possible career opportunities. It is a good idea to ask a more experienced colleague for pointers. For instance, readers normally assume that the failure to mention some particular attribute or aspect of work is a deliberate omission, and is to be read as such. Readers of references are accustomed to 'read between the lines', and to decode the reference. The writer and would-be sponsor therefore needs to understand the code's conventions. Omission of something as a consequence of oversight, or because it is thought unimportant, may inadvertently disadvantage the candidate. Equally, careless references can be damaging. It is a good idea to read the further particulars of the post being applied for: a reference that makes no reference to teaching competence when the candidate is to be interviewed for a lectureship may not cut enough ice. Equally, failure to stress the originality of someone's research and the importance of its contribution to the discipline may also be damaging.

The supervisor will not just be a referee for the candidate's first job. The obligation may continue for many years. There is often a continuing relationship, changing subtly from that of student/supervisor, to junior colleague/ senior sponsor to a collegial relationship between equals. The successful supervisor of successful graduate students may have to provide suitable references throughout their careers, up to consideration for readerships, chairs and fellowships. It is important for successful supervisors to be aware of the various demands and conventions that are brought to bear on such documents, and to respond accordingly. It is equally important for graduate students to be taught to understand the process involved, encouraged to keep their supervisors and other senior staff up-to-date with their plans, current curriculum vitae and so on. Students may need explicit statements from you about whether, for example, you will always, routinely do references or wish to be asked afresh each time an application is made. Whatever you decide, it is important to ensure that you have accurate, up-to-date information on the student or former student before you provide a reference, that you have some idea of why the student wants the job, so that you can angle the reference accordingly, and that you know how it will be used in the future.

There is also an issue about providing open or closed references. This is a matter of personal choice, but if you do show the reference to the student you should tell the potential employer you have done so. And, of course, you and the subject of the reference must recognize that it may be disregarded if the candidate has seen it. There may also be times when you can, and should, decline to be a referee, or warn the student that if they use you, then you will not be able to be positive. If a student applies for an inappropriate post with a department who will value your opinion, you have to refuse to be a referee or write a negative reference: the damage to your reputation if you lie will carry over to future candidates for other jobs, and might even harm you.

There is no doubt at all that career development for aspiring young academics should include advice on referees and potential sponsors. It is not necessary to encourage Uriah Heap-like behaviour, but you should encourage graduate students and post-docs to think constructively about who they will be using in that capacity, and how to ensure that they are fully acquainted with their work, and have a favourable view of them as potential researchers or lecturers.

Job seeking

The research student may need your help if he or she wants to stay in academic life. If they want a job outside universities, the careers service may be able to provide what they need, although careers in private sector firms with whom there is research collaboration may also depend on the supervisor and other members of the research group. If you and your colleagues routinely hear from postgraduate students that the careers service is 'not much help', then it may be sensible to talk constructively to the relevant staff there, and explain what your postgraduates might need – and see how the careers service and the department can cooperate on it.

As far as academic jobs are concerned, students may need help in discovering where opportunities are advertised – if they are in specialist journals, general weeklies such as *The Times Higher, The Economist* or *New Scientist*, newsletters produced by learned societies, or newspapers, or on the World Wide Web. Point out that with the financial constraints on universities posts may be advertised in only one national newspaper, and so students may have to scan several. If you have been settled in your own job for several years, you yourself may be out of date, and need to work with students to rediscover where the opportunities are to be found advertised.

Graduate students may well want careers counselling in various ways – or at least to talk over with you various options. While the academic labour market is very tight in many disciplines, and becoming increasingly so in the wake of renewed financial constraint, jobs do arise with a fair degree of regularity in most general disciplines, and graduate students are sometimes faced with choices. The answers to their dilemmas cannot be reduced to simple formulae, and must depend on a host of individual considerations. But students need to be aware of, and be able to talk over, the relative merits of different kinds of appointment (such as a lectureship versus a postdoctoral fellowship) in different kinds of institution ('old' versus 'new' university). Preferences will not always be straightforward: a permanent lectureship in a decent, but not outstanding, university and against a fixed-term appointment in a highly regarded department is not an easy choice to make. Personal choices may depend on a host of circumstances, such as relative geographical mobility, family commitments, tolerance of insecurity and so on. It is, however an important part of a supervisor's general mentoring role to be able to provide students with the kind of general advice they need in order to make informed choices. They may rarely have the luxury of choosing between job offers, of course, but they may avoid making inappropriate applications, and wasting their own and others' valuable time. For graduate students attempting to enter the job market, dummy selection interviews may be useful preparation. It is easy to forget that students may have very little experience of being interviewed or of other aspects of job selection – such as the requirement to make a brief presentation about their research and career plans. For some students, practice in a familiar environment, with a small number of academic staff role-playing a selection committee, may prove a valuable investment of time and effort.

In order to come to sensible career-building and job-seeking strategies, therefore, students need to gain a sensible understanding of the job market at any given time, and a realistic appreciation of their own strengths and weaknesses. The may need – especially towards the end of their initial registration period – the equivalent of 'appraisal' interviews when they assess the kinds of skills and areas of competence they have to offer. Throughout their graduate student career, they will need to consider the kinds of experience they can amass with a view to their future employability. The narrow areas of specialization encouraged by research degrees will often be supplemented by summer schools on specific research methods and techniques, staff development sessions, areas of teaching and demonstrating experience and so on. In other words, the specific focus on one's own research can usefully be complemented by a broader portfolio of competences, with a view to enhanced employability in the academy or elsewhere.

Employability is, of course, enhanced through publication, and it is never too early to be thinking about that aspect of academic career development.

Publication

Graduate students and their supervisors have joint interests and responsibilities towards publication in the promotion of the research itself and sponsorship of the student.

Sponsoring publication

One of the key areas in which the supervisor and the graduate student can work together in sponsoring and mentoring that student – often to mutual advantage – is in the general area of publication. For the purposes of general career development, graduates, especially those with aspirations to academic and research careers, need to recognize that the thesis is not the only product of the research, and certainly not the end-point of the process. The thesis is an important part of the work, and energies and intelligence must be focused on it. But career development will be furthered by publication as well as by a higher degree. It appears to be the case that graduate students who think about themselves and their work professionally in general will develop a professional attitude to publication in particular. Long-term success is likely to be based on attitudes and work practices that are established early in the academic career: the period of time spent as a graduate student is certainly not too soon to learn important lessons. For those reasons, the work of the successful supervisor or graduate committee is likely to involve some element of sponsorship in publication.

One area where graduate students benefit from a supervisor who is an active researcher is that of publication. A supervisor who is writing, publishing, refereeing for journals, vetting manuscripts for publishers, and editing the work of fellow scholars will be more able to offer informed practical help to graduate students, and will be better placed to hear about opportunities for students to start publishing.

The actual practices of publication and the associated expectations differ markedly from discipline to discipline, and within disciplines there are differences in emphasis as between different departments or centres. In our own discipline we have worked with younger colleagues who have come from one highly regarded department in which graduate students are not specifically encouraged to publish: the view they internalize is that they should definitely finish the thesis first, before thinking specifically about publication. Our own view, that we try to instil in our students, is that while the thesis is their first priority, its prime importance does not preclude constructive thought about publication on the way. In some experimental sciences, publication of results of key experiments may be almost taken for granted – especially if the graduate student's work is part of a larger ongoing research programme, generating a more or less constant stream of research publications. In such research groups, joint publication of results is a collective undertaking, and an integral part of the research culture. In other disciplines, most notably in the humanities, early publication is less common, as is joint publication.

We also run career development workshops for early career scholars, attended by PhD students, post-docs, and even new lecturers. Imagine that you are in one such session and hear the following:

Vignette H: Blocked publications?

Lennox Kemp says he has a problem with publication. He is a post-doc with Professor Mappenstone, and there are some papers coming through, but all the potential papers from his PhD are stuck. He has drafted three articles, given them to his supervisor, Dr Pigeon, who leaves them in his in-tray and does not vet them, add to them, or signal that they can go off to journals. Karl Alberg gets animated: he has a similar problem. His PhD was funded by industry and has been embargoed for commercial reasons. He now works as a post-doc for Professor Thanet, who is only interested in sending papers to the top two journals in the world, and so far Karl says, nothing he has done has met Professor Thanet's criteria for submission to such journals. He wants to get some papers out for his own CV: what can he do?

Notwithstanding the fact that cultural differences are marked, and very important, as between the different academic disciplines (Becher 1989, 1990; Becher and Trowler 2001), we believe that it is no bad thing for students to be encouraged to begin publishing as soon as it is practical for them to do so, given their subject matter, the disciplinary and local intellectual traditions, and the practical constraints within which they are working. The discussion of a publication strategy may, therefore, be a useful basis for aspects of general career development and socialization into an academic culture or subculture.

There are, for instance, background issues that novices can usefully learn about the processes of academic publication. All experienced academics are familiar with the hierarchies of esteem that are attached to different kinds of output (refereed journals, conference proceedings, edited collections, textbooks, monographs, etc.). Equally, they will be aware of the finer discriminations that may be drawn within those categories. The research active academic (and nobody should be doing this if they are not active) will be well versed in the fine gradations that can be used to distinguish journals: to be able to identify the 'blue chip' or 'diamond' list of international journals, for instance, and the solidly respectable journals in the second rank, and separate them from the low-status, meretricious or local. Likewise, in disciplines that progress by means of monographs, they will be able to rank publishers – distinguishing among and between the university presses, the commercial publishers and others. These discriminations are part of the intellectual stock-in-trade of the successful academic. Judgements based on such criteria are brought to bear on individuals, when their CV is scrutinized for appointment or promotion, on research groups, and on entire departments. The recurrent pressures of Research Assessment Exercises lend ever greater urgency to an informed awareness of these niceties. It is therefore important to ensure that graduate students begin to understand the nature and consequences of these issues.

The correct response to such awareness is necessarily variable. But in our experience, and the experience of others, one should certainly not assume that graduate students, however successful and well motivated, will necessarily be aware of the issues involved. It is all too easy to take for granted how these judgements and processes operate, let them remain at an implicit level, and find that students go all the way through their careers muddled or in the dark. A lack of awareness is, one suspects, most likely in disciplines where solitary publication is the norm, and students are not being socialized into research groups that routinely and frequently publish their results.

Students need to be aware, for example, not only of the personal and collective value of publishing. They also need to be given the kind of information that will allow them to make sensible decisions and construct feasible plans. Our own graduate students need to know, for instance, not just which are the most highly esteemed journals; they also need to have a broad sense of their rejection rates, the likely length of time it takes to get reviewed, and the typical delay between acceptance and publication. Graduate students can turn out to have rather vague understandings of the whole process of academic publishing, with little or no awareness of how academic journals operate, the responsibilities of editors, editorial boards, reviewers, and the like. While it might be thought that novices and junior members of the profession do not need to have detailed understandings of these and similar areas, if they are going to commit their career prospects to the vagaries of academic publication, then we are in no doubt that they need systematic introduction to the general issues concerned. Graduate students cannot be told exactly what to publish, or exactly when to publish it. For any individual student there is always a potential tension between pressing ahead with the thesis, and publishing aspects of the research as they go along, and general prescriptions cannot cover all the contingencies of research timetables, time and other resources. They do need to have the right kind of background information to make informed decisions, however – whether to concentrate on conference papers and conference proceedings, whether to go for 'research notes' and letters, whether to attempt to get into the top journals or try to place their papers with slightly less glittering outlets with lower rejection rates. They need to be helped to think strategically and pragmatically about what is publishable, and when to do it.

The issue of joint publication with a supervisor or a larger number of collaborators in a research group is, as we have indicated, very largely coloured by the conventions and traditions of particular disciplines. Beyond those, and especially in disciplines where collaborative publication is not necessarily the norm, graduate students and their supervisors need to establish some basic expectations and working agreements. Even in the humanities and social sciences, joint publication between student and supervisor may be a productive and beneficial strategy. There are always worries about the intellectual and moral exploitation of the junior partner in this process. Some academics and students in the humanities harbour stereotyped views of natural sciences, in which professors and research directors have their names on research papers solely by virtue of their position and with no regard for any actual work that has gone into the research and the ensuing paper. By contrast, they assume that any joint output must necessarily reflect the asymmetrical power relationship, must be exploitative and oppressive, and that the practice of joint publication is to be avoided in most cases. Such views are based on culture-specific views of authorship and publication, and are based on specific views of collaboration. Experimental scientists are likely to have quite different views about what authorship and co-authorship actually signify, and of the nature of the 'collaboration' that justifies such patterns of co-publication. Equally, one must acknowledge that there are always grains of truth in myths and stereotypes, and some graduate students and junior researchers do feel themselves exploited in the common patterns of collaboration and co-authorship. The point of our discussion here is not to attempt to adjudicate on these issues for individual students and supervisors. Everything we have said hitherto would render general precepts unrealistic. Rather, we advocate that supervisors, and/or those responsible for more general mentoring and training of graduate students should pay attention to explicating these and other considerations that relate to publishing plans and procedures. The emerging scholar should be able to think clearly about what to publish, when to publish, how to publish, with whom to publish, as part of the growing cultural competence of becoming a productive academic.

We have already suggested in Chapter 2 that exploring the conventions of citation is one way of opening the research student's eyes to the politics of publishing. This should be followed up in a graduate class, or in individual supervisions, with a clear account of the stages through which a potential article moves from the author's word processor to the editor, out to referees, back to the editor, and back to the author with a verdict. It can be extremely useful to set up a 'dummy' exercise where a group of students practise refereeing an article for an 'editor'. Such exercises go along with the tasks we have proposed to improve judgement in Chapter 7.

We move on now to some specific guidance that can be given to graduate students on how to prepare their work for publication. In Figure 10.1 we provide an outline for possible handouts or advice for graduate students on the process and obligations of getting into print.

Figure 10.1: Advice on getting published

There are two main ways of publishing your research: as a monograph (i.e. a book), or as journal articles. Not all theses make books, but every successful thesis ought to have at least one journal article in it. If you want the world to know about your research, then try to publish it. Theses themselves are read by very few people and lie forgotten on library shelves.

Just as you have used your intelligence to do your academic research, so too you should research possible outlets. If you have spent a lot of time and effort collecting data and writing them up, then spend a bit more time and effort preparing the ground for publication.

That advice applies to journals and to book publishers, and means that you should think about the following:

1 Who publishes your area of specialization? Do any publishers have special lists or series in your area? Have any publishers already published similar studies? What specialized journals exist for your area? What more general journals are there that might welcome your sort of approach?

2   What sort of audience are you trying to reach? Fellow academic
    social scientists? Practitioners? The lay public? There will obviously
    be different outlets for different readerships, which will call for
    different styles of writing.
3   Are there any special or new outlets? Sometimes new journals
    appear, which put out calls for papers: they may be less heavily
    subscribed with papers than old-established journals. Sometimes
    journals announce special issues and call for papers: if your topic
    fits, then you may have a better chance of publishing than in
    general competition.

Journals

Once you have done your basic research and identified possible journals, then you will need to prepare your paper(s). There are no guar-
antees of success, but the following will help:

1   Get the format right. Journals have 'notes for contributors', at least
    once a year, which specify basic requirements for submissions.
    Check them and make sure your paper complies with them.
2   Get the length right. Many journal submissions fail because they are
    far too long. Check the guidelines, look at the run of issues and get
    your own word-count right.
3   Write each paper about a clearly defined topic or issue. Many submis-
    sions fail because they are ill-focused, diffuse and incoherent. Do not
    write a paper which has several different papers struggling to get out.
4   Get the editor and the referees on your side by submitting a clear,
    readable typescript. Scruffy typescripts and faint xeroxes do not add
    up to successful self-presentation.
5   If the journal has such a section, you may have a chance of getting a
    small, modest piece published as a 'research note' – especially if you
    are reporting empirical findings.
6   Do not send the same article to more than one journal at a time.
    Most journals have a policy of refusing to consider papers submit-
    ted to more than one editor simultaneously, and multiple submis-
    sions are almost always detected.
7   However, if you do get rejected by one journal, don't give up: try
    another one.

Books

Once you have identified possible publishers, you will need to have something to send them. The editor will *not* want to be sent a copy of your
precious thesis; and will not give you a contract without detailed review
of what you've got to offer. So, prepare a prospectus which incorporates
all the information an editor will want to know. If you follow these guidelines, you will look very professional and will get off on the right foot.

1   Working title;
2   author's name and mailing address;

3 brief synopsis of the book: background, aims, content.

4 Market: who is the book aimed at? Students? Practitioners? What level? A level? Postgraduates?

5 Style: What degree of difficulty is the text to represent? What level of readership, in other words;

6 Will the book be designed for specific courses or types of course (e.g. does every student in the country doing this subject have to do a course in your area)?

7 Competitors: Are there any other books on the market with which you will be competing? If so, you will probably need to persuade the editor that yours is different and better (after all he or she will have to persuade other people of that).

8 Chapter outline: You need to present the chapter-by-chapter outline. You need to indicate the chapter sections and contents briefly. If you can't work that out yet, then you are not yet ready to plan and write the book.

9 Length: You should indicate the approximate length of each chapter, and the total length overall (expressed as thousands of words). This is important, as it will have a direct bearing on the marketability and pricing of the final product.

10 Indicate if there will be any special typesetting requirements (figures, tables, photographic plates). They are expensive and should be kept to a minimum. In our line of work they are rarely needed.

11 Biographical details: Brief outline of who and what you are. Nationality is important (for copyright reasons).

12 Timetable: You should indicate a realistic date for the completion of the manuscript. A publisher will be more impressed by realism than over-optimism.

13 Specimen chapter(s): You should have some specimen material ready – and indicate that it can be supplied. It is probably unnecessary to send it with the initial proposal, however.

In general, make sure the proposal is clearly presented, well typed and attractive. If you can't get the typescript or the proposal right, what chance is there for a book-length manuscript?

Be prepared to be rejected. It is very hard to get published. Theses are not popular material with commissioning editors. You will have to do a fair amount of work to transform a successful thesis into an acceptable book. If you plan to publish a specialized monograph, then you may need to look to less commercial publishers and imprints. Major commercial publishers are not normally enamoured of detailed empirical research reports.

Do you need a literary agent? No. It is not necessary for this sort of book. You are unlikely to get involved in delicate negotiations for the film rights; if you are doing this for the money, forget it. In any case, as an unpublished academic you may have more trouble finding a decent agent than finding a publisher.

Information of the kind packed into Figure 10.1 may seem dry and abstract to students, so we also use a set of vignettes to stimulate discussion among our graduates about publishing. These are given in Figure 10.2. While ours are very specific to our kind of social science, they can easily be adapted for other disciplines.

Figure 10.2: Publication case studies: Vignettes for group discussion

1   Kyra Keaton has successfully completed her EdD thesis which evaluated two different intervention schemes designed to raise the GCSE performance of African-Caribbean boys. Her external examiner said, rather vaguely at the end of the viva, 'You should publish this for heads and for academics.' What should Kyra do to follow up this advice?

2   Connor Westphal is on a PhD programme with a one-year MA followed by a three-year thesis stage. His MA thesis was a literature review which received a distinction. His supervisor mutters that he should publish it: what could he do?

3   Sonora Blair is keen to publish a paper or two while she writes up her PhD, because she wants to be ready to apply for jobs. Her supervisor keeps trying to dissuade her, while her housemate, a PhD in chemistry, already has two publications *with* her supervisor. Who is right?

4   Betty Armstrong had sent an article to *Sociology*. It has come back with a letter four sides long from the editor, and comments from three referees. The letter says the paper 'can't be accepted in its present form' and the three referees seem to disagree. Betty feels sick. You're her best friend in the department – what do *you* do?

5   Richard Tucker wants to get a paper into an American journal – they want eight copies, a handling fee of 20 dollars, American spelling, and they have an unfamiliar house style – but it is *the* journal on mental handicap. Richard's boss is hassling him to publish quickly – and his friend at the medical school edits a local, regional journal which wants two copies, no handling fee, and is in a style Richard regularly uses. What would you do?

6   Jim Winterlake was at a conference. His supervisor introduced him to Phoebe de Vine, who works for Peabody and Brodribb, a major publisher in social policy. Phoebe talked to him about his research, and said, 'Let me see a proposal – we might fit that into our ageing series.' What should Jim do next?

Conclusions

We have outlined in this chapter a variety of ways in which a supervisor can help a graduate build an academic career. This is satisfying for the supervisor, and career-enhancing too, because one's own reputation grows if one's post-graduates are competent and successful. In the next, and final, chapter, we deal with the supervisor's enlightened self-interest and the development of a productive graduate culture.

11

A rather unpromising consignment: selecting successful students and building a research culture

His eye roving over a group of Shrewsburians a-sprawl under the beeches, like that of a young Sultan inspecting a rather unpromising consignment of Circassian slaves.

(Sayers 1972: 342)

Introduction

Hitherto in this book we have written implicitly as if the process and outcomes of higher-degree supervision were solely matters of individual students and their individual supervisor. While many of the problems and their solutions that arise in day-to-day academic work are as we have described in the preceding chapters, it would be wrong to ignore some of the wider and more collective aspects of supervision and the sponsorship of graduate students. In this concluding chapter it is not our intention to recapitulate all of the contemporary policy and organizational issues that confront the contemporary institution of higher education. To do so would require another book, and would take us well beyond the specific remit of supervisors and their work. Nonetheless, one must pay some attention to more general issues, as a supervisor, and as a member of a department, a research group or centre. Those issues include several, all related, that are concerned with the maintenance and betterment of a research culture, and the promotion of graduate studies. They are explored at greater length in Atkinson and Delamont (2004). Here we shall deal with the selection of students; the promotion of a graduate student culture; and the collective responsibility for the training of research students. All relate to how a department or centre is going to set about building and supporting a graduate division or graduate school – and how therefore it will reproduce itself. When we refer here to the promotion of a graduate school, we do not necessarily mean a university- or faculty-wide organization with its own physical space, staffing and so on. Of course, some institutions have such arrangements, and they can be very successful. But the kinds of things we want to raise are not entirely predicated on such formal arrangements, whatever their strengths and weaknesses. Rather, we mean to convey the institutional and individual interest in building and fostering a collective responsibility for research student training, and a collective identity on the part of the graduate students. Such a graduate student culture will help to maintain the flow of research problems and interests from one generation to the next, to promote coherent research orientations, and to overcome the feelings of personal and intellectual isolation that so often assail the graduate student.

Selecting students

Selecting successful doctoral students is the first problem facing any university department and any individual supervisor. When a department and the individual supervisor get the selection right, everyone wins. The department gets a completed thesis, the supervisor has a satisfying three-year supervisory relationship, a junior colleague, and a friend for life. The student has a happy three years and the platform for a career.

When the wrong students are selected, the results are serious for all parties. Nothing is more frustrating than pouring time into a research student who fails to respond, to settle to work, to cope with the poverty and isolation, to gather data, to analyse them, to write them up, and to submit the thesis. The time, intellectual energy, emotional commitment, and general all-round effort that has to be put into a doctoral student is awesome. To pour all that into a person who drops out, especially two, three or four years into the doctorate, is one of the most miserable things that can happen to an academic. There are few other things which can take an hour or two nearly every week of the year and ultimately produce *nothing*. A department wants higher-degree students who will complete as a group, the individual needs individual students who will fit in to his or her own style.

There is very little research available on selection, and none on whether the changing policy context has altered the selection criteria used by funding bodies and departments, or, indeed, by individual supervisors. Certainly for much of the twentieth century the only criterion for acceptance as a PhD candidate was possession of a first-class degree. One of our social science informants, Professor Hakapopoulos, drew a vivid caricature of the British PhD in the past in order to contrast it with prevailing arrangements at Gossingham at the time we interviewed him:

> one still has the vague idea that this chap got a First in whatever field he's in, he has an intellectually-orientated mind, he has an interesting idea that he wants to pursue, he can sit down in the library and occasionally chat to members of the Senior Common Room and lo! a thesis will appear.

Here Professor Hakapopoulos identifies an important dimension of contrast. The point of reference is an image of the PhD which is from time to time offered as having been dominant in the past: something based on the personal qualities of individuals, with little or no structure, highly dependent on implicit criteria. In Professor Hakapopoulos's account it carries overtones of a leisured and privileged past. Today, all universities, all departments and most supervisors are keen to provide a much more structured context in which the student proceeds smoothly through the stages of the higher degree. If it becomes normal for students to do a taught Masters with a short thesis before embarking on the PhD, then selection processes will become easier for departments.

Hudson (1977) offers a vividly written argument about how to select PhD students who will finish their higher degrees, which is about Paul Atkinson and Sara Delamont's cohort of fellow higher-degree students at Edinburgh in the 1968–73 era. Hudson argues that the most important characteristic of those students who submit higher-degree theses is self-confidence and an academic variety of 'killer instinct': the same kind of quality soccer managers want to have in strikers. While this may be true, it does not help the supervisor to select the students. First, because these are hard to define and identify. Second, because characteristics that may exist in the undergraduate context can vanish like smoked salmon on a buffet table when the doctoral blues set in.

David Pearson's (2002) respondents offered a range of characteristics they looked for in a prospective student:

> Professor Eyers (musicologist): Someone who has some vision of what they want to do. That's fairly obvious but it isn't always the case that you find that in an applicant; someone who knows how to work by themselves or gives the impression of being really curious and unaccepting of things that are handed to them; these are quite bolshie characters often . . . who won't accept anything without testing it. . . . But someone who clearly has intellectual stamina because they have to work by themselves for three years and it's quite a difficult shift from undergraduate level. And you're looking for someone who's actually bright, but not necessarily the type of person who gets a brilliant first: they're not always the best researchers. Someone who worked to a peak at undergraduate level isn't necessarily going to be able to apply himself or herself across three years of drudgery, which is often what it is. So there's a sort of balance to be struck.

This can be contrasted with Professor Robinson, a chemist, whose desire for clubbable, soccer-playing team members was quoted earlier in the book (p. 98), and Dr Pinnock, a physicist, who also wanted to select students who would quickly settle into the research group and the laboratory:

> Dr Pinnock: If they're coming from outside then I want them to settle into the department and feel at home there because that's obviously the only way they're going to get on with the work satisfactorily. In a physics background, I'd like them to get familiar with the techniques – do quite a bit of background reading – but get familiar with the experimental techniques that we employ.

Settling in is both personal and scientific. New students have to learn the local research techniques efficiently.

The most important thing for a selector to do is to think carefully about the skills and abilities a student needs to produce a PhD in that department, and then separate which of these can be taught during the PhD. So if a student needs to be particularly deft and not clumsy at the laboratory bench, it is important to decide whether this can be taught and learned, or not. If not, then you need to ask applicants to carry out an experiment while you are interviewing them, and/or explicitly ask their referees about their dexterity and bench skills. If the student needs good IT skills, then you need to decide whether you can provide teaching in IT, or need a candidate who already has the skills. If a student needs palaeographic flair, then you must either choose someone who has done well in a specialist palaeographic training, or provide such training, or look for evidence of relevant abilities in the references. In other words, when you ask for references, be explicit about the specific qualities you are looking for, so that you can get information on what you need to know.

Second, we do believe that doctoral students need to be highly motivated, and not just drifting into higher-degree work. To complete a PhD a person needs to be passionate about the discipline and want to advance knowledge in it. The student also needs to be able to stick at tasks. If the student's CV shows many false starts and abandoned courses, then the selector needs to be very wary.

Third, doctoral students need to be able to work independently: the CV and references need to be scrutinized for evidence of working autonomously. If the student's first degree included a dissertation or project, or if they have done a Masters degree, then the selector should explore how much the student enjoyed the dissertation or project element, and especially how they approached the independent work involved.

Fourth, successful doctoral students need to have intellectual creativity, or at least some ideas of their own. Testing this will be very discipline-specific, but it should be possible to invite applicants to display their ideas about where a particular line of research might go next.

Fifth, doctoral students need to be able to write. Again, it is important to ask students about their experiences with writing and their feelings about those experiences, and to ask the referees about students' writing abilities. Evidence may usefully be gathered from relevant examples of students' own written work – a report, a dissertation, a Masters thesis, or whatever is appropriate to the discipline, and is available. Many departments will ask for a research proposal as part of the application process, and much can be learnt from that: not just about the candidate's specific ideas, but (probably more importantly) about her or his ability to express them cogently. In the absence of other evidence, it may be useful to ask some candidates to write a brief paper for the selectors.

Sixth, students who are going to be able to do doctoral work need to be critical of previous work, so it is worth exploring with candidates – through written work, through an oral presentation, or at interview – if they can provide reasoned, critical commentary on key work in the discipline. One is not looking for a gratuitously negative view of existing theory, or of received wisdom in the research field, but the ability to use a critical faculty, and the willingness to offer an independent perspective.

In summary, therefore, we recommend that prospective doctoral students should have the specific skills to carry out the proposed research project, or be clearly able to benefit from research training, be highly motivated and able to persevere with academic tasks, be able to work independently, be able to write, and be able to exercise critical judgement. These are the individual qualities we recommend searching for in applicants, and the ideal applicant would have all of them. However, we are rarely able to select ideal applicants. For the most part, we find ourselves balancing strengths and weaknesses – as we do in most contexts. It is, however, clear that clever undergraduates who get good degree results do not automatically become good doctoral students without some of the personal and intellectual qualities we have just discussed.

There are two distinct aspects to the selection of students: selecting them for the department and selecting them for one's own personal supervision. Both may be beyond your control: you may work in a place where others choose the students and then assign them to you, and you may be unhappy with the students you get. If you suffer from that problem, it is probably wise to argue for a departmental review of advertising, applications and admissions policies and practicalities, and a thorough discussion of sources of support for student funding, using the rationale that a review could lead to increasing the total numbers. Most departments need *more* PhD students, particularly overseas candidates, and research council funded people: a departmental working group or discussion ostensibly focused on how to increase the total number may well be a wedge to open up discussion about who is doing the selecting, why, how, and on what criteria. Most people can persuade colleagues that a review designed to increase the quality and/or quantity of doctoral students is a good idea.

Dissatisfaction with the allocation of particular individuals to you is a rather different problem and may need careful diagnosis and then even more tactful resolution. The causes of the problem are likely to be different in science departments and non-science ones. In many science and engineering departments the allocation of studentships to research groups, and to particular supervisors may be based on money, the status and power of professors and group leaders, rather than issues of 'choice'. In an arts or social science department it may be impossible to contemplate supervising any student unless one has volunteered to do so because of their topic, except when someone else has left/died/gone off sick/gone on sabbatical/ quarrelled irreconcilably with the candidate.

If you are in a department where other research groups, or the senior staff in your own group, seize the 'best' candidates and/or allocate to you people you find hard to supervise, you have to learn how the department works, what the power structures are, and seek advice on how to change them. The most productive strategy is probably to raise your own funds, and publish a good deal, so your reputation rises and you can attract students to your specialism. In an arts or social science department, if you are not getting any doctoral students to work on topics you really care about, you probably need to be more proactive among the best undergraduates: are your lectures and seminars suffused with your excitement about the frontiers of your research area? It is also worth exploring whether your department's recruiting policies stress your specialism enough, and make it sound exciting. If the difficulty is getting ESRC funds to support the bright students, then two investigations are needed. First, ask someone in your field, ideally someone who has vetted such applications, to go through one of your potential applicant's forms with you, and help you sharpen the presentation. Second, ask yourself if you are currently being 'research-active' in the area. If not, then you need to get research funds and ongoing publications in your own right so you are contributing to the field yourself. The current policy consensus is that doctoral students are best placed with staff who have research funds, and are actively building their disciplines. Therefore, if you are not being allocated, or are not attracting, the type of doctoral student you want, it is probably because you are not active enough in research. In an arts or social science discipline you may be able to attract self-funding part-time students to supervise, and it is clearly better to have active supervision of part-timers than no doctoral students at all.

If you are allocated students to supervise whom you have not chosen, you need to see if you can work with them. If you cannot, they need to be placed elsewhere, for their own sake. There are two kinds of student who can be a problem: those who you do not feel able to supervise because they lack some fundamental quality(ies) or because of their topic/method/theoretical position, and those you just do not like. It is hard to imagine seeing someone everyday in your lab or for about an hour every week for four years if you actively dislike them/are afraid of them/or find them maddening.

It is important to know and recognize some characteristics of potential students that will make them hard, or even impossible for you to supervise. Here, the qualities of the individual which may make supervision hard are dealt with first, and then the issues around academic matters such as topic, method, and theoretical position.

Example 11.1: One woman's meat . . .

Sara has problems with two types of student: very shy females who whisper and nervously agree to everything she says, and those who are careless about punctuality and attendance at departmental events. The former lead her to be a bully: 'For heaven's sake, speak up and get a grip', the second violate her sense of order and make her too irritated to focus on their academic work. She tries to steer both types to more appropriate colleagues.

One of the issues that can come between a supervisor and student is that of gender. Scholarly relationships between males and females are not necessarily easy, as the research on women in science (see Gornick 1990 and Zuckerman *et al.* 1991) and on gender roles in higher education generally (e.g. Aisenberg and Harrington 1988; Carter 1990; Delamont 1989c; Lie *et al.* 1994) reveal. It is important to recognize a whole set of issues around this issue which we can gloss as 'chaperonage'. Many male scientists and engineers have never had a woman PhD student, or colleague; many women in arts and social science have never had a male PhD student. Coeducational higher education is a relatively new phenomenon, and one we are not all used to in everyday life, when some staff groups and some research groups are still entirely male in composition.

When we read accounts of the first women to be students or staff in universities they seem antique and quaint. The period described seems much further into the past than 50 or 100 years (see Dyhouse 1994; Delamont 1989c). In some cases, women *are* relative newcomers. Women were only admitted to the University College of Lampeter in 1961. When many of today's senior male academics were students or junior faculty, not only were they undergraduates in single-sex colleges or halls, they experienced male-only social spaces such as men's unions or, as at King's College London when Crick and Watson visited Maurice Wilkins in the 1950s, *men's* senior common rooms (see Delamont 2003). The relations between the sexes in the white middle classes in Britain have changed so much in the past 50 years, and the sexes are now so routinely 'mixed' together, that many people in higher education can be ignorant of, outraged by, or discourteous to, other cultures when they find people who want to segregate the sexes or practice chaperonage. This can be found in three quite separate ways, two 'traditional', one 'modern'.

Class extremities in the UK. The British upper class, and much of the working class in the UK adheres to segregated sex roles more strictly than the liberal middle class. Students from upper-class homes, especially men from public schools, or working-class homes where a strong division of labour by sex operated may be less comfortable with egalitarian relations between the sexes than those from liberal middle-class, dual-career, homes. Women supervisors may find male students from such homes are uncomfortable with the prospect of a woman in authority over them, with accepting females as academically serious, and with the day-to-day relationships of supervision. If you are a man who grew up in either of those class milieux, you may find it harder to work with women students. In either case, the shrewd supervisor recognizes the potential tensions and either brings them out for discussion and resolution, or passes the student to a more compatible colleague.

'Other' cultures. Both inside the UK and in many countries which send students to the UK to do higher degrees, particularly those with strong Islamic influences, sex segregation is much stricter than many supervisors are used to. Men doing PhDs may be genuinely appalled at the prospect of a woman supervisor, and vice versa. It may be impossible for women students from some cultures to have unchaperoned supervisions with a male supervisor. Handling these problems needs sensitivity: it may be that the latter

problem (female student, male supervisor) can be resolved by agreeing to keep the door open, having a female secretary or technician in earshot, or supervising students in pairs.

In contrast to the 'traditional' groups described above, there is also a new kind of student around, the woman who is a separatist feminist.

Separatist feminists. There are women in higher education who are only interested in working on a feminist research agenda with a woman supervisor. Most of these will choose a woman's studies programme, but it is important to be sensitive to such perspectives.

Gender is not the only personal quality of students that can impede establishing a working relationship. People with strong prejudices and antipathies, whatever their targets and origins, are unlikely to get the best out of higher-degree students they find it hard to get along with. There is no excuse for prejudices against women or ethnic minorities, nor indeed against particular intellectual styles and interests. The most important thing to do if you know that you harbour any such biases is to do something about your own attitudes and values. Likewise, if you have a colleague who is disadvantaging applicants or students, then you or the director of graduate studies, or the head of the department, need to do something about it. In the interim, it may be best to avoid direct clashes of styles, personalities and attitudes through the careful allocation of students to supervisors. It is, of course, a particular benefit of having supervisory panels, rather than reliance on the lone supervisor, that direct personal confrontations and differences may be less stark. Apart from characteristics of the student, such as sex, religion or sexual orientation, there can also be people who are personally compatible, but whose topic, methods or theoretical position is a cause of disagreement. Potential disagreements about thesis topic, methods, or theoretical position may not be apparent at the selection stage, and it is probably best to choose good candidates and ensure that there are clearly specified procedures for students to change supervisor within the department, and that all students are aware of them. If your department does not have any such procedures, then getting some agreed is a sensible step. Many personality conflicts can be resolved by a change of supervisor, as can disputes over the ways that projects are developing. The cases of Magdalena and Catherine are examples of this.

Example 11.2: Changing horses

Magdalena Yoder was an EdD student who had been allocated to Dr Hoyland. They started well, but Magdalena ground to a halt and Dr Hoyland felt defeated. A switch to Dr Sibley reinvigorated Magdalena. Dr Hoyland felt only relief and gratitude. In contrast when Catherine Le Vendeur wanted to change PhD supervisors away from Dr Maglione he felt insulted and angry which caused Catherine some guilt. The head of department had to intervene, to reassure Catherine that she had a right to change.

While this book is designed for supervisors it is important to recognize that students have a range of motivations to do postgraduate work, and may end up registered for a higher degree in places they did not choose, working on topics in which they have little interest. Before we turn to building up a research culture, we have presented some material on how candidates end up on doctoral programmes, in order to show how a range of different factors influence their 'choices'.

The view from the candidates

We know relatively little about what motivates students to do a higher degree, or how they decide where to apply and which supervisor(s) to approach. Our geography PhD students offered us mixed motives. Most had chosen to carry on and do a PhD in their undergraduate specialism because of their enthusiasm for the subject. Nineteen of the geography respondents specifically mentioned a love of geography, and this was the commonest motivation. Rick Moliner was typical when he said, 'It sounds a bit daft really. I've just got a thing about geography. I love the subject.' Jason Ingersoll, also at Boarbridge, expressed the same view:

> I've always loved geography since school, and I've always wanted to carry
> it on, go as far as I can with it. I can't think of anything I enjoy more than
> geography, I just love all sorts of geography.

Students from other places were equally enthusiastic about the discipline. For example, Sam Verney, at Tolleshurst, said he had: 'discovered geography was the thing I really wanted to do' and that led him to do a PhD. Vicky McQuaid at Ottercombe, said: 'I've always loved the subject I was doing, I was completely fascinated by it, really enjoyed it and wanted to do something more with it.' Eric Severance, at Hernchester, talked in the same way:

> I've always been interested in geography, I've always liked writing, and
> I was interested in economics, people, industry, that sort of thing, travel
> – and I thought it would be a nice thing to study.

Other motivations mentioned were, in descending order, that the person did not feel ready to enter the labour market and/or wished to stay a student, that the challenge of the PhD was appealing, that the respondent wanted a job in research or higher education which required a doctorate, and that none of the alternatives appealed except a doctorate.

Once the student had decided to seek a place and funding to do a doctorate, he or she had to find a department, money and a supervisor. At the time of our fieldwork, the ESRC and NERC policy of sanctioning departments with poor completion rates was in force. Most of our sampled departments had been 'blacklisted' by the NERC and ESRC for some part of the preceding five years and so could not offer government grants for doctoral study.

Bill Staley, a physical geographer at Hernchester, described his 'choice' of that university. He had done his undergraduate degree at Tolleshurst.

> I did second and third year options with Professor Cassands on physical hazards. I enjoyed Professor Cassand's work and the kind of fieldwork involved in doing his courses . . . When I decided I wanted to do a PhD . . . Professor Cassands gave me four names – of people he thought it would be interesting to study under . . . I was interested in three of them – Luftkin in London, Professor Lisle-Chevreuse at Reddingdale and Professor Barsington at Hernchester . . . Reddingdale was blacklisted, so I couldn't get any money, and Luftkin retired. So therefore I was only left with Professor Barsington . . . I came to the interview and liked the look of it here.

The availability of an ESRC or NERC studentship was the most powerful 'pull' factor reported by our respondents. Julian Perini had graduated from Tolleshurst, did an MA, abroad, and then came back to the UK.

> I went to the geography department at Tolleshurst, and I was talking to one of my old teachers, and he suggested I apply here (Hernchester) for various reasons. They weren't blacklisted for a start, they'd just got off the blacklist.

Elvira Tilley, at Boarbridge, answered our question, 'Why did you choose Boarbridge?'

> It was blackmail really. I came here for an interview and it was a competition award, the ESRC one. I was trying to get money to go to either Southersham or Tolleshurst. Here the ESRC award goes with the place. I got the place. I couldn't say no to this one at the time because I didn't have the guarantee of anything else.

Other students had been offered studentships funded by the institution or attached to specific projects, which had determined their 'choice'. Patsy Shroeder had hoped to go to another Scottish university, but Wellferry offered her a bursary so she returned to the place she had done her undergraduate degree.

Theo Karras, a physicist at Ottercombe, told us he had applied for 'numerous' PhD grants and places, then he took 'the only one' he was offered. Yves Bisson had remained at Ottercombe because 'I like it here, it is a friendly department . . . they seemed keen to keep me if they could have the money, and in the end they offered me funding.'

Although departmental interests were obviously important to them, geography respondents highlighted funding as the most crucial determining factor in their choice of department. Sheridan Ireland, at Hernchester:

> I did my undergraduate degree at Ebbfield . . . Why Hernchester? The supervisor of my choice was here, it's got a good reputation, the facilities are good, you get a lot of support, it's a big department. There are also

social reasons – it's a good location. Hernchester and the department got a good UGC rating – also I saw the advertisement, NERC funded: Hernchester had the funding, other places didn't.

Given such data – and there is no reason to believe that students in other disciplines are very different from geographers – it is important to try to select the best candidates, and to mould the students you do get into membership of a research group and participation in a shared research culture.

Building a research group

The opportunity to recruit successful students in a particular specialism, and to make them part of a collective research group, differs widely between the academic disciplines. In the natural sciences it is commonplace for research to be conducted in groupings, and for there to be a regular allocation of doctoral students to such groups. The doctoral students work on projects that fall within the scope of the existing research programme – often on topics prescribed by the senior members of the group – and are part of a substantial grouping that includes postdoctoral researchers as well as tenured members of the academic staff. In the humanities, by contrast, research students and studentships may be much thinner on the ground. They may be few and far between for any given supervisor, and group-building may be a much less natural kind of activity in such contexts. The long-standing tradition of individual scholarship in the humanities militates against a collective view of the graduate enterprise. While the traditions and resources are different as between different departments and different disciplines, however, there is – as we have seen – ample evidence to suggest that social and intellectual isolation is a recurrent phenomenon for many graduate students, and that some degree of collective culture and orientation can be a valuable part of the postgraduate experience.

In the contemporary UK department there are external factors that push the individual supervisor and the department towards a more strategic and collective view of the matter. In the first place, as we mentioned earlier, the 'graduate division' or 'school' is regarded as an indicator of esteem and success in its own right. As UK academics have become more and more attuned to the requirements and pressures of external review, they have also become more aware of graduate students, and the health of recruitment, as a performance indicator. For those kinds of reasons, the majority now recognize that the recruitment and training of research students, the provision of adequate facilities for them, monitoring of their progress and the promotion of their intellectual well-being are central functions of the academic department or research centre as a whole. They cannot be left to individualistic interest and sponsorship alone. We have written extensively about this elsewhere (Atkinson and Delamont 2004).

Some people believe that if they have shared social events with graduate students, the research culture will build 'naturally' and spontaneously. If the graduate students are homogeneous – usually all young, childfree British men – and the supervisors match the students socially too, then this may well be true. Whatever the student body is like, social events, both spontaneous ones like going for a drink after a seminar, or pre-arranged things such as a theatre trip, pre-planned walk, or the Christmas dinner, can be useful in building social solidarity. However, certain categories of student such as those with small children, or those (like Muslims) who do not drink, may be unable or unwilling to come to some such events, or unable to participate. Staff need to be sensitive to the dynamics of such events, and try to ensure that vital matters are not exclusively dealt with at such social events, excluding (unintentionally) those who cannot attend them, or feel uncomfortable at them. The autobiographical writings of women and ethnic minority graduate students frequently report feelings of exclusion from the group culture caused by well-meaning but insensitive behaviour. To ensure that everyone is involved in building a research culture, it is necessary for it to have some more formal and planned characteristics.

Our suggestions on this score are in two parts: first, ideas to make the work of the research students a matter of general concern in the department; and second, strategies to weld the research students into a coherent group. Both are desirable in building a research culture. In a very big department, with 50 or more lecturing staff, the strategies we outline below will probably be better implemented at a section level: in an engineering department with 100 academic staff, for instance, it may be sensible to build one research sub-culture around the graduate students in civil engineering, another in mechanical engineering, and another in electronics. At the other extreme, in a department of history with fifteen staff, the whole department will need to cooperate in building one research culture.

There is a variety of ways in which a lecturer can encourage a *generalized* concern for the welfare and performance of the research students. First, it is important that the recruitment, progress, and achievements of the research students are public, and are routinely discussed. This means having regular reports at the staff meeting and the more specialist sub-committees such as the research committee, or the teaching-and-learning committee. Ghettoizing graduate affairs in a graduate committee can allow some staff to ignore the research students. If there is a post of 'graduate coordinator', or equivalent, the person holding that post needs to report regularly in a way that interests the rest of the staff. Spreading the concern about research students among staff, so that people care about all the research students and not just their own supervisees, can be done by having a sub-committee to look at the graduate students' annual or termly reports (and if your university does not require such reports from research students and their supervisors, then you should institute them at the departmental level). The upgrading from MPhil to PhD can be a useful occasion to involve a range of staff beyond the individual supervisor. The internal examiner system can also spread the general concern about the graduate students. A staff discussion about recently examined theses, led by the internal examiners, can be a useful forum for the review of collective achievements, standards, criteria for success and so on.

Regular training for supervisors, and regular training for examining, are ways of spreading the culture of 'graduate school' activities. If the university has a published set of guidelines for supervisors, then discussion of them every eighteen months or so is useful. If the university does not have such a list, then developing some for the department or faculty is a good way of focusing colleagues' minds on the work of research students.

It can be helpful for staff to have a list of the research students registered in the department, what their topics are, and who is supervising them. Such information – regularly updated – can be included in department's internal newsletters, on their Web homepage, and other sources of information. The dissemination of such information can be especially helpful if there are many part-time students who are not regularly visible in the department. It can also help graduate students find out about each other, while making research supervision a more visible part of the department's work.

Research students should be giving seminar papers regularly to the research group closest to their project (the medievalists, the French history group, the cliometricians, the feminist history seminar) and to the whole department. However good this is for them, it will not spread the culture of the research group unless staff and other students are encouraged, or even required, to attend.

To build camaraderie among the students we suggest the following. First, the department should provide the best facilities it can afford, ensure that all the research students are aware of them, and encourage them to use them. Second, have clear policies on supervision, ensure that these are known to students, and monitor them. Third, provide training and development opportunities for the research students throughout their registration period: apart from any formal courses required in the first year of registration, it is helpful to arrange classes on teaching (perhaps even the opportunity to do a diploma or certificate in teaching), classes on career-building (on getting published, giving conference papers, preparing the CV, job searching, raising research funds) and updating of skills (library skills, IT skills, writing, changes in the university or higher education policy). The mock viva (see Chapter 9) can be a useful developmental and social event: we find students choose to attend all three or four of the 'performances' that take place while they are enrolled.

As well as encouraging or requiring graduate students' attendance at departmental seminars given by staff, fellow students and visiting speakers, it is particularly good to allow and encourage the graduates to choose some of the outside speakers (and even have a budget to invite some speakers to come and address them without staff involvement). When visitors are in the department, it is important to ensure that graduate students meet them, and are not just passive members of the audience, left to slip away unobtrusively at the end of the seminar.

All these activities will only work if the people organizing them make it clear why they are important and that the benefits are general. If a department has post-docs and other research associates and assistants, then they too should be included in these events. Their contribution to the overall promotion of a departmental research culture is invaluable. Experienced research workers can do a great deal to provide day-to-day advice to graduate students, while also helping to inculcate research awareness and research values among the group.

12

The very loftiest motives: institutional frameworks and audit cultures

> She is a splendid person, but hasn't much sense of humour. She can't bear anything to be done except from the very loftiest motives.
>
> (Sayers 1972: 37)

In this final chapter we address the institutional framework, national policies, and audit cultures which overshadow, and underlie, the personal relationships of supervisors and students. These frameworks, policies and audits have been put in place from the loftiest of motives, but they do not suggest that those who drafted them had much of a sense of humour. Dealing with these frameworks, policies and audits can be depressing unless supervisors feel confident about their own practices, and retain some documentation. This is a new chapter, which addresses the changing institutional and national frameworks that underlie, or occasionally overshadow, the individual relationships between students and their supervisors in academic departments. For readers in Britain the whole chapter is relevant. For those elsewhere, the brief history of policy changes may not be of interest, but the rest of the chapter addresses the big themes such as accountability and the audit culture which are now pervasive in the Anglophone world.

The British policy context

The first edition of this book went to press before the Harris Report (1996) had been published. We wrote an account of policy changes from 1986 to 2000 in Delamont, Atkinson and Parry (2000). Here we have concentrated on the Harris Report itself and developments since, rather than earlier debates.

The Harris Committee was set up in 1995 by the Higher Education Funding Council for England (HEFCE), the Committee of Vice-Chancellors and Principals (CVCP) which is now called Universities UK (UUK) and the Standing Conference of Principals (SCOP) which represents all the higher-education institutions which offer degrees but are not full universities. The chair of the committee, Martin Harris was at the time Vice-Chancellor of Manchester University. The remit was a review of all taught post-graduate courses and qualifications, and of higher degrees by research. The committee produced a two-volume report in 1996, containing a great many recommendations. Areas covered included how universities should be funded to teach postgraduates, responsibility for better quality assurance for postgraduate provision, the clearer codification of the titles of postgraduate degrees across the UK, and the importance of institutional codes of practice covering postgraduate research degrees. The report was the subject of some fierce debate in higher-education circles, which quickly died away, because of the change of government after the 1997 election.

The main Harris recommendations

The main recommendations concerned standardizing and codifying taught postgraduate courses, quality issues, a written code of practice for research students, funding taught courses, and concentrating publicly-funded doctoral students in units with a 'critical mass' of high quality research activity.

1   Harris proposed (paragraph 5.38) that public funding for research students should only go to institutions that have signed up to a code of practice for doctoral education.
2   Harris recommended that there should be a directory of postgraduate courses which makes it clear what their level, status and type are, then a standardization of degree names, so that potential students know exactly what a diploma or a specific or a generic masters degree is (Recommendations 4.23–4.37).
3   Harris made a range of recommendations on quality issues (4.38–4.57), these included calling for one unified quality agency for England, and for separate Teaching Quality Assessment (TQA) reports for undergraduate and postgraduate courses.
4   Harris recommended (5.23) that institutions in England should not be allowed to use undergraduate funding to support taught postgraduate courses, which should be transparently funded in their own right.
5   Most controversially, Harris proposed (5.37–5.42) that HEFCE *research* monies (as opposed to teaching funds) should not reward doctoral students in units with an RAE grade below 3 unless there was a great deal of externally funded research activity, and that teaching monies for doctoral studies should be concentrated in places with a 'critical mass' of research activity.

Neither the subsequent report of the Dearing inquiry into higher education (1997) nor the government has diluted the force of these comments. Dearing was mainly an inquiry into undergraduate issues, and did not make proposals for postgraduate issues which differed significantly from those of Harris.

The issue central to Harris's treatment of research students which we found most interesting was the proposal that government funding for PhD students should only be made available to outlets where there is 'a critical mass of research activity'. We have explored this idea elsewhere (Delamont,

Atkinson and Parry 1997a, 1997b). Its importance here is that this proposal was aligned with a whole series of measures and policies before 1996 and since that date designed to concentrate government funding for all aspects of research, including PhD students, in a small number of elite institutions. In this respect The Harris Report was insensitive to the deep differences between disciplinary cultures (Becher 1990; Becher and Trowler 2001; Delamont, Atkinson and Parry 2000).

Since the publication of Harris, the main policy statement has come from the Quality Assurance Agency for Higher Education. They conducted an inquiry chaired by another Vice-Chancellor, Ivor Crewe, and then published, in 2001, *The Framework for Higher Education Qualification in England, Wales and Northern Ireland*, and an equivalent for Scotland. These set out the basic standards for all degrees, up to and including the professional doctorate and the PhD. This was, and is, the first time that any such generic statement had or has been made about any degree across the whole nation. Before, each university could define its degrees in its own language. So, there is now a common standard across higher education about what a person with an MPhil, a professional doctorate, a PhD or a DPhil should be able to do. There is a parallel publication covering Scotland, which recognizes that the undergraduate degree there is an MA, with consequences for the titles of the qualifications intermediate between first degree and doctorate.

Paralleling the codifications done by the QAA the past decade has seen a plethora of inquiries and reports on postgraduate issues by disciplinary bodies and learned societies. The UK Council for Graduate Education (UKCGE 2000), a body founded in 1994, conducted an inquiry starting in 1998 into the vexed issue of research training for humanities postgraduates. The British Academy (BA 2001) carried out an investigation into graduate studies in humanities and social sciences. The Council of University Deans of Arts and Humanities (CUDAH 2002) researched the career destinations of doctoral students in arts and humanities. The Higher Education Funding Council for England presented the report of an inquiry into the supply of scientific manpower (Roberts 2002) with strong recommendations on the PhD. The Rhind Commission (2003) included some discussion on social science PhD students in its inquiry into the state of UK social sciences. We have not summarized the findings and recommended actions of these bodies here, but do advise our readers to get up to speed on the reports that relate to their discipline, whether earth sciences or sculpture.

During 2003 the four higher education funding councils set out to produce 'threshold standards' and 'framework of good practice' for postgraduate degrees. They consulted during 2002/2003 (HEFCE 2003) about establishing these basic levels of institutional practice, to ensure that students not only did good projects but also gained skills useful outside academia. The threshold standards proposed in 2003 were:

1 A code of practice throughout the institution covering seven areas as follows:

2 (a) Measures to combat intellectual isolation.
  (b) A completion rate of 70 per cent within four years for full-time students, and eight years for part-time students.

3 Entry requirements of either an upper second or equivalent, a relevant Masters or accredited prior learning.

4 Supervisory arrangements
  (a) all new supervisors to be trained,
  (b) a supervisory team of a least two people, both active researchers, one designated the main supervisor,
  (c) the main supervisor should have had at least one previously successful completion,
  (d) the main supervisor should not have more than six students,
  (e) regular structured interactions to focus on personal and academic progress with recorded outcomes.

5 Reviews of progress
  (a) annual, formal progress reviews of full- and part-time candidates, with at least one reviewer who is not part of the supervisory team,
  (b) final examination by viva by at least two examiners who are research active, at least one of whom is an external.

6 Feedback mechanisms
  The institution must gather feedback data from all parties.

7 Appeals procedures
  There must be procedures to handle appeals and complaints which must be publicised.

8 Skills
  The institution must provide students with access to training in research and other skills (see below).

There are 36 skills which the student should have mastered. These are in seven subsets, covering skills to do their research, an understanding of the research environment, research management, personal reflexivity and open-mindedness, communication, networking and team working, and career management.

Many universities have all, or almost all, of these eight areas in place: and social science students funded by the ESRC have been required to obtain most of the 36 skills since 1987. However, there is no doubt that if this code is adopted throughout the UK there will be less institutional variation in future, and the lives of doctoral students will be less subject to the whims of their supervisors. However there are many academics, and many graduate students who chafe under this regulatory and audit culture.

The perceptive sociologist, Basil Bernstein (1996) objected strenuously to the introduction of generic skills training into the PhD programme, complaining it transformed what had been 'a license to explore' into 'a driving

198   *Supervising the doctorate*

licence' (p. 135). We are finalizing this edition of the book before it is clear how much of the proposed framework will be mandatory, and it is not at all clear how much of it will be applied to students at the thesis stage of the professional doctorate. However, most of the framework appears to us to mandate things which all higher-degree students deserve to have anyway and things which will not disturb a productive student–supervisor relationship. Such a framework should hold no terrors for our readers.

Further reading

This list is in two parts: first we have listed further reading for supervisors, and second we have listed useful books for students.

Further reading for supervisors

This section is divided into subsections: on supervision, on the research. There are three types of literature on supervision: guidelines produced by specific learned societies dealing with appropriate behaviour for supervisors in that discipline; general guidelines; and reports of social science research on supervision. We have not listed examples of the first type of literature, but we strongly advise supervisors to find out if their learned society produces such guidelines, and if it does, to get hold of them and publicize them in their department.

General guidelines

In the UK the research councils produce guidelines on good supervisory practice, available from each separate Research Council's website. The National Postgraduate Committee (1995) also produce *Guidelines for Codes of Practice for Postgraduate Research.*

In your own university, there are probably some guidelines available, at institutional, faculty or departmental level which you should get hold of. If the higher education funding bodies in the UK implement the code of practice being advocated by the four UK funding councils in 2003, public money will only support higher-degree students in institutions with a written code of practice governing supervision.

Australia has produced two useful sets of guidelines for supervision by Connell (1985) and Moses (1985). From the UK there is helpful advice in Chapter 6 of Brown and Atkins (1988), and it is salutary to read the chapters on supervisors in the advice books for students by Cryer (2000), Leonard (2001) and Phillips and Pugh (2000). Ryan and Zuber-Skerritt (1999) is an invaluable set of papers on the issues that arise when supervising students whose first language is not English. The collection on quality in postgraduate education edited by Zuber-Skerritt and Ryan (1994) is also worth consulting. In New Zealand, Sue Middleton has produced a CD-Rom of supervision training workshops. http://www.waikato.ac.nz/education/edstudies/middleton/CDWeb/start.html.

There is a useful video produced by Rowena Murray from Strathclyde University: details from The Centre for Academic Practice, University of Strathclyde, Graham Hills Building, 50 George Street, Glasgow G1 1QE.

Research studies

Empirical evidence on postgraduate research students and their supervision has been accumulating rapidly in the last decade. The research on France, Germany, Japan, the UK and the USA can be traced from Burton Clark (1993). The American scene can also be explored from Bowen and Rudenstine (1992). The British research can be found in Becker *et al.* (1994), Burgess (1994) and the evidence volume of Harris (1996). The Australian research can be traced in Zuber-Skerritt and Ryan (1994).

Further reading for students

This section is divided into six subsections:

General guidelines,
Finding and reviewing the literature,
Preparing for examination,
Grammar and style,
Writing,
Confessional and autobiographical texts.

1 General

Cryer, P. (2000) *The Research Student's Guide to Success* (2nd edn)
Phillips, E. and Pugh, D. (2000) *How to get a PhD* (3rd edn)
Rudestam, K.E. and Newton, R.R. (2000) *Surviving your Dissertation* (2nd edn)
Leonard, D (2001) *A Woman's Guide to Doctoral Study*
Graves, N. and Varma, V. (eds) (1997) *Working for a Doctorate*
Potter, S. (ed.) (2002) *Doing Postgraduate Research*

Allan, G. and Skinner, C. (ed.) (1991) *Handbook for Research Students in the Social Sciences.*
Burton, D. (ed.) (2000) *Research Training for Social Scientists*

2 Finding and reviewing the literature

Hart, C. (2001) *Doing a Literature Search*
Gash, S. (2000) *Effective Literature Searching for Research* (2nd edn)
Booth, Wayne C. *et al.* (1996) *The Craft of Research* (Chapter 5 and 6) is good on this.

3 Preparing for examination

Murray, R. (2003) *How to Survive your Viva*
Tinkler, P. and Jackson, C. (2004) *The Doctoral Examination Process*

4 Books to help students with grammar and style

In Chapter 8 we divided these into four broad categories: technical manuals, general books on how to write books on thesis writing and reflexive books on how texts are produced and received in academic disciplines.

Technical Manuals: This area has continued to produce good new books, but there seems to be a problem with excellent texts going out of print fast, too. We *strongly* advise buying copies of these for the library while they are available.

For library use only we recommend: R.M. Ritter (2002) *The Oxford Guide to Style* which replaces the trusty *Hart's Rules*. *The Chicago Manual of Style* (2003) (13th edn) should also be in the libraries of all institutions where PhDs are done.

For student purchase: The Bloomsbury Press produce *The Encarta Concise Student Dictionary*, which has been compiled after research on students, and is designed so they can use it, and corrects the mistakes contemporary students make.

Robert Allen (2002) *Punctuation*
Robert Allen (2002) *Spelling*
John Seely (2002) *Words*
John Seely (2002) *Writing Reports*
Jo Billingham (2002) *Editing and Revising Text*
Jane Dorner (2002) *Writing for the Internet*

and the rest of the OUP 'One Step Ahead' series are all splendid. They have cartoons, lots of diagrams, and are friendly.

E.P. Bailey and P.A. Powell (1987) *Writing Research Papers* is an American book for advanced undergraduates and people on taught Masters courses. The UK equivalent is Cuba and Cocking (1994).

A.A. Berger (1993) *Improving Writing Skills* deals with producing memos, letters, reports, proposals and 'business documents', and would help any graduate student.

Diane Collinson *et al.* (1992) *Plain English* is an excellent book for graduate students, which includes an introductory quiz, and chapters on the central topics such as punctuation, each with exercises.

Lee Cuba and John Cocking's (1994) *How to Write about the Social Sciences* is aimed at advanced undergraduates and people doing taught Masters courses, but many doctoral students have found it helpful because it deals with searching the literature, framing an argument, and technicalities in one slim volume.

Michael Dummett's (1993) *Grammar and Style* is extremely helpful to postgraduates in humanities and social sciences, because it combines ideas on good grammar with clarity of style. As Dummett hates much contemporary social science writing he includes many 'classic' sociologists in his negative examples.

John Kirkham's two books, *Good Style* (1992) and *Full Marks* (1993) are specifically for science and technology graduates, and are excellent.

M.H. Manser's (1990) *Bloomsbury Good Word Guide* is our reference work of choice because it addresses most of the confusions found in postgraduate writing.

Turabian's classic *Manual for Writers of Research Papers, Theses and Dissertations*, originally produced in 1937, is an essential reference work, but is not designed to be read. There has been a separate British version since 1982, and the most recent edition, the sixth, should be in all university libraries and on student's reading lists.

John Whale's (1984) *Put it in Writing* is a cheerful text which would improve anyone's writing.

The vexed question of non-sexist writing also needs some guidance. Marilyn Schwartz (1995) *Guidelines for Bias-Free Writing* was prepared for the Association of American University Presses. It carefully explains the derivations and current acceptability of terms like Chinatown (but not the offensive use of Welsh as a verb), seminal, and dwarfism.

F.W. Frank and P.A. Treichler (1989) *Language, Gender and Professional Writing* is a thorough guide to non-sexist usage published by the American Modern Language Association.

Books on writing strategies
The book we recommend above all others is Howard Becker's (1986) *Writing for Social Scientists* which is funny, inspiring and packed with ideas that help experienced scholars as well as novices. The companion volume *Tricks of the Trade* (Becker 1990), is less amusing, but very useful.

Eviatar Zerubavel (1999) *The Clockwork Muse* is very helpful. A group of American graduates recently voted it their 'most useful' book.

Wayne Booth *et al.* (1995) *The Craft of Research* has five chapters on writing (11–15) which are extremely helpful.

Pechenick and Lamb's (1995) *How to Write about Biology* does exactly what it suggests: guide young scholars in the biological sciences towards professional text production.

Laurel Richardson's (1990) *Writing Strategies* is an autobiographical study of how she wrote about her own research – on women who were having affairs with married men – which was published as a best-selling non-fiction book and as an academic journal article. On the way through this account a student can learn a great deal about writing.

R.A. Day's (1995) *How to Write and Publish a Scientific Paper* is a clearly written book which would help any novice academic in science and engineering submit material for publication.

Harry Wolcott's (1990) *Writing up Qualitative Research* is short, well written and emphasizes the need to build writing into research from the beginning. It will be of value across a range of disciplines – notably sociology, anthropology, education, health research, human geography and cultural studies.

5 Writing the thesis

Since the first edition of his book, there have been several texts specifically on writing a thesis. We have bought and read the following.

Rowena Murray (2002) *How to Write a Thesis* is British, and comes from the well-established centre at Strathclyde, which also produces helpful videos.

Patrick Dunleavy (2003) *Authoring a PhD* is by a political scientist from LSE, and we found it very dull.

The American books include
Rita S. Brause (2000) *Writing your Doctoral Dissertation* which actually covers a range of survival issues as well as writing.

Allan A. Glatthorn (1998) *Writing the Winning Dissertation,* is by a social scientist who has chaired over 100 dissertation committees (in UK terms, supervisory teams).

Jean Bolker (1998) *Writing your Dissertation in Fifteen Minutes a Day* is hard to obtain in the UK, but is by an author who runs writing clinics, and is excellent.

Reflexive texts on academic reading and writing
There is now a large literature dealing with the rhetoric and poetics of academic writing. Key references include: Edmondson (1984) and Atkinson (1990, 1992) on sociology; Clifford and Marcus (1986) and Wolf (1992) on anthropology; Cameron (1989) on history; Ashmore, Myers and Potter

(1994), Bazerman (1988) and Myers (1990) on the natural sciences. Some students find this somewhat introspective material liberating (and it helps them to read and write) while other find it inhibiting because it makes them too self-conscious about their own drafts. This is an area where you need to know your own students before despatching them to the library. Gilbert's (1993, 2001) paper on writing about social research is a useful test to see if your students will find this reflexive literature helpful.

6 Confessional and autobiographical accounts

Eggleston, J.F. and Delamont, S. (1993) *Supervision of Students for Research Degrees* (esp. Chaps. 2 and 3) or Eggleston and Delamont (1981) *A Necessary Isolation?*
Vartuli, S. (ed.) (1982) *The PhD Experience*
Walford, G. (ed.) (2002) *Doing a PhD in Educational Research*

References

Aisenberg, N. and Harrington, M. (1988) *Women and Academe: Outsiders in the Sacred Grove*, Amherst, MA: University of Massachusetts Press.

Allan, G. and Skinner, C. (eds) (1991) *Handbook for Research Students in the Social Sciences*, London: Falmer.

Allen, R. (2002a) *Spelling*, Oxford: Oxford University Press.

Allen, R. (2002b) *Punctuation*, Oxford: Oxford University Press.

Ashmore, M., Myers, G. and Potter, J. (1994) Discourse, rhetoric and reflexivity, in S. Jasanoff, G. Markle, J. Petersen and T. Pinch (eds) *Handbook of Science and Technology Studies*, London: Sage.

Atkinson, P.A. (1981) *The Clinical Experience: The Construction and Reconstruction of Medical Reality*, Farnborough: Gower.

Atkinson, P.A. (1984) Wards and deeds: Taking knowledge and control seriously, in R.G. Burgess (ed.) *The Research Process in Educational Settings*, London: Falmer.

Atkinson, P.A. (1990) *The Ethnographic Imagination*, London and New York: Routledge.

Atkinson, P.A. (1992) *Understanding Ethnographic Texts*, Thousand Oaks, CA: Sage.

Atkinson, P.A. (1996) *Sociological Readings and Re-Readings*, Aldershot: Avebury.

Atkinson, P.A. and Delamont, S. (1985) Socialisation into teaching: the research which lost its way, *British Journal of Sociology of Education*, 6 (3): 307–22.

Atkinson, P.A. and Delamont, S. (2004) *Building Research Careers and Cultures*, Maidenhead: Open University Press.

Atkinson, P.A., Reid, M.E. and Sheldrake, P.F. (1977) Medical mystique, *Sociology of Work and Occupations*, 4 (3): 243–80.

Bailey, E.P and Powell, P.A. (1987) *Writing Research Papers*, New York: Holt, Rinehart and Winston.

Barr, B. (1984) *Histories of Girls' Schools and Related Biographical Material*, Leicester: The School of Education of the University of Leicester.

Barzun, J. (1986) *On Writing, Editing and Publishing* (2nd edn), Chicago: Chicago University Press.

Bazerman, C. (1988) *Shaping Written Knowledge: The Genre and Activity of the Experimental Article in Science*, Madison: University of Wisconsin Press.

Becher, T. (1989) Physicists on Physics, *Studies in Higher Education*, 15 (1): 3–21.

Becher, T. (1990) *Academic Tribes and Territories*, Milton Keynes: Open University Press.

Becher, T. and Trowler, P. (2001) *Academic Tribes and Territories* (2nd edn), Buckingham: Open University Press.
Becher, T., Henkel, M. and Kogan, M. (1994) *Graduate Education in Britain*, London: Jessica Kingsley.
Becker, H.S. (1986) *Writing for Social Scientists*, Chicago: Chicago University Press.
Becker, H.S. (1990) *The Tricks of the Trade*, Chicago: Chicago University Press.
Becker, H.S., Geer, B., Hughes, E.C. and Strauss, A.L. (1961) *Boys in White*, Chicago: Chicago University Press.
Berger, A.A. (1993) *Improving Writing Skills*, Newbury Park, CA: Sage.
Bernstein, B. (1996) *Pedagogy, Symbolic Control and Identity*, London: Taylor & Francis.
Billingham, J. (2002) *Editing and Revising Text*, Oxford: Oxford University Press.
Blaxter, L., Hughes, C. and Tight, M. (1998) *The Academic Career Handbook*, Buckingham: Open University Press.
Bolker, J. (1998) *Writing your Dissertation in Fifteen Minutes a Day*, New York: Henry Holt.
Booth, W.C., Colomb, G.G. and Williams, J.M. (1995) *The Craft of Research*, Chicago: Chicago University Press.
Bourdieu, P. (1988) *Homo Academicus*, Cambridge: Polity Press.
Bourdieu, P. and Passeron, J.-C. (1977) *Reproduction*, London: Routledge.
Bourdieu, P. and Passeron, J.-C. (1979) *The Inheritors*, London: Chicago University Press.
Bowen, G. and Rudenstine, N. (1992) *In Pursuit of the PhD*, Princeton, NJ: Princeton University Press.
Brause, R. S. (2000) *Writing Your Doctoral Dissertation*, London: Sage.
British Academy (2001) *Review of Graduate Studies in the Humanities and Social Sciences*, London: The British Academy.
Brown, C. (1982) *The Education and Employment of Postgraduates*, London: Policy Studies Institute.
Brown, G. and Atkins, M. (1988) *Effective Teaching in Higher Education*, London and New York: Methuen.
Brown, P. and Scase, R. (1994) *Higher Education and Corporate Realities*, London: UCL Press.
Burgess, R.G. (1984) *In the Field*, London: Allen & Unwin.
Burgess, R.G. (ed.) (1994) *Postgraduate Education and Training in the Social Sciences*, London: Jessica Kingsley.
Burton, D. (ed.) (2002) *Research Training for Social Scientists*, London: Sage.
Cameron, A. (1989) *History as Text*, London: Duckworth.
Carter, I. (1990) *Ancient Cultures of Conceit*, London: Routledge.
Chicago Manual of Style (2003), Chicago: Chicago University Press.
Clark, Burton R. (ed.) (1993) *The Research Foundations of Graduate Education: Germany, Britain, France, United States, Japan*, Berkeley, CA: University of California Press.
Clifford, J. and Marcus, G.E. (eds) (1986) *Writing Culture: The Poetics and Politics of Ethnography*, Berkeley: University of California Press.
Coffey, A. and Atkinson, P.A. (1996) *Making Sense of Qualitative Data*, Thousand Oaks, CA: Sage.
Cole, J. (1979) *Fair Science*, New York: The Free Press.
Collinson, D., Kirkup, G., Kyd, R. and Slocombe, L. (1992) *Plain English*, Buckingham: The Open University Press.
Connell, R.W. (1985) How to supervise a PhD, *Vestes*, 2, 38–41.

Cook, I. (2001) You want to be careful you don't end up like Ian, in P. Moss (ed.) *Placing Autobiography in Geography*, Syracuse: Syracuse University Press.

Cross, A. (1970) *Poetic Justice*, New York: Avon.

Cryer, P. (2000) *The Research Student's Guide to Success* (2nd edn), Buckingham: Open University Press.

Cuba, L. and Cocking, J. (1994) *How to Write about the Social Sciences*, London: Harper & Row.

CUDAH (2002) *Doctoral Futures*, Leicester: De Montfort University for the Council of University Deans of Arts and Humanities.

CVCP (1985) *Report on Academic Standards* (The Reynolds Report), London: Committee of Vice-Chancellors and Principals.

Day, R.A. (1995) *How to Write and Publish a Scientific Paper*, Cambridge: Cambridge University Press.

Dearing, R. (1997) *Higher Education in the Learning Society* (The Dearing Report), London: National Committee of Inquiry into Higher Education.

Deem, R. and Brehony, K. (2000) Doctoral students' access to research cultures, *Studies in Higher Education*, 25 (2): 149–68.

Delamont, S. (1976) The girls most likely to, *Scottish Journal of Sociology*, 1 (1): 29–43.

Delamont, S. (1989a) Gender and British postgraduate funding policy, *Gender and Education*, 1 (1): 51–7.

Delamont, S. (1989b) Citation and social mobility research, *Sociological Review*, 37 (2): 332–7.

Delamont, S. (1989c) *Knowledgeable Women*, London: Routledge.

Delamont, S. (2002) *Fieldwork in Educational Settings* (2nd edn), London: Falmer.

Delamont, S. (2003) *Feminist Sociology*, London: Sage.

Delamont, S. and Atkinson, P. (1995) *Fighting Familiarity*, Cresskill, NJ: Hampton.

Delamont, S. and Atkinson, P. (nd) Who's Complaining? Narratives and research on the doctoral viva. Unpublished paper.

Delamont, S., Atkinson, P. and Parry, O. (1997a) Critical mass and pedagogic continuity, *British Journal of Sociology of Education*, 18 (4): 533–50.

Delamont, S., Atkinson, P. and Parry, O. (1997b) Critical mass and doctoral research, *Studies in Higher Education*, 22 (3): 319–32.

Delamont, S., Atkinson, P. and Parry, O. (2000) *The Doctoral Experience*, London: Falmer.

Delamont, S., Atkinson, P., Coffey, A. and Burgess, R.G. (2001) *An Open Exploratory Spirit? Ethnography at Cardiff 1974–2001*. Cardiff: School of Social Science Working Paper 20 http://www.cf.ac.uk/socsi/publications/index.html

Diamond, P. and Zuber-Skerritt, O. (1986) Postgraduate researchers: some changing personal constructs, *Higher Education Research and Development*, Vol. 5, 161–75.

Dorner, J. (2002) *Writing for the Internet*, Oxford: Oxford University Press.

Dummett, M. (1993) *Grammar and Style*, London: Duckworth.

Dunleavy, P. (2003) *Authoring the PhD*, London: Palgrave.

Dyhouse, C. (1994) *No Distinction of Sex*, London: UCL Press.

Edge, D. (1979) Quantitative measures of communication in sciences, *History of Science*, 17: 102–34.

Edmondson, R. (1984) *Rhetoric in Sociology*, London: Macmillan.

Eggleston, J. and Delamont, S. (1981) *A Necessary Isolation? a Study of Postgraduate Research Students in Education*, Cardiff: Social Research Unit, Department of Sociology, University College, Cardiff.

Eggleston, J.F. and Delamont, S. (1983) *Supervision of Students for Research Degrees*, Kendal, Cumbria: Dixon Printing Company for British Education Research Association.

Eickleman, D. (1978) The art of memory, *Comparative Studies in Society and History*, 20 (4): 485–516.

Eickleman, D. (1985) *Knowledge and Power in Morocco*, Princeton, NJ: Princeton University Press.

Encarta Concise Dictionary (2001) Student edition, London: Bloomsbury.

Evans, C. (1988) *Language People*, Milton Keynes: Open University Press.

Evans, C. (1993) *English People*, Milton Keynes: Open University Press.

Fleck, L. (1979) *The Genesis and Development of a Scientific Fact*, Chicago: Chicago University Press.

Fox, M.F. (ed.) (1985) *Scholarly Writing and Publishing*, Boulder, Colorado: Westview Press.

Frank, F.W. and Treichler, P.A. (1989) *Language, Gender and Professional Writing*, New York: The Modern Language Association of America.

Galton, M. and Delamont, S. (1976) *Final Report on PhD/PGCE Chemistry Courses*, Leicester: Leicester University School of Education, for the DES.

Gash, S. (2000) *Effective Literature Searching for Research*, Aldershot: Gower.

Gilbert, N. (1993) Writing about social research, in N. Gilbert (ed.) *Researching Social Life*, London: Sage.

Gilbert, N. (2001) Writing about social research, in N. Gilbert (ed.) *Researching Social Life* (2nd edn), London: Sage.

Gilbert, N. and Mulkay, M. (1984) *Opening Pandora's Box*, Cambridge: Cambridge University Press.

Glatthorn, A. (1998) *Writing the Winning Dissertation*, Thousand Oaks, CA: Corwin Press.

Goode, G. and Delamont, S. (1996) Opportunity denied, in S. Betts (ed.) *Our Daughters' Land*, Cardiff: University of Wales Press.

Gornik, V. (1990) *Women in Science*, New York: Simon & Schuster.

Gowers, E. (1986) *The Complete Plain Words* (revised edn prepared by S. Greenbaum and J.Whitart), London: HMSO.

Graff, G. (2003) *The PhD in English*, Menlo Park, CA: Carnegie Essays on the Doctorate http://carnegiefoundation.org/CID/essays/CID_engl_Graff.pdf

Granfield, R. (1992) *Making Elite Lawyers*, New York: Routledge.

Graves, N. and Varma, V. (eds) (1997) *Working for a Doctorate*, London: Routledge.

Gumport, P. (1993) Graduate education and research imperatives: Views from American campuses, in R. Burton Clark (ed.) *The Research Foundations of Graduate Education*, Berkeley: University of California Press.

Hacking, I. (1992) The self-vindication of the laboratory sciences, in A. Pickering (ed.) *Science as Practice and Culture*, Chicago: University of Chicago Press.

Hammersley, M. and Atkinson, P. (1995) *Ethnography: Principles in Practice* (2nd edn), London: Routledge.

Harris, M. (1996) *Review of Postgraduate Education, Volume I: The Report, Volume 2: The Evidence*, Bristol: The Higher Education Funding Council for England.

Hart, C. (2001) *Doing a Literature Search*, London: Sage.

Hartley, J. and Jory, S. (2000) Lifting the veil on the viva, *Psychology Teaching Review*, 9, 76–90.

Hartley, J. and Fox, C. (2004) Assessing the mock viva, *Studies in Higher Education*, 29 (2) forthcoming.

Hayhoe, R. (1984) The evolution of modern Chinese educational institutions, in R. Hayhoe (ed.) *Contemporary Chinese Education*, London: Croom Helm.

HEFCE (2003) *Improving Standards in Postgraduate Research Degree Programmes*, Bristol: HEFCE.

Heyl, B. (1979) *The Madam as Entrepreneur,* New Brunswick, NJ: Transaction Books.

Hockey, J. (1991) The Social Science PhD, *Studies in Higher Education,* 16 (3): 319–32.

Hockey, J. (1994a) Establishing boundaries: problems and solutions in managing the PhD. supervisor role, *Cambridge Journal of Education,* 24 (2): 293–305.

Hockey, J. (1994b) New territory, *Studies in Higher Education,* 19 (2): 177–90.

Hudson, Liam (1977) Picking winners: a case study in the recruitment of research students, *New Universities Quarterly,* 32 (1): 88–106.

Jones, D.J.H. (1993) *Murder at the MLA,* Athens, Georgia: Georgia University Press.

Kadushin, C. (1969) The professional self concept of music students, *American Journal of Sociology,* 75: 389–404.

Katz, J. and Hartnett, R.T. (eds) (1976) *Scholars in the Making,* Cambridge Mass: Ballinger.

Kirkman, J. (1992) *Good Style,* London: Spon.

Kirkman, J. (1993) *Full Marks,* London: Ramsbury.

Lathen, E. (1982) *Green Grow the Dollars,* London: Gollancz.

Lather, P. (1991) *Getting Smart,* London: Routledge.

Latour, B. and Woolgar, S. (1986) *Laboratory Life* (2nd edn.), Princeton, NJ: Princeton University Press.

Leonard, D. (2001) *A Woman's Guide to Doctoral Studies,* Buckingham: Open University Press.

Lie, S.S., Malik, L. and Harris, D. (eds) (1994) *The Gender Gap in Higher Education,* London: Kogan Page.

Lodge, D. (1984) *Small World,* London: Martin Secker & Warburg.

Lynch, M. (1985) *Art and Artefact in Laboratory Science,* London: Routledge.

Manser, M.J. (1990) *Bloomsbury Good Word Guide,* London: Bloomsbury.

Middleton, S. (2001) *Educating Researchers: New Zealand Education PhDs 1948–1998.* NZARE: Wellington.

Miller, C.M.L. and Parlett, M. (1976) Cue-consciousness, in M. Hammersley and P. Woods (eds) *The Process of Schooling,* London: Routledge & Kegan Paul.

Morley, L., Leonard, D. and David, M. (2002) Variations in Vivas, *Studies in Higher Education,* 27 (2): 261–73.

Moses, I. (1985) *Supervising Postgraduates,* Kensington, NSW: Higher Education Research and Development Society of Australasia.

Mosley, W (2000) Holiday is not an option, *The Guardian,* 26 July, 12–13.

Mullins, G. and Kiley, M. (2002) It's a PhD not a Nobel Prize, *Studies in Higher Education,* 27 (4): 369–86.

Murray, R. (2002) *How to Write a Thesis,* Buckingham: Open University Press.

Murray, R. (2003) *How to Survive Your Viva,* Buckingham: Open University Press.

Myers, G. (1990) *Writing Biology: Texts in the Social Construction of Scientific Knowledge,* Madison: University of Wisconsin Press.

Nyquist, J. and Wulff, D.H. (nd) Recommendations from National Studies on Doctoral Education: Re-envisioning the PhD. http://grad.washington.edu/ envision/project_resources/national_recommend.html

Olesen, V. and Whittaker, E. (1968) *The Silent Dialogue,* San Francisco: Jossey-Bass.

Pearson, D. (2002) *Pressure Points in Academic Life,* Unpublished PhD Thesis, Cardiff University, Cardiff.

Pechenick, J.A. and Lamb, B.C. (1995) *How to Write About Biology,* London: Harper Collins.

Pert, C. (1997) *Molecules of Emotion,* New York: Simon & Schuster.

210   *Supervising the doctorate*

Phillips, E.M. (1994) Quality in the PhD, in R.G. Burgess (ed.) *Postgraduate Education and Training in Social Sciences*, London; Jessica Kingsley.
Phillips, E.M. and Pugh, D.S. (2000) *How to Get a PhD* (3rd edn), Buckingham: Open University Press.
Phillips, S.U. (1982) The language socialisation of lawyers: acquiring the 'cant', in G. Spindler (ed.) *Doing the Ethnography of Schooling*, New York: Holt, Rinehart & Winston.
Porter, M. (1984) The modification of method in researching postgraduate education, in R.G. Burgess (ed.) *The Research Process in Educational Settings*, London: Falmer.
Potter, S. (ed.) (2002) *Doing Postgraduate Research*, London: Sage.
QAA (2001) *The Framework for Higher Education Qualifications in England, Wales and Northern Ireland*, London: The QAA.
Rhind, D. (2003) *Great Expectations: The Social Sciences in Britain*, London: The Academy for the Learned Societies in Social Sciences.
Richardson, L. (1990) *Writing Strategies*, Newbury Park, CA: Sage.
Ritter, R.M. (2002) *Oxford Guide to Style*, Oxford: Oxford University Press.
Roberts, G. (2002) *SET for Success*, London: HEFCE.
Rudd, E. (1984) Research into postgraduate education, *Higher Education Research and Development*, 3 (2): 109–20.
Rudd, E. (1985) *A New Look at Postgraduate Failure*, Guildford SRHE and NFER Nelson.
Rudestam, K.E. and Newton, R.R. (2001) *Surviving your Dissertation* (2nd edn), London: Sage.
Ryan, Y. and Zuber-Skerritt, O. (eds) (1999) *Supervising Postgraduates from Non-English Speaking Backgrounds*, Buckingham: Open University Press.
Salmon, P. (1992) *Achieving a PhD*, Stoke on Trent: Trentham Books.
Sayers, D.L. (1972) *Gaudy Night*, London: Gollancz.
Schwartz, M. (1995) *Guidelines for Bias-Free Writing*, Bloomington: Indiana University Press.
Scott, S. (1985) Working through the contradictions in researching postgraduate education, in R.G. Burgess (ed.) *Field Methods in the Study of Education*, London: Falmer.
Scott, S. and Porter, M. (1980) Postgraduates, sociology and cuts, in P. Abrams and P. Leuthwaite (eds) *Transactions of the BSA*, London: British Sociological Association.
Scott, S. and Porter, M. (1983) On the bottom rung, *Women's Studies International Forum*, 6 (22): 211–21.
Scott, S. and Porter, M. (1984) Women and research, in S. Acker and D. Warren-Piper (eds) *Is Higher Education Fair to Women?*, London: SRHE.
Seely, J. (2002a) *Words*, Oxford: Oxford University Press.
Seely, J. (2002b) *Writing Reports*, Oxford: Oxford University Press.
Smith, D. (1994) A Berkeley Education, in K.P.M. Orlans and R.A. Wallace (eds) *Gender and the Academic Experience*, Lincoln, NE: University of Nebraska Press.
Spradley, J.P. and Mann, B.J. (1975) *The Cocktail Waitress*, New York: Wiley.
Spradley, J.P. (1979) *The Ethnographic Interview*, New York: Holt, Rinehart & Winston.
Spradley, J.P. (1980) *Partipant Observation*, New York: Holt, Rinehart & Winston.
Startup, R. (1979) *The University Teacher and His World*, Farnborough: Saxon House.
Tesch, R. (1990) *Qualitative Research: Analysis Types and Software Tools*, London: Falmer.

Tinkler, P. and Jackson, C. (2000) Examining the Doctorate, *Studies in Higher Education*, 25 (2): 167–80.

Tinkler, P. and Jackson, C. (2004) *The Doctoral Examination Process*. Maidenhead: Open University Press.

Torrance, M.S. and Thomas, G.V. (1994) The development of writing skills in doctoral research students, in R.G. Burgess (ed.) *Postgraduate Education and Training in the Social Sciences*, London: Jessica Kingsley.

Traweek, S. (1988) *Beamtimes and Lifetimes*, Cambridge, Mass: Harvard University Press.

Turabian, K. (1937) *A Manual for Writers of Research Papers, Theses and Dissertations*, Chicago: Chicago Press.

Turabian, K. (1982) *A Manual for Writers of Research Papers, Theses and Dissertations* (British edn), London: Heineman.

Turabian, K. (1995) *A Manual for Writers of Research Papers, Theses and Dissertations* (6th edn), Chicago: University of Chicago Press.

UKCGE (2000) *Research Training for Humanities Postgraduate Students*, Leeds: Dialhouse for the UK Council for Graduate Education.

UKCGE (2002) *Professional Doctorates*, Leeds: Dialhouse for the UK Council for Graduate Education.

Valli, L. (1986) *Becoming Clerical Workers*, New York: Routledge.

Vartuli, S. (ed.) (1982) *The PhD Experience*, CBS: New York.

Wakeford, J. (1985) A director's dilemmas, in R.G. Burgess (ed.) *Field Methods in the Study of Education*, London: Falmer.

Walford, G. (ed.) (2002) *Doing a PhD in the Sociology of Education*, London: JAI Press.

Wallace, R. (1994) Transformation from sacred to secular, in K.P.M. Orlans and R.A.Wallace (eds) *Gender and the Academic Experience*, Lincoln, NE: University of Nebraska Press.

Whittlesea, C. (1995) *Pharmacy doctoral students: thesis writing skills and strategies*. Unpublished MScEcon thesis, University of Wales College of Cardiff.

Wilkinson, R. (1964) *The Prefects*, London: Oxford University Press.

Winfield, G. (1987) *The Social Science PhD* (2 volumes), London: Economic and Social Research Council.

Wiseman, J.P. (1994) New perspectives, new freedoms, in K.P.M Orlans and R.A. Wallace (eds) *Gender and the Academic Experience*, Lincoln, NE: University of Nebraska Press.

Wolcott, H.F. (1990) *Writing up Qualitative Research*, Newbury Park, CA: Sage.

Wolf, M. (1992) *A Thrice Told Tale: Feminism, Postmodernism and Ethnographic Responsibility*, Stanford: Stanford University Press.

Woods, P. (1986) *Inside Schools*, London: Routledge.

Woods, P. (1996) *Researching the Art of Teaching*, London: Routledge.

Wright, J. (1992) *Selection, Supervision and the Academic Management of Research Leading to the Degree of PhD*. Unpublished PhD thesis: University of Nottingham.

Young, K., Fogarty, M.P. and Mcrae, S. (1987) *The Management of Doctoral Studies in the Social Sciences*, London: Policy Studies Institute.

Young, L.J. (2001) Border Crossing and Other Journeys, *Educational Researcher*, 30 (5): 3–5.

Zerubavel, E. (1999) *The Clockwork Muse*, Cambridge, MA: Harvard University Press.

Zuber-Skerritt, O. and Ryan, Y. (eds) (1994) *Quality in Postgraduate Education*, London: Kogan Page.

Zuckerman, H., Cole, J.R. and Bruer, J.T. (eds) (1991) *The Outer Circle*, New York: W.W. Norton.

Hunter, F. and Jackson, C. (1990) Examining and Documenting Skills in the Community, *Nursing* 39(22): 16-36.

Hylton and Johnson, C. (2001) *The General Contractor: Owner Atifs*, ahead, Open University Press.

Payne, M.S. and Thorne, S.V. (1984) The Development of Writing Skills in doctoral research students, in K.C. Burgess (ed.) *Postgraduate Education and Management in the Social Sciences*, London: Jessica Kingsley.

Powell, S. (1985) Recruitment and Training, Cambridge: Men, Mentors Press.

Pritchard, F. (1997) *A Manual for Writers of Dissertations, Theses and Doctoral*, Chicago: Chicago Press.

Pritchard, L. (1988) *A Manual of Referral of External Papers*, Prentice: Dissertation (Prince ed.) London: Robertson.

Prondozo, L. (1990) *Guidance Manual for Research, Papers, Theses, etc.*, 2nd edition, Open University Press: Buckingham.

UKCGE (2000) *Research Training for the Humanities*, Providence: Stratton, Leeds: Database for the UK Council for Graduate Education.

UKCGE (2002) *Postgraduate Research for the Profession for the UK Council for Graduate Education.*

Willis, C. (1996) *Becoming Critical Writers*, New York: Routledge.

Winter, S. (ed.) (1990) *Letters to Research Students*, New York.

Wildford, L. (1986) A discursive dilemmas, in B.C. Burgess (ed.) *New Methods in the Sociology of Education*, London: Falmer.

Wisker, G. (ed.) (1996) *Enabling a PhD: the psychology of Research*, London: JAI Press.

Wisker, K. (1997) Communication, Reflection and supervision, in K.C. (ed.) *Who and Research*, London: Research in Education and the Disciplines of writing, Edinburgh: Falmer Literature of Edinburgh Press.

Wilson, D., C. (1990) *PhD thesis development: Doctoral study topics, changes in Republished Mind for Single Improvement in the UK*, Office of the UK, Milton.

Wilkinson, R. (ed.) (1997) *Support Schools Buckingham Press.*

Wittering, G. (1987) *The Social Science Policy volume 6*, London: Economic and Social Research Council.

Worsham, J.B. (1997) *New perspectives: New Methods in the RPM Course*, 2nd, P.V. Walker (ed.) *Power and the Academic Workforce*, Lincoln: NE: University of Nebraska Press.

Wilson, H.R. (1990) *Principles Qualitative Research*, Reading, Park: Sage.

Wolf, A. (1995) *A learn the Key*: employers expectations and their psychological development, London: School of Education Press.

Wolf, R.L. (1993) *Writing the real Thinking Learners*, London: Routledge.

Woods, T. (1996) *Re-making the Great Teaching*, London: Routledge.

Wright, G.H. (1987) *Dilemmas, Supervision and the Women Researcher in Research Training*, in K.C. (ed.) *Supervision of Postgraduates in Buckingham UK.*

Yin, R. (1994) *Case Study Research: Design and Method*, (2nd ed.) A framework of Case Studies: Applied Social Research Series, London: Sage Publications.

Young, J. (2000) *Research Theories and Other Techniques*, Buckingham: Research.

Zuckerman, H. (1977) *The Conference in the Cambridge, Massachusetts: University Press.*

Zuber-Skerritt, O. and Ryan, Y. (eds) (1994) *Quality in Postgraduate Education*, London: Kogan Page.

Zuckerman, H., Cole, J.R. and Bruer, J.T. (eds) (1991) *The Outer Circle*, New York: W.W. Norton.

Index

The Society for Research into Higher Education

The Society for Research into Higher Education (SRHE), an international body, exists to stimulate and coordinate research into all aspects of higher education. It aims to improve the quality of higher education through the encouragement of debate and publication on issues of policy, on the organization and management of higher education institutions, and on the curriculum, teaching and learning methods.

The Society is entirely independent and receives no subsidies, although individual events often receive sponsorship from business or industry. The Society is financed through corporate and individual subscriptions and has members from many parts of the world. It is an NGO of UNESCO.

Under the imprint *SRHE & Open University Press*, the Society is a specialist publisher of research, having over 80 titles in print. In addition to *SRHE News*, the Society's newsletter, the Society publishes three journals: *Studies in Higher Education* (three issues a year), *Higher Education Quarterly* and *Research into Higher Education Abstracts* (three issues a year).

The Society runs frequent conferences, consultations, seminars and other events. The annual conference in December is organized at and with a higher education institution. There are a growing number of networks which focus on particular areas of interest, including:

Access	FE/HE
Assessment	Graduate Employment
Consultants	New Technology for Learning
Curriculum Development	Postgraduate Issues
Eastern European	Quantitative Studies
Educational Development Research	Student Development

Benefits to members

Individual

- The opportunity to participate in the Society's networks
- Reduced rates for the annual conferences
- Free copies of *Research into Higher Education Abstracts*
- Reduced rates for *Studies in Higher Education*

- Reduced rates for *Higher Education Quarterly*
- Free online access to *Register of Members' Research Interests* – includes valuable reference material on research being pursued by the Society's members
- Free copy of occasional in-house publications, e.g. *The Thirtieth Anniversary Seminars Presented by the Vice-Presidents*
- Free copies of *SRHE News* and *International News* which inform members of the Society's activities and provides a calendar of events, with additional material provided in regular mailings
- A 35 per cent discount on all SRHE/Open University Press books
- The opportunity for you to apply for the annual research grants
- Inclusion of your research in the *Register of Members' Research Interests*

Corporate

- Reduced rates for the annual conference
- The opportunity for members of the Institution to attend SRHE's network events at reduced rates
- Free copies of *Research into Higher Education Abstracts*
- Free copies of *Studies in Higher Education*
- Free online access to *Register of Members' Research Interests* – includes valuable reference material on research being pursued by the Society's members
- Free copy of occasional in-house publications
- Free copies of *SRHE News* and *International News*
- A 35 per cent discount on all SRHE/Open University Press books
- The opportunity for members of the Institution to submit applications for the Society's research grants
- The opportunity to work with the Society and co-host conferences
- The opportunity to include in the *Register of Members' Research Interests* your Institution's research into aspects of higher education

Membership details: SRHE, 76 Portland Place, London W1B 1NT, UK Tel: 020 7637 2766. Fax: 020 7637 2781. email: srheoffice@srhe.ac.uk
world wide web: http://www.srhe.ac.uk./srhe/
Catalogue: SRHE & Open University Press, McGraw-Hill Education, McGraw-Hill House, Shoppenhangers Road, Maidenhead, Berkshire SL6 2QL. Tel: 01628 502500. Fax: 01628 770224. email: enquiries@openup.co.uk
web: www.openup.co.uk

SUCCESSFUL RESEARCH CAREERS
A PRACTICAL GUIDE

Sara Delamont and Paul Atkinson

This book provides practical advice on key aspects of higher education research activity including:

- Building successful research teams
- Mentoring in order to foster a research culture
- Publishing in academic journals and writing books
- Obtaining research grants

Written in an informative and accessible style, it addresses all the issues involved in building a research group and creating a research culture. Key strategies are outlined that will empower researchers by illuminating how the system works and where opportunities are to be sought. Most importantly, the book not only outlines approaches to research activity but motivates the reader to succeed.

Successful Research Careers takes a radical, unstuffy look at higher education and is of interest and relevance to anyone working in the higher education sector. Based on the authors' research on research groups, and on their experience in education management, the book provides advice for younger academics making their way in the system, and for more senior people who need to mentor research staff, build research groups and shape research-led careers.

Contents

Preface and acknowledgements – Introduction: 'plain words by a truth-telling friend' – Building a research culture and a research group: 'holding their place' – Supervising and mentoring: 'taken under the wing' – Research funding: 'the maieutic instinct' – Writing: 'superogatory contributions to scholarship' – Publishing journal papers: 'some marvellous things to say' – Publishing books: 'a kind of apocalyptic romance' – Other dissemination: 'expeditious diffusions' – Research assessment exercises: 'the susceptibilities of scholars' – Conclusions: 'stoking a modest imagination' – Appendix 1: Further reading on writing and publication – Appendix 2: CVCP publication categories – Appendix 3: Book proposal – References – Index.

224pp   0 335 21208 1 (Paperback)   0 335 21202 6 (Hardback)

THE DOCTORAL EXAMINATION PROCESS
A HANDBOOK FOR STUDENTS, EXAMINERS AND SUPERVISORS

Penny Tinkler and Caroline Jackson

- What is the viva and how can students prepare for it?
- What should supervisors consider when selecting PhD examiners?
- How should examiners assess a doctoral thesis and conduct the viva?

The doctoral examination process has been shrouded in mystery and has been a frequent source of anxiety and concern for students, supervisors and examiners alike. But now help is at hand. This book sheds new light on the process, providing constructive ways of understanding the doctoral examination, preparing for it and undertaking it.

This book stands alone in the field due to the extensive research undertaken by the authors. During a four year project, interviews were conducted with candidates and academics from a wide range of disciplines through the United Kingdom. Outcomes and ideas from the research have been united to provide the most comprehensive information available.

Real life accounts and case studies are combined with useful advice, tasks and checklists to create an illuminating handbook. This user-friendly book is a vital resource for anyone involved in the doctoral process. No doctoral candidate, examiner or supervisor should be without it.

Contents

192pp   0 335 21305 7 (Paperback)   0 335 21306 5 (Hardback)

HOW TO WRITE A THESIS

Rowena Murray

This is the book that all PhD supervisors and their students have been waiting for: the first comprehensive overview of the many different writing practices, and processes, involved in the production of a doctoral thesis. Crammed full of explanations, shortcuts and tips, this book demystifies academic writing in one fell swoop. Everyone who reads it will be massively enabled as a writer.

> Professor Lynne Pearce, Associate Dean for Postgraduate Teaching,
> University of Lancaster

Rowena Murray's down-to-earth approach both recognises and relieves some of the agony of writing a PhD. The advice in this book is both practical and motivational; sometimes it's 'PhD-saving' too. By using Rowena Murray's techniques of regular snacking, instead of occasional bingeing, I managed to rescue my PhD from near-death at a time of work overload.

> Christine Sinclair, Part-time PhD student and lecturer in
> Educational Development, University of Paisley

This book evolved from fifteen years' experience of teaching thesis writing. The contents have been tried and tested with postgraduates and academics. Early chapters explore the ambiguities and subtleties of thesis writing in detail. Later chapters are more compact, listing steps in the writing process. All chapters provide examples to illustrate techniques and activities to progress writing.

When you write a thesis be ready to develop new modes of writing. The harsh reality is that:

> If you like to work to goals, you are likely to have to submit to floundering around, reconstructing your well laid plans;

Whilst if you are the kind of person who hates to be driven by goals, or does not see the point of them, you will have to submit to deadlines and milestones that may seem like millstones. This book will help you cope with the challenges inherent in writing your Thesis.

Contents

Introduction – How to write 1000 words an hour – Thinking about writing a doctorate – Starting to write – Seeking structure – The first milestone – Becoming a serial writer – Creating closure – Fear and loathing: revising – It is never too late to start – The last 385 yards – After the viva: more writing? – References – Index.

304pp   0 335 20718 9 (Paperback)   0 335 20719 7 (Hardback)